REVIEWS FOR

THE UNTOUCHED PART:

The Untouched Part is a manual for life for the 21 Century Christian adult. The writer brings to the open vulnerabilities which we as Christians encounter but sometimes are too scared to discuss. Certainly, a must read for every Child of God.

—Seye Sandey

***

A book for today that speaks to this generation by someone who is not only authentic but has lived the life from both sides of the fence. This is a project from the heart.

How could Eunice say she had nothing to write about?

—Captain Bunmi Sandey

***

This is a classic evangelical work made possible by the inspiration of the Holy Spirit on the Author. It is an express call for Christians to return to the 'Old Time Religion,' the Christianity of righteousness, that which renews the body, soul and spirit, that which brings about a complete change from inside out, that which produces the new creature.

This book will meet the needs of those struggling to be Christians and those Christians who need the reassurance that they are still standing in the faith.

—Folasade Oluwatoyin Phillips. Executive Director, *Vine Crest College, Iperu-Remo. Ogun State. Nigeria*

***

It is particularly heartening to attest to a book birthed by months of dwelling in God's presence. I recommend it for all searching for answers for the often-neglected part of the Christian Faith, for those seeking for something different which is vital for the 21st Century Christian. It is a must read!

—**Tunde Olanipekun (MFA)**, Senior Pastor at *The Redeemed Christian Church of God.*

***

When the veil is taken away, only then you see clearly. This is a simple-to-read, yet deep and thought-provoking book. It strips you of all the different layers you have skillfully used to cover yourself and leaves you naked as you make a self-assessment of your life as a Christian. This is a must read for everyone who desires what the Bible calls 1 Peter 1:4, **'an inheritance incorruptible and undefiled and that does not fade away, reserved in heaven.'**

—**Attah Ogbole**

***

The Untouched Part is an essential and valuable piece of work detailing the intricacies of being a Christian, a masterpiece that makes today's Believer more aware of the dangers of conformity to the world. It serves as a guide which encourages the reader to examine oneself as a Follower of Christ...

—**Thomas Booth**

The Untouched Part

Eunice-Pauline Olatunji

Published by KHARIS PUBLISHING, imprint of KHARIS MEDIA LLC.

Copyright © 2020 Eunice-Pauline Olatunji

ISBN-13: 978-1-946277-94-7
ISBN-10: 1-946277-94-0

Library of Congress Control Number: 2020950520

All KHARIS PUBLISHING products are available at special quantity discounts for bulk purchase for sales promotions, premiums, fund-raising, and educational needs. For details, contact:

Kharis Media LLC
Tel: 1-479-599-8657
support@kharispublishing.com
www.kharispublishing.com

God, The Creator of Heaven and Earth, The Creator of time and seasons, The Just One, The Righteous One, The Merciful One, The Consuming Fire, The Giver of ALL good things, The Fighter of my battles, My Love that would not, cannot and will never let me go.

I apologize on behalf of my generation and myself for how we have treated You, how we have reduced You in our hearts to a set of rules, sects and religions, to a topic of contention and debate, and for how we have been spending the time You have given to us on earth, trying to prove Your existence, rather than worshipping and serving You. I apologize, too, for how we have misused the gifts, resources, knowledge, freedom and much more, which You have given unto us. Father of Mercy, Lover of all souls - even the wicked souls - please have mercy upon us all.

Words will never describe how I feel about You... I love You.

Jesus Christ, The Darling of Heaven, Your name brings smiles to my face. Thinking about You fills me with excitement. You are The Champion, The One who gave His life for all men alike; The Savior, The Word, The Wiper of my Tears, my Coxswain, my Comfort, my Hope, my Friend, my Mentor, my Lover, my Husband, my Brother, my Sanctifier, my Purifier, my Redeemer. You are The Commander of my destiny! You saved me and I thank You for saving me. Thank You for caring for me. Thank You for praying even for those who crucified You with their own hands. Thank You for the gift of Your Precious Blood. Jesus, My Breath. My Lifeline, You are Everything to me and I do not know the first thing I will do when I see You. Hug You? Kiss You? Roll and Cry? No power of hell and no scheme of man will ever pluck me from Your Hands.

I am in love with You. I have fallen so deeply in love with You. You are all and more than enough for me.

Holy Spirit, The Truth! You are the real and only deal! You! You! You! My Prayer Partner and Enabler, thank You for putting up with me. Thank You for the Leadings, the Promptings, the Alignments, the Directions, the Enlightenment, the Patience, the Wisdom, the Counsel, the Lightbulb Moments, the Gifts and the Fruits. You are the most effective Life Administrator there can ever be. I love our Secret Place moments.

Thank You.

My Brothers and Sisters in Christ, all readers of this book, I love you. We will finish strong.

~Notice~

As all individuals are warmly welcome to read this book, the intended audience is those who identify as Christians and accede to the authority of the Holy Scripture and its effectiveness as a Life Manual, which is *"God-breathed and is useful for teaching, rebuking, correcting and training in righteousness."* 2 Timothy 3:16

The content of this book is Scripture-heavy. All views of the author are backed up and inspired by Biblical exegesis, and as such, are intended to encourage the reader to refer to the Holy Bible for views perceived as unnecessarily stringent or conservative.

On that ground, there will be no appeal.

Contents

Acknowledgement

- **The Holy Spirit**. When You laid this on me, it was a "wow moment" like no other! I had all sorts of questions, went through different emotions, stopped, continued, stopped, continued… but You led me through it all. You inspired every single letter of this book. You are the real Author and I am grateful to be a vessel. I am honored. I am humbled. Thank You.

- **The Great Men and Women of history who have shaped the world we live in today**. Thank you. I wept reading some of your stories and the sacrifices you paid on our behalf so that we enjoy them so freely today. Faithful servants of God, continue to rest in the joy of our Lord. Thank You.

- **The Great Men and Women of God still with us at the writing of this book**. Thank you. There are too many of you to list individually, all you who have mentored and inspired me personally and vicariously on this pilgrimage. I pray that you all finish strong in Jesus' name. Amen. Thank you. God bless you.

- **My Biological Parents**. Practical Christians. Christians in every sense of the word. Thank you for being the perfect role models as individuals and as a couple. Thank you for investing in and nurturing me over the years, and for inspiring me to be better every day. Thank you for your sacrificial and relentless love to my siblings and me. Thank you for being adopted parents, mentors, and outstanding leaders to many others. Thank you. God bless you.

- **All creators of the various Bible applications and websites.** You have made the best and most unbeatable contribution to technology. Thank you. God bless you.

- **The Redeemed Christian Church of God.** My birthplace and Physical Tabernacle. God bless this great Church of God. It is an honor to be a seed of this family. God bless you.

Foreword

I have known the author of this book for as long as she has lived on the face of this earth, even when she wasn't aware of my existence. In other words, I knew her before she knew me. This makes reading this book and endorsing it a real pleasure.

Oftentimes, we have seen businesses trying to lure us into buying their latest slimming products, presenting us with a "before" and "after" picture of the effects of their product on their customers. They want us to believe that when we try out their product, we will have the same experience. We will achieve our goal. This is exactly how I feel as I read this book. I examine the subject matter and deliberate over the contents of the book, and when I consider the young lady I've known over the years who has authored the book, I can tell there's a before and after picture in the narrative. It is a narrative from someone who has had an encounter with the Living God. As I read this book, I perceive that her desire is to bring other young adults like her to the place of encounter with God, where He will radically change their perception about life and the things that matter most in life.

One is not surprised to see that the author has issued a "notice" to whoever picks up this book. It is not a book for just anyone. You really have to be in the place of the deer panting after the water brooks (Psalm 42:1) to appreciate the message the author is trying to convey. Is it desirable for this generation of young adult believers? My answer is a big "Yes!" I would to God that every believer, whether young or not, will get to "the place in God" where the author has been. It is only when the Holy Spirit leads you there that you can truly appreciate the message being conveyed in *The Untouched Part*. As one who has had the experience of walking with God for over five decades, and still desperately longing for more of Him, I can relate very much with the message of the book.

There's a hunger and thirst after righteousness that we must understand; there is more to our walk with God than going to church on Sunday and having nothing to show for it from Monday to Sunday. In many Christian circles today, the majority speak "Christianese," as if that is all that is required to offer us a free admission into God's eternal kingdom.

Jesus makes it clear that there is a cross to bear to follow Him, and a denial of self or anything that will take His place in our lives. There is knowing Him and the power of His resurrection, and the fellowship of His sufferings that the Apostle Paul talked about, which we can discover as we immerse ourselves in the Word of God.

This is the message the author conveys in this book, which also lends credence to Jesus' words in Matthew 7:21, which says, "not everyone who calls me, 'Lord, Lord' will enter into the kingdom of heaven, but he who does the will of My Father who is in Heaven."

Anyone reading this book will also be aware of Jesus' admonition in Matthew 7:13-14 that "wide is the gate and broad the way that leads to destruction, and there are many who go in by it. Because narrow is the gate and difficult is the way which leads to life, and there are few who find it."

The Untouched Part is a sure read for anyone who truly wants to discover the narrow but exhilarating and liberating way that leads to life, and I wholeheartedly recommend it to all spiritually "hungry" believers who want to experience the extraordinary and superabundant life that we have been called into.

Elewechi Ngozi M. Okike,
PhD, MPhil, MSc, BSc, FHEA, FRSA, FICG, MNIM
Publisher and Award-Winning Author.

Preface

I don't mean to say that I have already achieved these things or that I have already reached perfection. But I press on to possess that perfection for which Christ Jesus first possessed me. No, dear brothers and sisters, I have not achieved it, but I focus on this one thing: Forgetting the past and looking forward to what lies ahead, I press on to reach the end of the race and receive the heavenly prize for which God, through Christ Jesus, is calling us. **Philippians 3: 12-14**

Ever been to a wedding and seen a magnificent cake? I mean, the most breath-taking, mouth-watering, eye-catching edible edifice you could ever imagine right in front of you? And have you ever been waiting patiently until the bride and groom finally cut and share that cake with their guests? Surely, it must taste even better than it looks.

As the wedding party winds down and the hall empties, you notice that this wonder of a creation that you've had your eyes on all the while, has still not been cut. It is just there, sitting pretty, untouched, unshared. Suddenly, you see this cake, which is about seven layers tall, being packed up, just as it is. You are wondering, "Why would they spend money, time, and effort on that cake and not share it among the guests?" Then you go over and ask someone why the wedding cake is being packed up without being shared, and they laugh at you saying, "Dummy, it's just a dummy cake! It's not real."

A dummy cake!? Until that day in 2015, I was not aware that such a thing existed, such a beautiful piece of nothing! That experience became one of the most anticlimactic memories of my adult history. However, God will have nothing happen in our lives, no matter how random or insignificant it may be at the time, which is not a piece of a big picture.

...Hear ye indeed, but understand not; and see ye indeed, but perceive not.

xiii

Isaiah 6:9

A few years later, five years to be precise, in the landmark year of 2020, the message in "The Parable of the Dummy Cake," as it had become, suddenly came alive.

Then He opened their minds so they could understand... Luke 24:45

I realized that I was that cake! I was exactly what that dummy cake embodied – beautifully set up, perfectly laid out, sitting-prettily, eye-catching and …. that was all there was to me; that was all there was to see on this pretty (as I'd been called) young lady.

Our beauty should not come from outward adornment, such as braided hair and the wearing of gold jewelry and fine clothes. Instead, it should be that of your inner self, the unfading beauty of a gentle and quiet spirit, which is of great worth in God's sight. 1 Peter 3:3-4

In an age of the rise of self, self-love, self-care, self-worth, selfies, self-help, self-affirmation, self-awareness and more self, self, self.....**self-destruct**, we are experiencing and living complacently in the spiral of the greatest, silent, deadliest virus in history.

The Epidemic of Personal Branding: The Pandemic of Self!

Introduction

SoulTune: O God of Bethel by Whose Hand[1]

Did you know, in the 1500s, most people got married in June? That was because they took their yearly baths in May and still smelled pretty good by June. However, they were starting to smell a little, so the bride carried a bouquet of flowers to mask the body odor. Thus, we have the convention of carrying a bouquet to this day when getting married!

Did you know this or were you just going with a trend? Are brides still a bit smelly when walking down the aisle? And that's the last you will read about marriage in this book, as it is *not* a book on marriage.

History is life. It gives meaning to everything we see today, do today, hear today and believe today. Many people assume they are enlightened because they have gathered surplus information in a certain field, have substantial years of experience in their vocation, discovered advanced knowledge about a subject matter or perhaps and probably the most asinine of them all, because they consider themselves exposed either by possession of money and investments or some form of travel. Unfortunately, that is simply fantasy and quite mistaken belief.

There is only one path to true enlightenment and that is by going down the dark paths of history and into awareness of the sacrifices of many who have brought us to where we are today.

The lockdown period of 2020, due to the Coronavirus pandemic, introduced a wave of new trends, businesses, lifestyles, habits, and more. A terrific period of time that will certainly go into the annals of history, should the Lord tarry. It brought in the fashionableness of face masks; the normalcy of 10-guest weddings *similar to what the Wedding of the Lamb will be like – a scanty feast - whilst the jamboree in hell will be an overcrowded torment*; important business meetings held over the internet, with *some* joining in from the comfort of their toilet seats; online church, and online learning. We have gained new buzzwords and phrases, including: "new normal," "stay at home," "wash your hands,"

---

[1] Philip Doddridge; O God of Bethel by Whose Hands; (1737).

"lockdown," "social distancing," "sanitize," "send the link," and "stay safe." What a time to be alive!

It was also a year in which there have been many shocking deaths of precious children, women, and men. May all their souls continue to Rest in Peace. Amen.

For me, one of the blessings of the season has been time to know God more by studying His Word, the Holy Bible. As I read, studied, meditated, and dug deeper, I discovered new and fascinating gems. The realness of the Bible is mind-blowing. From discovering random facts, such as Luke was not a disciple of Jesus; to seeing there was first a Deborah *before Deborah*, who is probably never acknowledged in any context; to finding out that Ahithophel, the "Judas Iscariot" of David, was the grandfather of Bathsheba, with whom David committed adultery, ostensibly giving Ahithophel motive for his unsuccessful betrayal of David.

I also noticed the trend between fathers and sons, particularly in the life of Isaac, who told the same lie (*his wife was his sister*) that his father *Abraham* told for the same reason, which was *fear of being killed*; Isaac's son *Esau* got married at the same age (*40*) as Isaac did, to seeing that trickery might have been in Jacob's bloodline. For Jacob did to his father, what his uncle Laban did to him.

The distinction between Pharisees and Sadducees was finally understood: the latter do not believe in resurrection, angels or in spirits, while the former do. Also, the Holy Spirit finally opened my eyes to understand the Book of Jeremiah! I love that book.

The most intriguing part of these discoveries was learning the intricacies about the characters of some of these Biblical figures. I began to play this game where a Biblical figure comes to mind and then I had to say, out loud, one word describing them. For instance: **God** – wow! **Abraham** – sweet! **Jacob** – free-spirit! **Israelites** – stressful! **Moses** – bold! **Daniel** – committed! **Jonah** – ridiculous! **David** – passionate! **John** – cheeky! *My favorite two*: **Peter** – funny, predictable, life-of-the-party, open-book, courageous (it's simply impossible to describe the Apostle Peter with one word!)*;* **Paul** – me! And most importantly, **Jesus** – Love!

I completely fell in love with studying The Word. It gave me the gift of new life *and* enlightenment!

The intrigue heightened my curiosity about some facts which were not in the Bible. For instance, how did my personal favorite, the Apostle Paul, die?

Where are all the churches today, to which he wrote in his time, Rome, Corinth, Galatia, Ephesus, Philippi, Colossae, Thessalonica? One of the most exciting things to do was to carry out further research on some of the Biblical figures and places, to see which of the places still exist today, and how they have evolved: Damascus is now the capital of Syria, Ephesus and Galatia are now Turkey, and Corinth is now Greece, and so on.

At this point, join me in taking a moment of silence and saying a prayer for Turkey, once the grounds on which the Ephesian church lay. Today, as forewarned, Turkey has become a **candlestick out of his place. (Revelation 2:5)** Bishop Hilarion of the Russian Orthodox Church described their recent but *lowest of the-low* action of turning the UNESCO World Heritage site, Hagia Sophia, into a mosque as "a major blow to global Christianity."

You see, Hagia Sophia was specifically constructed some 1,500 years ago as a cathedral under the Christian Byzantine Empire. The World Council of Churches wrote to the Turkish President expressing their "grief and dismay" at such a deplorable action. Pope Francis said turning the revered site into a mosque "saddened" him.[2]

Meanwhile, terrorist organizations, such as the Palestinian Hamas and Muslim Brotherhood, sent their congratulations to the Turkish government for this disheartening move, indicating that the Turkish government must be oblivious to the dire fact that when known and declared terrorist organizations are congratulating them for its "historic achievement", such events can only be the devil's smiling face of approval of stealing, killing and destruction with expedience.

More fascinating discoveries were made which proved that Christianity isn't just the only way to eternal life but it is Truth. Everything we read in the Bible happened exactly as stated. To see that relics such as fragments of the Cross, the sandals Jesus wore on earth, the robe He wore and even a tear drop from His weeping at Lazarus' death still exists was satisfying.

It was also interesting to discover that terms we commonly use today, such as "Trinity," "Sacrament," and "Old and New Testament," were all coined by a scholar called Tertullian, and not by God, as many might instinctively assume.

With the early Christians, martyrdom was a thing of pride. There was an overzealous, competitive attitude towards Christian martyrdom and in

---

[2] https://www.bangkokpost.com/world/1950184/pope-joins-criticism-of-turkey-turning-hagia-sophia-into-mosque

finding joy and fulfilment in obtaining what was called the "Martyr's Crown." For those martyrs, being able to confess Christ in the face of death was the highest accolade of approval. As a matter of fact, the day of a martyr's death was recognized as their birthday, and rightly so, for do we really live for Christ unless we die – to self and to "life?"

A great number of once wealthy people found Christ, and upon their conversions, renounced their earthly wealth and inheritances to focus on spreading the Gospel; some even took oaths of poverty. I began to wonder why, with all these sacrifices and transformative effects, this same Holy Word of God was not having such radical effects on our generation.

Now, why is Christianity merely about amusement, empowerment, nice outfits on a Sunday, self-satisfying Bible verses picked in isolation from the context of their chapters, some charity here and there, but no *actual* effect in the lives of individuals?

Can Christianity be just the same appearance; same dressing-styles; same places visited; same character; same friends; same music, and basically the same lifestyle from before and after? Today, supposedly finding Christ consists in nothing notably different from an addition of God's love and our glorious destinies which He has planned for us. Nor is finding Christ today apart from everyday conversation, with maybe a Bible verse in a profile section to indicate we identify somewhat, albeit nominally, as Christian. Perhaps those are all great acknowledgments, *but* what about **us?**

Of our very selves, our inner-men, our inclinations, desires, thoughts, aspirations, ambitions, reactions, priorities, interests, time-spending patterns, *what* has changed? Why has this once passionate zeal and somewhat fanatical outcome of the Gospel on individuals' lives ceased to have results in our lives? Why, among the young and old, women and men, rich and poor, strong and weak, great and ordinary, boy and girl alike, with no exception, have we not had changed outcomes in our lives? Why has this not occurred among those of us in the "Information Age," when there has been no change in the Word? The same Bible those read long ago is the same Bible we read; it will be the same Bible in posterity for ages to read, until the Lord comes. It is the same Word which *will* remain when this world eventually passes away.

I found the answer as I discovered parts of the Bible I had never seen or heard in my few years of listening to sermons, or my church attendance, or even in counselling. What's more, these people took the Word of God in its entirety and literally. They did not attempt to rationalize, or to align any part with any culture, evolution, or "human freedom." They were *automata* for the

Word. Even centuries and millennia later, the result of this unwavering dedication has produced lasting fruits which we are still studying, which still inspire us, and by which we are being transformed.

What we do in life when we are alive is great, but nothing matters apart from what is remembered of us when we are gone. We are not our lives. Our lives do not last. We are our legacy. Every day we live is a building block of our legacy. If what we do today has no effect on tomorrow, we have merely existed today, but we have not lived. It is not uncommon to hear timeless quotes such as, "Make every day count," "Make hay while the sun shines," and these all point to an inevitable end. Every day is a building block to a firm legacy, which will either last ages or will be forgotten as the few number of guests at our funeral walk away. Not every legacy is good, however, but legacy *is* legacy. Being known for no legacy is *also* a legacy like world famous oldest man, Methuselah of 969 years whose legacy is that he died.

We must appreciate history, for history teaches, history saves, history corrects, history enlightens, and when deeply reflected upon, history humbles. What is more important, we must be grateful to those who have given their time, talents, skills, resources, and lives in recording and preserving these precious records for our undeserved and free learning.

A lot of parts of the Holy Bible have been left untouched, gathering dust over the years. There have been few to no people touching these parts. As time continues to pass and we continue to spiral down the roads of darkness, we are at risk of completely untouching the Word of God; that has no effect on the Word itself, but it is self-driving to death. This untouching of necessary-to-be-touched parts has caused the intended effect of the Word of God, which is a double-edged sword, to produce in our generation a somewhat table knife effect. As a table knife, the Word is just good enough to cut off some unwanted parts and 'spread some butter' on us, as we desire, with us holding the knife as we remain fully in control but that knife is far too blunt to have the effect of the sharpness of a double-edged sword, with its overpowering effect of killing the flesh, will, and desire, with little to no input from the holder.

Welcome to, **"The Untouched Part."** In reading this, you will come across terms such as "SoulTune," the title of a song attached to every chapter of the book. I listened to each "SoulTune" repeatedly as I wrote each chapter, so it embodies the message carried in the chapter.

*Writer's Note refers strictly to thoughts of the writer when writing, and not that of the Author, the Holy Spirit. As the Apostle Paul puts it, *"I speak as a* *man,"* or *"I, not the Lord."*

In five simple *but* deep chapters, we will wipe off the long-gathered dust on some of the untouched but immensely vital parts of this living Word of God to restore its maximum, uncontrollable effect of transmogrifying our entire lives.

Ignorance of the law, in this sense, will not be an excuse for any one of us on *that* Day.

Apostle Paul declared,

> *And indeed, now I know that you all, among whom I have gone preaching the kingdom of God, will see my face no more.*
> *Therefore, I testify to you this day that I am innocent of the blood of all men.*
> *For I have not shunned to declare to you the whole counsel of God.* Acts 20: 25-27

PART A

CHAPTER 1

WHO?

Create in me a clean heart, O God; and renew a right spirit within me.
Psalm 51:10

SoulTune: For the Cause[3]

---

[3] Keith & Kristyn Getty; (2016); For the Cause; Nashville, TN: Getty Music Company, LLC.

HI! I'm Eunice. Very pleased to meet you. Who are you?

How do you answer that question, "Who are you?" Your name? An attempt to think outside the box for a more creative response? Not so quick, we are putting the superficial plateau on hold for a bit.

You see, when the thought of writing a book was laid in my heart, aside from all the brushing off I did, and the mental battles of listing all the reasons why I couldn't possibly write a book: Who am I to write a book? What do I have to say? I mean, I always knew I was going to write a book when I achieved "great" things in life. I knew I was going to write an autobiography, and even had a title for it when I became "successful" and people wanted to know the exciting story of my conquest and journey to victory. So, writing a book was not necessarily the issue. The issue was: Who am I to write a book *now*, at *this* stage of my life? I had not achieved anything extraordinary, there were no awesome inventions, nothing exciting, so why should I write a book?

As it became even clearer that this was something I *had* to do and was in fact *going* to do, I decided I was not going to put my name as the author. I was going to use a pseudonym. I mean, the book was not about me, so there was no need to associate my name with the book. I said, "Eunice," scoffing at myself. *That* same Eunice? Talking about God? What credibility? What track record? I have been, and am, described by different people in different ways, commonly but not limited to: repulsive, arrogant, proud, catty, rude, bipolar, mentally disturbed, lesbian (yes, someone once described me as this to another person), black sheep of the family, so different from her family members, disturbed, child of a pastor, problematic, and there are many labels I might have left out because I'm unable to bring them to memory at this time.

As the heaviness in my heart increased at putting down the message contained here, I decided that I would not put people off with the pressing issues herein by putting my name as the author of the book.

I was walking out of the bathroom on the morning of July 31, 2020, and it came, that voice we sometimes ignore, that voice we sometimes attribute to "something," that voice that makes us wonder if we truly hear it or if it's a figment of our imaginations. The voice of the Holy Spirit came palpably and said to me,

> *But you are a chosen generation, a royal priesthood, a holy nation, His own special people, that you may proclaim the praises of Him who called you out of darkness into His marvelous light.* 1 Peter 2:9

In "***The Parable of the Dummy Cake***" illustrated in the Preface, the Word of God exposed the dummy cake that was my "self." I was not a new believer, nor recently born again, but here I was, looking at the mirror that is God's Word. His Word is the mirror which is not a reflection of the beauty of our mortal bodies, but the mirror which reflects the state of who we really are: Our immortal selves, our hearts, our souls. As my meditation on the Scriptures deepened, the more exposed was the condition of my soul.

I picked up my phone one day and scrolled through pictures, saw times when I had been dressed to the nines, looking very well on-trend, "face beat," "hair laid," even as a "saved" person, and all I could feel was the dry heaves from true disgust, sadness, and confusion increasing in me. The more I saw beautiful pictures of me, the more my stomach turned.

As I reflected on some of the pictures I was looking at, I thought of how, on most Sundays, in getting ready for church, I had set aside two hours for my preparation routine, but still I would be almost running late for the Worker's Meeting, which began at 7:00 am at a church located just five minutes away from home. I recalled how there was no "off-day" for me at work in terms of my appearance. By no means are any of these things wrong. The issue here was that five months into a compulsory lockdown, I had survived without using makeup! I had seen how makeup and my appearance had become an unassuming idol in my life. What was more alarming was when I examined my "self" with Scriptures, I realized I truly had not been saved. "So, if the Son sets you free, you will be free indeed." John 8:32[4]

Could I say to myself that I was free from the need to always look good, to ensure that my physical appearance was in conformity to the beauty industry's standard? Was I free from the chains of materialism? Was I free from the bondage of daily social media usage? Was I free from self-gratification by way of food, TV shows, pampering days, and the like?

Even more alarming was that God, by way of His Word in the Holy Bible, was not seeing me as me. What He saw as me was my heart, my soul, my mind. I searched and searched for places in Scripture where our appearance was fundamental, but everything I found about appearance was directly incongruous with every criterion laid out as beauty standards of our generation. There was no provision for inference on this point, i.e., the Bible is explicit on this matter:

---

[4] Majority of Scripture quoted comes from the King James Version of the Holy Bible. Other versions are used where the translation is easier for a modern-day reader and no doctrinal issues might arise..

Charm is deceptive, and beauty does not last; but a woman who fears the LORD will be greatly praised. Proverbs 31:30

Proverbs 31 is, without contest, the most abused chapter of the Holy Bible by the 21st Century woman. To analyze the above Scripture by parts:

- *Charm is deceptive:* **Charm** (appeal, glamour, loveliness) **is** (certainly, closed to debate or dissent) **deceptive** (a lie, false, illusory).

  The infallibility of this statement is evident in *The Dummy Cake*.

  Test: What response do you get when you ask a lady in a gorgeous pair of high-heeled shoes about the comfortability of the shoes?

- *Beauty does not last:* **Beauty** (qualities pleasing to the sight) **does not** (tried and tested that it never will) **last** (remain, endure).

  The infallibility of this statement will be proven by different tests: *run a search for images of the "stars" of the 20th Century in their prime, placed beside their current appearance, or request a "before" picture from the survivor of a ghastly fire accident.*

- *A woman who fears The Lord:* **Fear** (a mixed feeling of dread and reverence). For anyone to be simultaneously dreaded and revered, the extent of each of those qualities in that person must be known, without illusions or guesses. Our Lord Jesus advised us thus, "And do not fear those who kill the body but cannot kill the soul. But rather fear Him who is able to destroy both soul and body in hell." Matthew 10:28 "and But I'll tell you whom to fear. Fear God, who has the power to kill you and then throw you into hell. Yes, He's the one to fear." Luke 12:5

It is nice to bask in the love, mercy, and faithfulness of our God. We will, however, be engaging in the highest and most irreversible form of delusion if we choose to only know the God who says, "*I have loved you with an everlasting love; I have drawn you with unfailing kindness*" Jeremiah 31:3, and gloss over or forget Deuteronomy 32: 19-20, *The LORD saw this and rejected them because he was angered by His own sons and daughters. "I will hide my face from them," He said, "and see what their end will be; for they are a perverse generation, children who are unfaithful."*

Again, remember that one minute, Uzzah was celebrating before the Lord, singing songs with diverse instruments, and the next minute, the Lord struck

Uzzah outright dead for his seemingly innocent/reflexive spur-of-the-moment act.[5]

Let us be without uncertainty about the attributes of our God and the justice of His Being. We should not mislead ourselves with the grace provided for us through the death of Jesus Christ.

> Hebrew 10:29-31 says *Just think how much worse the punishment will be for those who have trampled on the Son of God, and have treated the blood of the covenant, which made us holy, as if it were common and unholy, and have insulted and disdained the Holy Spirit who brings God's mercy to us. For we know the one who said, "I will take revenge. I will pay them back." He also said, "The Lord will judge His own people." (and reminded us yet again) 31. It is a terrible thing to fall into the hands of the living God.*

C.S Lewis lays it down beautifully:

> *God is the only comfort. He is also the supreme terror: the thing we most need and the thing we most want to hide from. He is our only possible ally, and we have made ourselves His enemies. Some people talk as if meeting the gaze of absolute goodness would be fun. They need to think again.*[6]

"The fear of the LORD is the beginning of wisdom" Proverbs 9:10. It is not the love of God, not the offerings to God, not the acceptance of Jesus Christ as our personal Lord and Savior. When we fear God, we enroll in the School of Wisdom – Level 1. *Until* we FEAR God, we are foolish, ignorant, and deluded.

We cannot fear God unless we know WHY we should fear God. We cannot know why we should fear God unless we know WHO God is. We cannot know who God is unless we dedicate our hearts to a deep, rigorous, daily, life-long, personal searching of the Scriptures, and commit ourselves to ceaseless prayers that we may know Him. He requires this of us and promises that we will find Him.[7]

However, for the most basic reason why we should fear God, Jesus gives us the hint in the verses above: He (God) has the power to kill our bodies *and* send our souls to hell.

Beyond beauty, beyond charm, the woman **worthy** (justified, deserving) to be **praised** (admired, lauded, influential) is that woman who FEARS the

---

[5] 2 Samuel 6:1-6 cf. 1 Chronicles 15:2.

[6] Lewis, C S. Mere Christianity. New York: Macmillan, 1960.

[7] 1 Chronicles 28:9; Jeremiah 29:13; Acts 17:27; Isaiah 45:19.

Lord. (Gavel pounded.)

With this knowledge, is it not rather harrowing that the global beauty/cosmetics industry is worth $507.8 billion US dollars, with a projected value of $758.4 billion US dollars by 2025?[8] Is it not startling that in 2020, the putative youngest self-made billionaire in history, aged 21, garnered a primary portion of this wealth from the sale of cosmetic products?

Do you feel the dry heaves when you ponder the meaning of the word, **Cosmetic**: "*affecting only the appearance of something rather than its substance?*" Synonyms include: superficial, skin-deep, and non-essential. Antonyms include: fundamental, essential, primary. This definition was not picked from a Christian dictionary or the Holy Bible but from the good old Oxford Dictionary of English.[9]

> *When with rebukes You correct man for iniquity, You make his beauty melt away like a moth; Surely every man is vanity. Selah.* Psalm 39:11

As said earlier, we live in an age where we feast and wine on a buffet of all things Self. Self-love, self-care, self-worth, selfie, self-help, self-affirmation, self- esteem and more self, self, self until we **Self-Destruct!**

On self-discovery, rather than God-discovery, Thomas á Kempis in his classic, *Imitations of Christ*, said:

> *You will quickly be deceived if you look only to the outward appearance of men, and you will often be disappointed if you seek comfort and gain in them. If, however, you seek Jesus in all things, you will surely find Him. Likewise, if you seek yourself, you will find yourself—to your own ruin.[10]*

That is noise to the ears of image positivity, self-confidence, and self-discovery preachers, promoting more destruction in an already destructive world.

We are so inebriated with everything "self" that even the celebrated icons of our mass media, with regularity, come forward to say they will need a "break" from it all to *find* themselves; this comes only after they realize they've become shadows of who they were before the lights, camera, and action. We are failing to deal with the growing epidemic of Personal Branding: The Deadly Pandemic of Self!

---

[8] https://www.statista.com/statistics/585522/global-value-cosmetics-market/

[9] 2010, Oxford Dictionary of English, Oxford University Press, España, S.A

[10] THOMAS, & RUELENS, C. (1879). The imitation of Christ; being the autograph manuscript of Thomas a Kempis, De imitatione Christi, reproduced in facsimile from the original preserved in the Royal Library at Brussels. London, Elliot Stock.

C.S Lewis says:

The moment you have a self at all, there is a possibility of putting yourself first—wanting to be the center—wanting to be God, in fact. That was the sin of Satan: and that was the sin he taught the human race…Satan put into the heads of our remote ancestors [was] the idea that they could 'be like gods'—could set up on their own as if they had created themselves—be their own masters—invent some sort of happiness for themselves outside God, apart from God. And out of that hopeless attempt has come nearly all that we call human history—money, poverty, ambition, war, prostitution, classes, empires, slavery—the long terrible story of man trying to find something other than God which will make him happy.[11]

Unfortunately, there was no official title for this malignant virus in the early part of the 20th Century in which C.S Lewis lived. A term was coined in 1997 by a man called Tom Peters. This man-made idol which is faithfully worshipped today is the 21st Century religion: Personal branding. Is it that, or did the Ancient Book have the original term for it? What's that? ***Pride of Life?[12]*** Must be. We will stick to the more familiar term, though.

Personal branding has eased its way into becoming a cultural phenomenon. Accessibility to full courses designed to train individuals in the dramaturgy of "personal branding" is limitless. For clarity, these definitions include:

- **Branding**: The marketing practice of creating a name, symbol or design that identifies and differentiates a product from other products.

- **Personal Branding**: The conscious and intentional effort to create and influence public perception of an individual by positioning them as an authority, elevating their credibility, and differentiating themselves from the competition, to ultimately advance their career, increase their circle of influence, and have a larger impact[13]. Personal branding defines success as a form of self-packaging[14].

Essentially, what we've done is to assume a persona which we reason to be the best presentation of ourselves to everyone *but* ourselves, and to the God who pays no attention to countenance or appearance but looks into the heart.[15] The *Saul Syndrome* as it is called. The response we receive from

---

[11] Lewis, C S. Mere Christianity. New York: Macmillan, 1960.

[12] 1 John 2:16.

[13] https://personalbrand.com/definition/

[14] https://journals.sagepub.com/doi/10.1177/0893318904270744

[15] 1 Samuel 16:7.

individuals who are as "flesh and blood" as we are, whether negative or positive, then determines a "value" we accept and attach to ourselves. It is not uncommon to hear statements like, "I know my worth," "Know your worth," and "I am an influencer."

An entire generation is on board the fast ride of a downward spiral into a non-existent delusion that there is more...more in a certain place, in a certain group of people, in a certain career, and as many more *"certains"* as there are. To look at the shoes of an individual comes with a reflex action of checking if the bottom is red, or if there is a symbol associated with a particular brand to determine whether the wearer is of some "value."

If it so happens that an individual is not living up to a perceived acceptable standard, it is not uncommon for that individual to fall into an emotional state where questions of self-worth and self-purpose are indignantly raised. The prescription for such self-sabotage mind-sets becomes "positive affirmations," or "self-affirmations," with statements creating even more delusions: "I am beautiful," "The world needs me," "I am generous," "I am happy," and a truckload of more philosophical and sophistic psychobabbles.

...Surely my brethren, this should not be. James 3:10

Friend, any solution offered by philosophy, self-help, affirmations, psychiatrists, psychologists, therapists, self-help guides, motivational speakers, transcendental meditation, science, influencers, friends, family, books, experiences, new-age cult etc., outside the foundation of the Solid Rock that is Jesus Christ, *is* sinking sand. It is a house of cards which will crumble. *Time is all it needs.* "*Beware* (be careful*), lest any man spoil you* (that you are not deceived) *through philosophy and vain deceit* (by seemingly clever but hollow ideas and solutions), *after the tradition of men* (they all came from the human minds of our ancestors), *after the rudiments of the world* (elemental spiritual forces of this world), *and not after Christ... for ye are complete in Him.*" Colossians 2:8, 10

How many of us have been taken captive by such seemingly normal ideas? We live in so much evil, but what we fail to realize is, we welcome it, carry it everywhere, spread it, share it, buy it, lie in bed with it, and delight in it. All seems well, so we assume all *is* well. A lot is NOT well. We are living in danger, physical, emotional, intellectual, spiritual, and most importantly, eschatological danger!

Affirmations, for instance, are not an invention of our intellects, neither by the greatest philosophers, nor by science. There is an express provision in the Holy Bible for affirmations. "*This is a faithful saying, and these things I will that thou affirm constantly*" Titus 3:8. What is this "faithful saying" that we are approved to affirm constantly? Found in Titus 2:11 – 3:7. In summary, **Jesus Christ!**

Anything outside of Him, unfounded in Him, attempted without Him, thought without Him, done without Him, tried without Him, not dedicated to Him, not surrounded by Him, not surrendered to Him, not covered by Him, not guided by Him, not sanctified by Him, not purified by Him, and/or not approved by Him, will fail. *Time is all it needs.*

How certain things will be, how unshakable things will be, how firm our lives will be, how fruitful and life-lasting our affirmations will be, if they sound like these: "I will not fail because Jesus Christ never fails;" "In Jesus Christ I live, I move I have my being;" "I am Jesus Christ's masterpiece;" "By the stripes of Jesus Christ, I am healed;" "I can do all things through Jesus Christ, Who gives me strength;" and "I am created by Jesus Christ to do good works." *When we are weak:* "I am strong because of what Jesus Christ has done for me;" "the Foundation of my Life is Jesus Christ;" "My relationships are built on the Solid Rock that is Jesus Christ;" and so on...

Without the "Jesus Christ factor," we are merely spitting into already-contaminated space. No matter how well-meaning we might be, or how *good* we might be, even if we think it in our heads and mean it *that* way in our *heads*, but *verbally* fail to profess the Name of Jesus Christ, we have merely set the hourglass of doom in place. And that hourglass is controlled by the prince of this world. There is only one "I am"[16] and "through Him all things were made; without Him nothing was made that has been made." John 1:3. To leave Jesus Christ out of every one of our *I's*, *am's* and *can's* is to think ourselves equal to Him, and to stand on the sandy foundation that is self. To honor Him as Captain of our lives, works and affairs, is the bold ability to march on, declaring, "greater is HE that is in me than he (it) that is in the world." 1 John 4:4.

With respect to our *personal brands*, why don't we imitate the Greatest Influencer alive? He trended through all of history and is still trending in this present age, just as He *will* in generations yet unborn. It has been 2,000 years and counting, *yet* His Name is called every single second of each day without fail, from the outermost to the innermost parts of the earth, in whatever capacity the utterer might intend. He is The One who lived a perfect, blameless, sinless, scandal-free, spotless life in this same depraved world in which we currently live: *The Man, Christ Jesus.*

---

[16] Exodus 3:14.

Whoever claims to live in Him must live as Jesus did. 1 John 2:6

He gives us the secret of His fame and the only personal branding standard we will ever need: *"Your love for one another will prove to the world that you are my disciples"* John 13:35. Love cannot be taught by any prestigious course: *"for God Himself has taught us."* 1 Thessalonians 4:9; love cannot be killed: for it is as strong as death (SOS 6:6); love cannot go out of fashion: *'Let brotherly love continue'* – Hebrews 13:1; love cannot be quenched even by the mightiest torrents (SOS 8:7), love cannot be faked so it needs no 'verification badge': *"it comes from a pure heart, a clear conscience and genuine faith"* -1 Timothy 1:5; love cannot be commodified (as in made into a commodity). You say 'money answers all things'[17] well, money answers ALL things *except* love. For love is <u>not</u> a thing. Love is life. Love is virtue (sic). Love is God. God is Love.[18] **If a man tried to buy love with all his wealth, his offer would utterly be scorned[19].**

> But anyone who hates a brother or sister is in the darkness and walks around in the darkness. They do not know where they are going, because the darkness has blinded them. 1 John 2:11

> Whoever claims to love God yet hates a brother or sister is a liar. For whoever does not love their brother or sister, whom they have seen, cannot love God, whom they have not seen. 1 John 4:20

Moving on to this fatal obsession with our looks, appearance, and self, what we *do* know from the Holy Scriptures about our image is this: *"Then God said, Let us make mankind in our image and likeness"* Genesis 1:26[20]; we also know, *"I am fearfully and wonderfully made: Your works are wonderful, I know that full well"* Psalm 139:14…. *Unless we don't?* There is absolutely nothing else we need to do for our body, our *fleshly suit,* but *"feed and care for it <u>just as Christ cares for the church</u>"* Ephesians 5:29 and *"exercise/physical training (which is of) <u>some</u> value."* 1 Timothy 4:8

Food, care, and exercise are all we "owe" to our bodies, but as straightforward as it might sound, it is worth determining exactly how we go about these

---

17 Ecclesiastes 10:19.

18 'God is Love' in this context does not intend to equate love as an attribute of God to the personality of God. Love will always be an attribute of God and not his essential nature. We don't worship love. We worship God. For more, see A.W Tozer's Chapter on 'The Love of God' in The Knowledge of The Holy.

19 SOS 8:7.

20 Some schools of thought suggest that 'image' in this verse doesn't refer to the physical but this school of thought and throughout the text adheres to Biblical literalism.

basic duties to our flesh. We again look at the life of *The Greatest Influencer*.

Food for The Body: *"My food is to do the will of him that sent me and to finish his work."* John 4:34. Food, as we know it, was not a priority to Jesus. His first priority was to do God's work, which He had been sent to do. Food should not be chosen over God's work. Again, in the *Sermon on the Mount* recorded in Matthew 5, Jesus tells us not to worry about what we will eat because our lives are more than food. How often do we go to restaurants and ponder and ponder and ponder on the menu? Sometimes we end up ordering it *all*, because we were unable to make a choice. Let us not worry about what we will eat. Jesus reminds us *"food doesn't go into the heart but into the belly and goeth out into the sewer"* Mark 7:19. What we physically eat to curb the stomach's hunger should not be cause for concern, other than what is available. The *Book of Wisdom*, written by King Solomon, in Proverbs 23:20-21 tells us to avoid gluttony and drunkenness. Eating to a state where you can't move is flesh-honoring and frankly, embarrassing.[21]

Again, in the quest to eat right, feel right, or look right, we can become intoxicated with healthy meal plans, eating right, or eating safe, but again, this is flesh-honoring and should be halted. In Luke 10:40-41, Jesus was warmly welcomed into the home of Martha. She was rightfully preparing a lovely meal for the most special Guest Who could ever walk the face of the earth, however, when it became a bother to her that her sister, Mary, was not assisting her, Jesus lovingly advised her, **Martha, Martha, ... you are worried about many things, but one thing is needful and Mary has chosen what is better, and it will not be taken away from her.** Jesus didn't stop her from cooking when He arrived, it was fine and surely would have been pleasing to Him, but the moment it became grounds for concern for Martha, He had to redirect her focus to the **one thing** that mattered, that which cannot be taken away.

Whatever is available to eat, so be it. In the post-Resurrection account of Luke, when Jesus appeared to the disciples, Jesus asks them, *"Do you have anything here to eat?"* Luke 24:41 and He ate what was offered. More than anything, it was to prove that He was human and not a ghost, for additional veracity that He was the same Jesus Christ they had known before He was crucified. He didn't demand a specific meal because it was His last meal on earth, or because He had done this unbeatable human act of dying for us and had to celebrate His victory by having a specific meal. He was offered baked fish and honeycomb. A translation suggests it was left over from what they had eaten. The disciples, in fairness to them being in a state of shock, did not

---

[21] Proverbs 25:16.

remember to offer any food to Him. He asked for it. Either way, He ate what was offered, because eating is a human thing to do, acceding to the fact that He was human. We eat because we are human and nothing else.

Above all else, when we are eating, two things *must* be observed. First, the poor must be remembered, not just in prayers but in action. If there is anybody around us who would be blessed by the food we offer them, we should give it to them. If there is nobody around us, we will need to go out of our way regularly to give food to people, the same quality of food we will eat. In the *Parable of The Rich Man and Lazarus* found in Luke 16: 19-31, this man who had all the earthly wealth one could have, and lived every day in luxury, offered nothing to the poor Lazarus who lay at his gate, wishing only that he could have the scraps left from the rich man's table. As he lay by the rich man's gate, dogs came and licked the open sores on his body, and he died.

The rich man also died and was sent to hell. There, in anguish, he recognized the earthly-poor Lazarus and needed a favor from him as he suffered in torment. The rich man needed a drop of water! Unfortunately, the great chasm that separated hell from Heaven made that impossible, even if Lazarus had wanted to do as the rich man asked. Guess who was earthly-poor Lazarus' spokesman? Father Abraham! The one who produced nations! The most influential man of religion and the one about whom we sing, "Abraham's blessings are mine!" He was the spokesman and host of earthly-poor Lazarus. We don't know whether the rich man was a sinner. We don't know if he lied, stole or was immoral. We don't even know if he donated to big charities and faithfully paid his tithe in the church, but what we do know is that he did not cater to the *poor* man at his gate while he was on earth.

Friend, *practically* and *directly* care for the poor, despite your earthly status, as King David did in 2 Samuel 6:19. David himself, after successfully bringing back the Ark of God into Jerusalem, "gave a loaf of bread, a cake of dates and raisins to each person in the whole crowd of Israelites, both men and women..." You must do so with the same, or even better quality of food *you* will eat.

About the Galatians, Apostle Paul in Galatians 4:14 wrote, "and even though my illness was a trial to you, you did not treat me with contempt or scorn. Instead, you welcomed me as if I were an angel of God, as if I were Christ himself." Jesus endorsed this in Matthew 25:42&45, "For I was hungry and you gave me nothing to eat, I was thirsty and you gave me nothing to drink...truly I tell you, whatever you did not do for one of the least of these, you did not do for me."

Remember, "But when you do a charitable deed, do not let your left hand know what your right hand is doing." Matthew 6:3

Finally, whenever we eat, we must give thanks to Jehovah Jireh. Jesus always began meals by giving thanks to God, at the feedings of the 4,000 and 5,000 (Matthew 14:19, Matthew 15:36), and at *The Last Supper* (Matthew 26:26, Mark 14:22). In the midst of a shipwreck, after going 14 days without any food, due to fear, Apostle Paul urged the people on board to eat rather than starve to death. Despite that they must have been famished and exhausted, "…he took some bread and gave thanks to God in front of them all. Then he broke it and began to eat" Acts 27:35. Sometimes, we get so excited about food, we forget to give thanks. Most times, we just forget and throw the food into our mouths. If thanks could be given to God before eating in a shipwreck, surely, we have no excuse.

A simple prayer of thanks to God who gives us food is all we need to do. We are to acknowledge and give Him glory in everything we do.[22] We don't need to cast and bind the food; Jesus already gave us assurance that as believers, even if we drink deadly poison, it will *not* hurt us Mark 16:18. Everything we could eat has been sanctified by the Word of Jesus, and if we eat with thankfulness, we cannot be condemned about food for which we have thanked God (1 Corinthians 10:30).

Exercise for The Body: The Bible does not tell us anywhere that Jesus had a workout session, but He walked everywhere He went. According to some schools of thought, He walked about 21,500 miles in His lifetime, which is the same as walking around the globe. Also, we know He was not aimlessly walking, "He went about doing good and healing all that were oppressed of the devil" (Acts 10:38).

In 1 Timothy 4:8, Apostle Paul acknowledges that physical training is "of some value but godliness has value to all things." Emphasis here is on *some* in contrast to godliness, which has value to all things *including* our physical bodies.

A workout routine to which we are more dedicated than we are to our spiritual exercises is simply a waste of time. There are benefits to the way we wish to appear, and in some cases, it supplements general health, but it ends right there. We are told that when we work out, our bodies release chemicals called endorphins which trigger a positive, happy feeling in us. Feelings are fleeting. What happens if we are seriously injured, or if we lose our legs and are unable

---

[22] 1 Corinthians 10:31.

to work out? What happens when we are old, gray, and bedridden?

Exercise is excellent for our bodies when done in moderation *and* simply (Jesus walked) through a regular dose of it, but we must not make exercise an idol for our enslavement. It surely must not surpass the amount of spiritual exercises/godliness to which we commit ourselves, because we know that *is* valuable for *all* things, *even* physical fitness: "I have told you these things so that you will be filled with my joy. Yes, your joy will overflow!" (John 15:11).

How then do we train ourselves to godliness? There are exercises for this, too. Just as in physical exercises, our mind tells us to stop at some point, when it gets tough. Still, we continue, because we know that our bodies will thank us later for the results, whether the goal was to achieve a desired appearance or the agility/endurance we've built.

The same principle applies to spiritual exercises. Our senses tell us to stop but our souls will thank us for it now *and* later. As physical exercises take from our inner strength but are good for our bodies, spiritual exercises will take from our flesh's strength and our natural desires but result in an intensive and beneficial spiritual formation.

> *Through suffering, our bodies continue to share in the death of Jesus so that the life of Jesus may also be seen in our bodies...That is why we never give up. Though our bodies are dying, our spirits are being renewed every day. For our present troubles are small and won't last very long. Yet they produce for us a glory that vastly outweighs them and will last forever!* 2 Corinthians 4:10; 16-17

We don't even have it 1% as tough as the Apostles and early Christians did in their days. They were physically beaten, dragged in the streets by bulls, mounted on stakes and burned to death, and living in constant danger for their Christian faith. Above all of them was Our Lord Jesus Christ, who suffered and died alone for the *whole* world. We are blessed not to have to go through those horrifying experiences, so the least we can do is to honor Our Lord Jesus Christ and these excellent men and women of God. We can build up our own spirits. Some of these spiritual exercises include daily study of the Bible, constant prayers in the Spirit, and in our mother tongue, fasting (*not for personal requests but as a regular exercise, just because*), daily reflections, waking up to pray, evangelizing, and periodic personal retreats with God in isolation from family, friends, social media, and so on; we should not regard these as one-off isolated events, but as the name says, exercise – regularly, spiritual exercise.

We must build stamina spiritually, just as in physical exercise, always going a level higher than the last. If we are willing to push harder and do another rep

14

or set at the gym or during our workout sessions, we must be willing to push harder in our godliness. These are things the average 21st Century Christian simply cannot cope with. If we are called by the name, Christians, we *must* live as Jesus did. "Christian" is not a *tick-the-box option* in the religion row of a form. "Christian" is called by Christ, "Christian" is to live like Christ did.

We are happy to justify and stand behind our personal acts that *seemingly* correspond to the fact that Jesus dined with sinners or turned water to wine, but we leave out such parts as, "Very early in the morning, while it was still dark, Jesus got up, left the house and went off to a solitary place, where He prayed"(Mark 1:35); or But Jesus often withdrew to lonely places ["the wilderness" is what the KJV says, but that will terrify the 21st Century Christian] *and prayed* (Luke 1:45); or "After he had dismissed them, He went up on a mountainside by himself to pray and when night came, he was still there alone" (Matthew 14:23); or "They went to a place called Gethsemane, and Jesus said to His disciples, "sit here while I pray" (Mark 14:32), or "After fasting forty days and forty nights, He was hungry"(Matthew 4:2).

To carry out any of these is abominable to us Christians in this age. At best, we might join a corporate fast with a church, or fast when we need something from God, as if fasting were spiritual blackmail by which we are *deceiving our own selves*, and then we negotiate the duration and frequency: "I'll fast until 12 noon." Let us learn, in these untouched parts, from the life of Jesus who went 40 days and 40 nights without food and water. What? 40 minutes *without* our mobile phones?

Care for The Body: "No one hates his own body but feeds and cares (cherishes) for it just as Christ cares for the church" (Ephesians 5:29). Why and how does Christ care for the church?

> *To make her holy, cleansing her by the washing with water through the Word, that He might present it to Himself a glorious church, not having spot, or wrinkle or any such thing but that it should be holy and without blemish.* Ephesians 5: 26-27

This verse is loaded in diverse dimensions. First, we need to *understand why*, as Christians, we *need* to care for the body. What is the goal? To make it holy for *presentation unto God,* Who truly owns it, and to make it *worth dwelling in for the Holy Spirit,* Who lives in us:

> *Or do you not know that your body is the temple of the Holy Spirit who is in you, whom you have from God, and you are not your own? For you were bought at a price; therefore, glorify God in your body and in your spirit, which are God's.* 1 Corinthians 6:19-20

15

It is quite overwhelming to receive and **understand** this free gift of God's mercies and love through the salvation of our souls. The understanding fills us with awe and wonder at how we wretched sinners can call upon the name of God and be saved from eternal damnation. We don't have to work for it. We welcome Him into our hearts, and we receive Him. There are no criteria, there is no standard, there is absolutely NOTHING we need to work at to receive[23] God's free gift of salvation. He promises that He will not, in any way, cast out whoever will come unto Him. We can never fully comprehend this love. (*Writer's note: As I attempted to write this, I was shaking and honestly at a loss for words to put down on the page. It cannot be explained. Help me, Holy Spirit.*)

John Newton calls it *Amazing* Grace. The Apostle Paul calls it, "the *exceeding riches of His grace in His kindness toward us through* Jesus Christ."[24] Charles Spurgeon (1834-1892) calls it *"graciousness ... not a covenant of works or merit which is enduring because grace is the basis, grace the condition, grace the stain, grace the bulwark, grace the foundation, grace the top stone."*[25]

Understand this: We were DEAD in sin. We were running into hellfire, grandly clothed with napalm and gasoline, cruising headlong into darkness and perennial destruction, and doing so, heedlessly and heartily. THEN the Father of all Lights, in Whom there is NO shadow of turning; the One brighter than the sun; the Creator of the universe, heavens and all the earth's land, seas, mountains, air, wind and oceans; the Almighty God; the I AM; the Alpha and Omega; the King of Heaven seated upon His throne, with earth as His footstool; the Holy One of Israel; the Undefeatable Warrior; the Giver of Life, and the wholly incomprehensible One True infinite God, OF-FERED us a gift!

> *What is man that You are mindful of him, And the son of man that You visit him?* Psalm 8:4

A gift? A gift! From Him to us, who are wretched, little, stinking, dead, hope-less, filthy, shameless, rude, entitled, walking dusts. We have a gift directly from Him to us. Written, wrapped, and sealed with His very own blood. A gift of new life. A license into His Kingdom to reign with Him, despite our filth! He gave us His own Son. He didn't give us Abraham or Moses or Elijah – all great men – but no, He gave us His own Bright and Morning Star. Morn-ing Star? MORNING STAR! Not stars as we know them that shine at night.

---

[23] Receiving is one part. Working to remain is a completely different dimension lest we receive in vain. (2 Corinthians 6:1).

[24] Ephesians 2:7.

[25] C.H Spurgeon; Morning & Evening Devotional.

He gave us HIS *Morning* Star, the very Darling of Heaven, Our Lord and Savior, Jesus Christ, to DIE for us. His was a graphic, gory, cursed death on a tree; He was murdered by our very own hands, yet He looked down at us and prayed up for us. His death for our salvation is a permanent, irretrievable gift, for, "*He hath commanded his covenant forever.*" Psalm 111:9

Thanks be to God for His indescribable gift! 2 Corinthians 9:15

"Thanks." Is that *all* we can say? That is all we can say. How do we say it? Do we just murmur, "Thanks," once and keep moving along? No, we absolutely do not.

Suppose you were to receive the best thing your individualistic self could ever desire, and receive, not once, but in a new supply every day. What if you woke up every morning and found your greatest wish was continually sent to you? How would you feel?

Now, what if that gift were given to you from someone to whom you have been so wicked, heinous, contemptible, and brutally mean? What if that were someone whom you stabbed, not in the back but right in their chest, as you looked into their eyes? How would you feel? Would you even be willing to accept the gift? Would you think, perhaps there's a catch to it? If it were food (*hopefully you can dream bigger than that*), would you not think it was poison?

What if you then realized that there was absolutely NO catch to it. The Giver just wanted to give it to you, because they love you and knew your wish (*need*), even if you did not ask for it or tell anybody about it. What if it were just a big wish you knew could never come to pass, so you just locked it in your daydreams and threw away the keys? What if it turned out your Giver just wanted you to be glad every day? What if, no matter how you try to chase after them to thank them, you can never *see* the Giver, because the Giver has travelled to a location you cannot reach? What if your Giver has set up a system through which you are able to receive this gift daily?

So, what about this gift? Every morning, *ta da*, new gift! You know the Giver but cannot get *hold* of the Giver; He's not around and cannot be traced. Even if you wanted to, you cannot even return the gift because there's no return address. What's more, you cannot give your gift to someone else because the Giver has largely and boldly engraved your name on the gift; He has customized it to suit you, and only you, so nobody can ever take it from you. If you decided to drop the gift then and there, never to use it, well, that doesn't change anything. It's still there. Your gift is piling up every day, and it's always that same gift of your greatest wish, delivered to you unfailingly, even before you get out of bed.

17

How do you suppose you will feel when you think retrospectively about all the lies you've spoken about this Giver? How will you feel when you look back and think about all the grief and pain you've caused? Will you feel guilty? Awkward? Ashamed? Sorry? Condemned? Dirty?

Know this: "There is therefore now no condemnation to those who are in Christ Jesus, who do not walk according to the flesh, but according to the Spirit." (Romans 8:1) The Giver loves you and has completely forgotten all that you have done to Him. There is no guilt, whatsoever. The Giver has both given you a gift, and also has taken away the entire burden of your life, past, present and future.

Now imagine that someone comes to you and tells you they had this same, overwhelming experience, and in fact, they are still experiencing it, just as you are. They tell you they've learned to just accept it, live with it, and show gratitude each day to the person who gave it, and the gift keeps coming, to you and to them. What would you do? *I don't know about you, but I would ask immediately*, "How do I show my gratitude? I have been trying to get a hold of Him to *at least* say thank you, because I really do not know what to do? I only know I can never pay the Giver back!"

Then the person laughs and tells you they were just like you, overwhelmed with confusion about how it could be even remotely possible that this was happening *every day*, but they finally found a way to show this gratitude. Then they tell you the way:

> *I beseech you therefore, brethren, by the mercies of God, that you present your bodies a living sacrifice, holy, acceptable to God, which is your reasonable* (reasonable because we can *never* repay what Jesus did for us. Good enough but not perfect) *service.* Romans 12:1

The person then tells you they know where this Giver of daily gifts is, and they are going there! *I don't know about you, but I would leave everything behind and declare*, "I am coming with you right away! I must meet this person!" I would add, "I want to at least have a conversation with Him and ask why and how all this was possible." The person would then tell you that the Giver is the Son of a very powerful and wealthy King. The other person would make it clear that there are strict criteria and procedures for entering their Kingdom, because once you get into their Kingdom, you become royalty, as well.

If all of that happens, you wouldn't have any thought about asking why He kept sending all those gifts to you, because once you enter into the Kingdom, you *will* be overwhelmed with desire and weak with love at what you see. You will be speechless! You will be overcome by the grandeur built with pearls and precious stones, by the brightness, by the perfection, by the splendor, and by the insurmountable wealth showing in streets paved with gold. Everybody will be adorned in pure, bright white, covered with natural glory.

Everything and everyone will be so completely clean; there will be neither stain nor speck in even the most minute places and all of this will happen because the Giver knew you had been looking for Him all along; He was expecting you, He Himself prepared a mansion for you; He is ready to grandly welcome you. Also, you will see many great people you've heard about, but could only dream of ever being near them. They are right there by you, eager to welcome you as a member of their Royal Family. You will also be completely transformed[26] in your appearance and receive your personal crown, customized to only fit your head.

Yet there is a standard to get into this Kingdom. Filth cannot and will not step into the Kingdom. *I don't know about you, but I would desperately inquire,* "What is this standard? I must get in. Please tell me." And you would learn:

> *...not having spot, or wrinkle or any such thing but that it should be holy and without blemish.* Ephesians 5:27

You learn this glorious standard, but *how* do you practically offer your body as a *living* sacrifice? This is a paradox; when something is sacrificed, it is dead, its life is taken. Does that mean you must kill yourself? Exactly *how* will you be able to offer your body as a *living sacrifice* to this Giver, so you can peacefully embrace the gifts He *has* continued to send you, even while you are trying to comprehend all you've heard? The person tells you:

> *Don't copy the behavior and customs of this world, but let God transform you into a new person by changing the way you think. Then you will learn to know God's will for you, which is good and pleasing and perfect!* Romans 12:2

And there you have it, Christian. Nobody is trying to punish you by denying you of your *enjoyment* because you have become a Christian. This is the bedrock of our Christian faith: A *personal* and *visual* understanding of what Jesus Christ did for us on the Cross of Calvary.

Every other thing that flows from this acceptance of Jesus will be "faith expressing itself in love." (Galatians 5:6) and not some burden or set of rules to follow. To become a Christian is to put on an entirely new identity. We do not physically die, but our old way of life and thinking, everything about it,

---

[26] 2 Corinthians 3:16-18.

must die. It is not just comatose; it must die.

Those who belong to Christ Jesus have nailed the passions and desires of their flesh to his cross and crucified them there. Galatians 5:24

Since we do not physically die as long as we are alive in the flesh and choose to be identified as Christian, in whom the Holy Spirit of God dwells, we must "put on the new self, created to be like God is true righteousness and holiness." (Ephesians 4:24) Do we tear our bodies apart? Do we undergo facial reconstruction surgery to have a "new" self? No, we don't, because we are "Not putting away the filth of the flesh but the answer of a good conscience toward God." (1 Peter 3:21). The true new self is a lifestyle change. It is "to be made new in the attitude of our minds."[27] We cannot have a mind of our own anymore, we have a transformed mindset which will, as a result, ultimately and undeniably lead to a change in our external appearance.

There would be an inexhaustible list if we had to name all the things amounting to *not* caring for the bodies entrusted to us, for **wide is the gate and broad is the way.**[28] On the other hand, each individual can carry out a simple, daily, personal litmus test against every activity we do with and to our Temple of the Holy Spirit, to determine if we are caring for it:

-Is it holy?

-Is it blameless?

-Is it without spot, wrinkle, or blemish?

-Is my conscience clear before God?

It is imperative to note that the Bible expressly states one unique and self-standing abomination to the body:

Flee (run away from) sexual immorality. Every sin that a man does is outside the body, but he who commits sexual immorality sins against his own body. 1 Corinthians 6:18

Again, with the distressingly vast assortment of sexual trends in the 21st Century, to list what sexual immorality entails would be impossible. Carry out the personal litmus test, keeping in mind: Sin is death. Sexual immorality is sin against your body. Sexual immorality is suicide. Sexual immorality, though we are yet still physically breathing, is to be a living dead, i.e. a zombie.

---

[27] Romans 12:2.
[28] Matthew 7:13.

The clothes we wear, how we sit down, our personal hygiene, the songs we sing and to which we dance, the places we go, the seemingly mundane things… we should determine if they are befitting the Temple of God's Holy Spirit.

With the use of makeup and cosmetics, clothing, and outward behavior, determine if the Holy Spirit will recognize you. Oh, He sees. The One who formed the eye sees![29]

Tattoos which read, "I love you, Jesus and will die for you," are NOT caring for the body.[30] We cannot love Jesus more than He loves us. If you want to scream *and prove* you love Him, go to the streets of Saudi Arabia with a megaphone and announce it. I *will* come along!

"My body, my choice!" to "feel comfortable" in the flesh, distorts the Temple of the Holy Spirit. Let us remember, the countdown timer began once we were born. We will be summoned, at *any* time, to give account for how we have used that which was loaned to us.

Let us offer it to God. The flesh is a prophet of doom, "Cursed is the one who trusts in man, who draws strength from mere flesh." (Jeremiah 17:5) Dishonorable management of our bodies will bring nothing but shame. "We are insulted and disgraced because the Lord's Temple has been defiled by foreigners." (Jeremiah 51:51) *Time is all it needs.*

Food, exercise, and care are all we owe to our bodies, so we who are called Christians *must* live as Jesus did:

> *He committed no sin, and no deceit was found in his mouth. When they hurled their insults at him, he did not retaliate; when he suffered, he made no threats. Instead, he entrusted himself to him who judges justly. He himself bore our sins in his body on the cross, so that we might die to sins and live for righteousness; by his wounds you have been healed.* 1 Peter 2:22-24

What shall we say about these? What then really matters? What are we here for? How do we use the years with which we've been blessed? Where do we find answers, rest, and fulfilment? What matters?

> *Beloved, I wish above all things that thou mayest prosper and be in health, even as thy soul prospereth.* 3 John 1:2

---

[29] Psalm 94:9.

[30] Tattoos prior to getting saved do not count against you (2 Corinthians 5:17). You are a new being and have come into the Light so do your diligence to stay in the Light (Ephesians 5:8).

Friend, this is the single answer to the problem of every human being on the face of this earth. Health and prosperity in what is our physical self, is a direct product of our soul's prosperity.

Prosper, prosperous, prosperity: *flourish physically, successful, flourish, thrive, go well, progress, advance, make one's mark, fly high.* These are some of the words the lexicon provides as the meaning of prospering.

Anything therefore, of a person, that might appear as such of these words above on the outside can only be disillusioned where the soul of such person is prospering. How do we know if a person's soul is prospering? First, we need to understand what the soul is.

Some confusion commonly arises about the difference between the soul and the spirit. Hebrews 4:12, and 1 Thessalonians 5:23 are parts of the Bible in which the soul and spirit are listed as two distinct parts of our being, so we can conclude that they are not the same. As Christians, we believe, when we accept Jesus into our hearts as our personal Lord and Savior, His Spirit dwells within us. What we know as our spirit, therefore, is the Spirit of God, the Holy Spirit, who is the link between God and ourselves. With regard to our souls, there is a wealth of relevant material out there, but in the simplest term, our soul is the part of us we cannot see or touch, yet it speaks so loudly and directs all our affairs; our soul comprises our conscience, will, emotions, and reflexes, and it is governed by the heart.

Charles Spurgeon expresses a prospering soul as a watered garden, cared for by the Gardener, the Holy Spirit, which is *"enclosed from the waste, walled around by grace, planted by instruction, visited by love, weeded by heavenly discipline and guarded by divine power, prepared to yield fruit unto the Lord,"*[31] but one which is susceptible to becoming parched when it lacks water; when it is parched, all its herbs die, which is the result of the Lord leaving a person.

What we *then* know from Scripture is this, "The human heart is the most deceitful of all things, and desperately wicked. Who really knows how bad it is?" (Jeremiah 17:9) We receive an answer in Jeremiah 17:10, "I, the Lord, search the heart, I test the mind…" and we are reminded in Revelation 2:23 "…I am He who searches the minds and hearts…"

So, we know our hearts are *desperately* wicked. This *"desperately"* connotes the feeling we get when we *really* need to use the restroom but cannot find one or there is not one around. We are then forced to hold in our bowels. You

---

[31] Jeremiah 31:12.

know how you feel? Yes, that is exactly how the heart is *constantly* pressed to do evil. We can hold it in as long as we want, but it *will* come out. When it *does* come out, it will be in the open, it will be embarrassing, and it will be out of our control.

We also know, of *all* things available, the heart is the most deceitful. So, if you've ever said, "The devil is a liar," this is true. He *is* a liar and the father of all lies, but it just might be *your* heart. In various places in the Bible, with regard to each of our hearts, we see such expressions as "Take heed!" "Guard above all else," "With all diligence," and other verses pertaining to our heart. This is because this fist-sized anchor of our earthly life has two parts. One part is the greatest source of evil, "For out of the heart come evil thoughts, murders, adulteries, fornications, thefts, false witness, slanders;" (Matthew 15:19) the other part is the gateway to God, "You shall seek me, and find me, when you shall search for me with all your heart." (Jeremiah 29:13)

We then discover two rather troubling mysteries:

1st Mystery: "Behold, You desire truth in the innermost being and in the hidden part [of my heart] You will make me know wisdom." (Psalm 51:6)

2nd Mystery: "Blessed are the pure in heart, for they shall see God" (Matthew 5:8)

So, our hearts are the most deceitful of all things but God desires truth from our hearts before we can get wisdom from Him who is the only Source of Wisdom! (Romans 16:27; 1 Timothy 1:17) It is not our lips, not our heads, but it is from this same most *deceitful*, heart! Wisdom is the principal thing in life,[32] so we *need* wisdom from God to stop walking in foolishness, but He will *not* give wisdom to a deceitful heart.

Our hearts are desperately wicked, as well, but *only* the pure in heart *will* see God. So, somebody can look clean, can play the part, can speak the part, can act the part, can be called the part, can seem the part, BUT only the pure *in* heart will see God!

> But the LORD said to Samuel, Do not consider his appearance or his height, for I have rejected him. The LORD does not look at the things people look at. People look at the outward appearance, but the LORD looks at the heart. 1 Samuel 16:7

Ultimately, we realize that we cannot assume we know anybody, despite the halo around them. As the saying goes, "Do not judge a book by its cover."

---

[32] Proverbs 4:5.

(Writer's note: Is this not how the Bible is judged? People see it's a Bible and then scorn it, calling it "a book of fiction," "the boring book," "the old people's book." Then they ignore it and walk in complete darkness, living their lives without the Manual for Life. This Holy Book of Truth, Wisdom, Food and Life! Have mercy, Lord). No one will **ever** truly know any other person but God. Why, then, do we waste our energies and distress ourselves with an already lost battle? Why do we focus on appearance, fall for appearance, envy appearance, adore appearance, judge appearance –rightly or wrongly? Are we not told this, repeatedly?

Let everyone guard against his neighbor; do not trust any brother, for every brother deals craftily, and every friend spreads slander. Jeremiah 9:4

She weeps aloud in the night, with tears upon her cheeks. Among all her lovers there is no one to comfort her. All her friends have betrayed her; they have become her enemies. Lamentation 1:2

Don't trust anyone—not your best friend or even your wife! For the son despises his father. The daughter defies her mother. The daughter-in-law defies her mother-in-law. Your enemies are right in your own household! Micah 7:5-6

Therefore, judge nothing before the appointed time; wait until the Lord comes. He will bring to light what is hidden in darkness and will expose the motives of the heart. At that time each will receive their praise from God. 1 Corinthians 4:5

Most importantly, why do we work so hard on our appearances, when the real work that *needs* to be done is solely on us and **in** us? The real work is on *our* own hearts - on this lethal ammunition within us. Seeing God depends on us knowing our hearts, purifying our hearts, turning our hearts to truth to see God. Yes, to see God depends on us!

O wretched man that I am! Who will deliver me from this body of death? Romans 7:24

Isn't this a true heart's cry? Who will deliver us from this prophet of doom? How do we see the Almighty God, YHWH[33]? How do we see this God, in His glory, robed in honor and majesty, this God whom we've believed in and some men say does not exist? We know, beyond all reasonable doubt, this

---

[33] Sic. Called the Tetragrammaton or Four Letters, YHWH is the exact way God revealed Himself to Moses as recorded in the Masoretic Text. Although we now spell and pronounce it as 'Yahweh', Adonai or Elohim, Biblical scholars agree that this was intentionally given to Moses this way *without vowels* to embody the manifestation of God's Holiness, making it hard for humans to pronounce His Name as none of us was worthy to call His name. 'Thou shalt not take the name of YHWH your God in vain' was best fulfilled if the name was NEVER spoken but thank God for JESUS!

God LIVETH, beyond circumstances and feelings.

I thank God through Jesus Christ our Lord. Romans 7:25

Excellent! We have found *the* Answer – Jesus Christ. How long do we have to do this? Can we begin when we have a bit more life experience and learning? We just got saved. Can we study our Bible a bit more because we are still struggling to understand it? We have the *most* demanding career and family, so can we have a schedule for this work that must be done in our hearts?

LORD, remind me how brief my time on earth will be. Remind me that my days are numbered— how fleeting my life is. Psalm 39:4

Let's recall this story from *2 Kings 9: 30 – 35*, using The Message[34] translation for its optimum visualization:

- EXPOSITION: **When Jezebel heard that Jehu had arrived in Jezreel, she made herself up—put on eyeshadow and arranged her hair—and posed seductively at the window. When Jehu came through the city gate, she called down, "So, how are things, 'Zimri,' you dashing king-killer?"**

- RISING ACTION: **Jehu looked up at the window and called, "Is there anybody up there on my side?" Two or three palace eunuchs looked out. He ordered, "Throw her down!"**

- CLIMAX: **They threw her out the window. Her blood spattered the wall and the horses, and Jehu trampled her under his horse's hooves.**

- FALLING ACTION: **Then Jehu went inside and ate his lunch. During lunch he gave orders, "Take care of that damned woman; give her a decent burial—she is, after all, a king's daughter."**

- ALAS: **They went out to bury her, but there was nothing left of her but skull, feet, and hands. They came back and told Jehu. He said, "It's God's word, the word spoken by Elijah the Tishbite: In the field of Jezreel, dogs will eat Jezebel. The body of Jezebel will be like dog-droppings on the ground in Jezreel. Old friends and lovers will say, 'I wonder, is this Jezebel?'"**

What a terrifying, tragic, anticlimactic, troubling, brutal, sickening, bloody,

---

[34] *The Message* (the Bible in contemporary language). 2005. Colorado Springs, CO: NavPress.

shameful, gruesome death to Queen Jezebel, the once-most-powerful woman in Israel! Born into royalty, this Phoenician princess, with just a threat, sent through a messenger by word of mouth *(not a letter, not evidence to prove she actually sent it)* to the great Prophet Elijah, who had called down fire from Heaven. Jezebel's message caused him depression and he prayed for the end of his life! What a miserable end for Jezebel, without even a decent burial. *The Tynedale Life Application Study Bible* comments adequately on this event:

> *Jezebel's skull, feet, and hands were all that remained of her evil life—no power, no money, no prestige, no royal finery, no family, no spiritual heritage. In the end, her life of luxury and treachery amounted to nothing. Power, health, and wealth may give you a false sense that you can live forever. But death strips everyone of all external security. The time to set your life's course is now, while you still have time and before you become set in your ways and your heart becomes hardened. The end will come soon enough.[35]*

How did the greatest King who reigned on earth summarize it again? "Vanity of vanities! All is vanity." (Ecclesiastes 1:2)

When we reflect on these rather petrifying but untouched parts of the Holy Bible, we realize that our plans, dreams, hopes, desires and even our lives are ALL at the mercy of God. Then we realize there is only one singular remedy we can apply to ourselves: sacrifice. Self-sacrifice.

How does one do self–sacrifice? We have two options:

> *Whosoever shall fall upon that stone shall be broken; but on whomsoever it shall fall, it will grind him to powder.* Luke 20:18

We either fall and be broken or stand and be crushed.

Basically, each human being on earth, Christian or non-Christian, *will* go through either of the processes above. We can make that intentional decision to fall by ourselves. It is less of a shock, the broken pieces are not wasted, they just need to be put back together by somebody other than us, because a broken vessel can do nothing of its own accord.

How do we fall on Jesus for this brokenness? With hot tears, we fall on our knees with hands lifted high or face flat down, crying out, 'Have mercy upon me, O God, according to thy loving-kindness, according to the multitude of Your tender mercies, blot out my transgressions." (Psalm 51:1)

---

[35] Life Application Bible: New Living Translation. Wheaton, IL. Tyndale House Publishers, 2004.

This life-transforming prayer is the first verse of the *Miserere*[36], the prayer King David prayed unto God after his legendary double sin – adultery and murder – which had offspring: lying, theft, leading another to drunkenness… He went on to plead, "Create in me a clean heart, O God, and renew a steadfast spirit within me." (Psalm 51:10) He had sinned with his body, but prayed for a new heart, not a new reproductive organ. He knew the solution to his wretchedness was a new heart. He went without food and lay all night on the bare ground, weeping nonstop for seven days, despite pleas from even the elders of his household.[37]

"I haven't committed murder or slept with any person's spouse!" This is the ultimate anti-God state of mind, resulting in spiritual death, because "all have sinned, and come short of the glory of God." (Romans 3:23) David knew well that it was not Uriah the Hittite whom he had sinned against, it was the Omniscient God, "against You, You only, have I sinned, and done this evil in Your sight…" (Psalm 51:4) If we measure our sin based on its visible effect upon our fellowmen, we will *never* be right with God. We must always plead for mercy from God. It is more than enough.

Before this incident, David had no cause to bitterly repent. He had been in considerably favorable standing with God since childhood. He had been anointed as King on a random day, unexpectedly. He had killed a lion and a bear with his bare hands at a young age and was a diligent shepherd. He was a good, caring son to his father. He had defeated the otherwise invulnerable, nine-foot tall Philistine, Goliath. He had ascended Saul's throne after God rejected Saul, even though he was not the rightful heir by custom.

David also had been delivered from Saul's sword multiple times, and God corroborated these blessings he enjoyed through Prophet Nathan, "I anointed you king over Israel, and I delivered you from the hand of Saul. I gave your master's house to you, and your master's wives into your arms. I gave you all Israel and Judah"…*and how spoiled was David by God? He added…* "and, if all this had been too little, I would have given you even more." (2 Samuel 12: 7-8)

There is nothing God would not have provided to satisfy David; despite that, David, like any other human, got entangled in multiple sins. No matter how well your life seems to be going, no matter how much God has blessed and lifted you, if you have never fallen on Jesus to be broken, even as a nominal Christian, beware! Your crushing might be ever so powdery.

---

[36] Psalm 51.
[37] 2 Samuel 12:16-17.

We must all go through this confession and genuine repentance episode *multiple* times in our lives. Not *just*[38] once by a mere mumbling of words repeated after someone. We must fall on Jesus and have our hard hearts broken into multiple, tiny pieces. Crying tears until we can barely breathe, while pleading for God's saving mercy.

If you have never done this, maybe because you found God early, or things seem to be going well, or you are a "good" person, beware! "Let him who thinks he stands take heed lest he fall." (1 Corinthians 10:12)

C.S Lewis has the perfect synopsis of this:

Now quite plainly, natural gifts carry with them a similar danger. If you have sound nerves and intelligence and health and popularity and a good upbringing, you are likely to be quite satisfied with your character as it is. 'Why drag God into it?' you may ask. A certain level of good conduct comes fairly easily to you…. Everyone says you are a nice chap and (between ourselves) you agree with them. You are quite likely to believe that all this niceness is your own doing: and you may easily not feel the need for any better kind of goodness. Often people who have all these natural kinds of goodness cannot be brought to recognize their need for Christ at all until, one day, the natural goodness lets them down and their self-satisfaction is shattered…If you are a nice person—if virtue comes easily to you—beware! Much is expected from those to whom much is given. If you mistake for your own merits what are really God's gifts to you through nature, and if you are contented with simply being nice, you are still a rebel: and all those gifts will only make your fall more terrible, your corruption more complicated, your bad example more disastrous. The Devil was an archangel once; his natural gifts were as far above yours as yours are above those of a chimpanzee.[39]

And I will destroy her vines and her fig trees, whereof she hath said, these are my rewards that my lovers have given me: and I will make them a forest, and the beasts of the field shall eat them. Hosea 2:12

Every good gift and every perfect gift is from above, and comes down from the Father of lights, with whom there is no variation or shadow of turning. James 1:17

Never mistake that anything "good" you have is from any source other than God Himself.

Even if it was a long time ago, you went through this bitter, yet life-renewing process, you must have cause to do it again. He will never reject a broken and

---

[38] Not just that but the added process of a genuine, personal and bitter repentance from our sin.

[39] Lewis, C S. Mere Christianity. New York: Macmillan, 1960.

contrite heart.[40] Never. Keep falling on Jesus to break you. His mercies are new every morning[41] so why rely on "stale" mercies? If you want to keep God close to you, remain broken-hearted in Christ as an offering to Him; "Then You shall be pleased with the sacrifices of righteousness, with burnt offering and whole burnt offering; then they shall offer bulls on Your altar." (Psalm 51:18)

There is absolutely no other process to this. Your offerings, tithes, good deeds, and ministry will be mere charity to men, but those are *certainly* no "credit deposit"[42] with God, because "the sacrifice of the wicked is an abomination to the Lord" (Proverbs 15:8) and He says, "Add your burnt offerings to your other sacrifices and eat the meat yourselves! For I did not speak to your fathers, or command them in the day that I brought them out of the land of Egypt, concerning burnt offerings or sacrifices." (Jeremiah 7:21-22)

Even more troubling is this glaring fact: Now - in our generation - more than ever in history is the increasing number of men and women 'of God' who are dropping like flies from grace. To be saved once is *not* to be saved all. To know God once is not to know God all. There is no doubt that they started on the right track with the right intent, the right call, and the dedication. However, as long as we are in this dust of a flesh, we must never forget, "woe is me! for I am undone; because I am a man." (Isaiah 6:5)

We must remember, at the time Isaiah made this statement, he wasn't a "sinner," he was already a great prophet of God, publicly denouncing sin and its consequences. Isaiah knew, however, that to be in flesh and blood without God is to be in ruin. This is the reason that consistently crying out to God, pleading for His mercy, is not only necessary, but it is the *only* way we can victoriously complete our earthly sojourn.

Throughout the Psalms, we see how much David depended on God's Word, mercy, grace, love, deliverance, and salvation. Of course, he was forgiven after his sin with Bathsheba, and he was given the precious gift of Solomon through her. The ultimate consequence of his sin - the sword in his home and amongst his sons - remains until this day in present-day Israel. *"All have sinned and fallen short of God's glory."* The world around us, everything we see, is a result of one man's sin, and we were born with that same blood (Acts 17:26). In John Bunyan's *The Pilgrim's Progress*, the protagonist, Christian, although a devout man of faith, bore the burden of his sin a very long way in

---

[40] Psalm 51:17.
[41] Lamentations 3:22-23.
[42] Philippians 4:7.

his pilgrimage, until he came to the cross, and he even had to face a final storm before entering the Celestial City. It is never over *until* it *is* over. It is not finished until, "It is finished."

This is why we must walk the face of this earth soberly, circumspectly, and introspectively, so we are not crushed (God forbid!) by the Cornerstone. There *will* be consequences for our sin because justice is an attribute of God's eternal Being. He is a true and righteous God. *"His justice upholds the order of the universe and guarantees the safety of all who put their trust in Him."*[43] If He were not just, He would not be trustworthy, but as just as He is, He *is* merciful. In *Jeremiah 16:14-15* we see God's beauty, not just in the power exhibited in His deliverance of the Israelites from Egypt, but much more in His ability and willingness, i.e., His *mercy* to restore them to the land He gave them after exile. God's grace is sufficient to see us through our pilgrimage. THIS and only this is the reason for the bountiful supply of God's grace: To see us through, not as a license to sin!

What shameful, blasphemous sermons are preached these days! We are not slaves to sin anymore, but since we live in the flesh, in a sinful world, ruled by the prince of the power of the air[44], we are susceptible to temptations from which we are to RESIST and FLEE! And God's grace *will* see us through the fleeing process because we are so weak in our human nature and can only do anything through God's grace! (Romans 6 [the whole chapter]; Galatians 5:13).

If the day you had this bitter repentance is now a somewhat distant and fond memory, the good old days of "being saved," take heed. *To be saved once is not to be saved all.* Many have departed from the faith and pierced themselves through with many sorrows.[45] The *joy of salvation* [46]should be renewed daily. It is just knowing that our hearts are in the hands of Jesus, and we have pleaded for and received God's refreshing mercies.

The writer of the classic Christian hymn, *Come Thou Fount of Every Blessing*, Robert Robinson, an 18th Century pastor, penned these words as part of that hymn, "Prone to wander, Lord I feel it.*"* He knew, as flesh and blood, that he was at the mercy of the vulnerability of wandering from the Faith. Unfortunately, this prophet, indeed wandered from the Faith. At first, he went from one kind of denomination to another, Methodist then Baptist, and then,

---

[43] Tozer, A W. The Knowledge of the Holy: The Attributes of God: Their Meaning in the Christian Life. Harrisburg, Pa: Christian Publications, 1961. Print.
[44] Ephesians 2:2.
[45] 1 Timothy 6:10.
[46] Psalm 51:12.

Unitarian. Alas, shortly before he died, as he was riding in a stagecoach one day, a lady sat next to him and she happened to be humming the very hymn this man penned at the age of 22.

She asked him what he thought about the hymn, not knowing he was the author. He responded with tears, "Madam, I am the poor, unhappy man who wrote that hymn many years ago, and I would give a thousand worlds, if I had them, to enjoy the feelings I had then."[47] How he eventually ended up before dying isn't clear, but what a testimony! In this world that is filled with roaming demons of darkness, we must stay very, *very, very* close to the semblance of beauty and light (2 Corinthians 11:4).

In Saul's case, God's spirit had rejected him, ejected him from his throne and departed from him, but Saul carried on business as usual, oblivious to the fact. His servant had to point out to him that an evil spirit was troubling him. (1 Samuel 16:15) Eventually, as it could only have happened, Saul died a weak, defeated, Judas Iscariot-style death; he took his own life.[48] What would have happened if tall, handsome, rich, powerful King Saul had acknowledged his sin before God, pleaded for mercy, genuinely repented, and humbly accepted the consequence of his sin by surrendering the throne to David? Even when he was reproved by Prophet Samuel, Saul was only concerned about his "personal brand," so rather than plead bitterly for mercy, he said to Samuel, "I have sinned; yet honor me now, please, before the elders of my people and before Israel" (1 Samuel 15:30)

This man, this King Saul, did not even care about himself, he only cared about how people viewed him. He was told in plain terms that God had rejected him from the throne and had given it to someone better than him but the sawdust of pride and personal branding had completely filled his ears. Saul still wanted to make that public appearance. What a shame to be so deeply-entrenched in a prideful, anti-God state of mind, entangled in a web of self, having chosen to stand to the end, rather than willfully falling for brokenness. Saul ended up getting ground to powder! These things are written for our sake, for our knowledge. We are blessed to have access to these timeless principles of life so that we can take heed.

Samson had a rather similar ideal, albeit with a different end from Saul. All was going well for undefeated warrior Samson, until *President Flesh* called him to work for it. So, he awoke from his sleep, and said, 'I will go out as before, at other times, and shake myself free!' But he did not know that the LORD

---

47 http://www.hymntime.com/tch/bio/r/o/b/i/robinson_r.htm
48 1 Samuel 18-30.

had departed from him." (Judges 16:20)

Samson was captured by his enemies, had both his eyes gouged out, and was paraded around as a ringmaster. However, "Samson prayed to the LORD, "Sovereign LORD, remember me. Please, God, strengthen me just once more, and let me with one blow get revenge on the Philistines for my two eyes." (Judges 16:28) Despite being saddled with the consequence of his sin with blindness and a great life cut short, Samson remembered his God and still finished strong, killing more men than he had ever killed in his lifetime at his death.

To be saved once is not to be saved all. To know God once is not to know God all. "If we confess our sins, He is faithful and just to forgive us our sins and to cleanse us from all unrighteousness." (1 John 1:8) He will cleanse us, for He is a God who is rich in mercy! His mercy is not for Him, His mercy is for us. He made us to exist within Him, not outside of Him. He needs no double-facedness, He needs no connoted personal brand. He needs no keeping up of appearances. He is the One who sees the heart and knows it all.

When He forgives, He forgets. He keeps no record of our sin, otherwise, none of us will or ever could stand. He wipes our slate clean, forever sees us with loving, tender eyes; He is a God of compassion. He is the Creator of all things and all men – good and evil. Like the Prodigal Son, when we come to our senses, our genuine repentance and cry warrants a Heavenly feast, a celebration of resurrection -from death to life, from lost to found.[49]

But If we claim to be without sin, we deceive ourselves and the truth is not in us... we make Him out to be a liar and his word is not in us. 1 John 1: 8 &10

When we are restored the joy of His salvation, the only way, like David, never to fall into that sin again is to promise God that we, "will teach transgressors Your ways, so that sinners will turn back to You" (Psalm 51:13), this serves as a personal testimony of our freedom from the bondage of sins we gladly partook and we permanently overcome by our testimony (Revelation 12:11). Paul testified, "Even though I was once a blasphemer and a persecutor and a violent man, I was shown mercy because I acted in ignorance and unbelief... But for that very reason I was shown mercy so that in me, the worst of sinners, Christ Jesus might display his immense patience as an example for those who would believe in him and receive eternal life." (1 Timothy 1: 13&16)

Broken or crushed? Fall or fallen upon? What happens when one is crushed

[49] Luke 15:11-32.

is simple: You are gone, never to be recognized or remembered. In contrast, when we fall and are broken into uncountable pieces, the joys, the slow, long-sustained process of perfection, are such a diverse, transforming, passionate, emotional, intense journey. That is why we cannot help but capture, in just a few inadequate words notwithstanding, that process done by the Great Potter, Himself. He is forever molding, ever breaking, ever re-shaping, ever re-filling, ever-redirecting us, His clay. His ways are beyond discovering; therefore, no flesh nor blood will ever fully explain this blossoming process; it is a joy that only a heart so broken can know. It is a joy unspeakable.

It is a rather humorous, yet paradoxical bliss. When one is in sin, the list is endlessly diverse. Mankind innovates new kinds of sin day after day. (Romans 1:30) To create a list of sins is impossible, but one could safely say, "Sin *is* sin," and will be wise to flee from all appearances thereof. The way is very wide, pluralistic, assorted, and luxurious; there is more than enough room to carry on. Still, at the end of it all, when all is said and done, they are destroyed in a second. It is as though they were never on earth. Their end is summed up as, *Eternal Destruction.* "For the wages of sin is death." (Romans 6:23)

Be that as it may, for the weary Pilgrim fallen on Christ, their way on earth is simple. Precisely, it is called Love to God and to men. That single word captures the Pilgrim's instruction on earth. However, the process of breaking in love, growing in love, being broken in love, pruning in love, loving on Love, overflowing with love, the end for those who finish strong, to describe it is yet impossible and will remain so for eternity but to safely ascribe a term, we declare, 'Glory to Glory'. A profound, terrifying, yet glorious mystery, as it is laid out in the Book of Truth, "No eye has seen, no ear has heard, no heart has imagined, what God has prepared for those who love Him." (1 Corinthians 2:9)

What is the effect on earth of this Holy falling on the heart of Man?

> *I will give you a new heart and put a new spirit within you; I will take the heart of stone out of your flesh and give you a heart of flesh.* Ezekiel 36:26

A new heart given, means death to the old heart. Not a physical death, an inner death. This is necessary because, "what you sow is not made alive unless it dies." (1 Corinthians 15:36) We sow our hearts to Jesus as a seed for Him to nurture, blossom, tend, prune, adore, and to completely own. A seed planted cannot care for itself. Someone needs to be dedicated to its nurturing.

It is the same way with our hearts. It is making our hearts "useless" for Jesus. It is abiding in Him blindly, hopelessly, foolishly, and helplessly. This is a mortification of our flesh and its desires, because we know that "flesh and blood cannot inherit the kingdom of God." (1 Corinthians 15:50) In essence, we are all born into this world dead, so until we surrender to the Source of Life, we remain *walking dead.*

As we sow our lives down in dishonor, bondage, weakness, tears, and shame, we are raised into honor, freedom, strength, joy and glory. Without fail, this has been the same result across earth for those who fall upon Jesus. It is the only consistent and common factor with His seeds all over the world.

> *They that sow in tears shall reap in joy. He that goeth forth and weepeth, bearing precious seed, shall doubtless come again with rejoicing, bringing his sheaves with him.* Psalm 127:5-6

Although this surgery called, "Circumcision of Heart,"[50] to which we submit ourselves, is only and all spiritual. We don't see the blood, knives, masks, or scissors; we don't even receive the anesthetic, yet the result is also a spiritual one called "Regeneration" (being 'born again[51]). Because we are completely exempt from the surgical process itself, having absolutely nothing to do with it, sometimes, we might wonder if it is happening, or if it has happened. There might be signs that it is happening in the physical world from time to time, through pain, loneliness, distress, brokenness, sadness, disappointment, loss, delay, and confusion.

When these occur after we have fallen on Jesus, we are going through a process. It is not happening physically, but His Spirit is at work in us. No surgery is without pain. The physical manifestations of this process are those things which leave us with pains in our hearts – Brokenness of Heart, Humility of Heart, Contrition of Heart – not physically, but spiritually.

However, the *proof* that this surgery took place is also *evidenced* in the physical world, rather shockingly, to us, and eventually to our fellowmen, *by* physical results. If the result of being born again is not evidently, clearly, and beyond all reasonable *doubt* seen in *some* measure, then *no* surgery has taken place. *Some* is emphasized because this is not a one-off process.

As Paul said, "being confident of this very thing, that He who has begun a good work in you will complete it until the day of Jesus Christ." (Philippians 1:6) There must be no pressure placed on ourselves nor accepted from external man, for perfection or for a complete work. Completion is to die. While we remain surrendered in Christ, and are in flesh and blood, we *will* be

---

[50] Romans 2:29.
[51] John 3: 1-10.

34

in the Operating Room (OR).

To be so uncomfortable during the surgical process, and to step out from the OR, is to come out mid-surgery. You are barely conscious; you are naked, bloodied, disillusioned, drugged and still sick. If anything, you are worse off than when you lay on that surgical table before the operation began. This is why we are reminded, severely and without mincing words, about the dangers of backsliding and our eventual fate if we do. By the Almighty God, Yahweh, the Lord God of Hosts:

Your own wickedness will correct you and your backslidings will rebuke you. Know therefore and see that it is an evil and bitter thing that you have forsaken the LORD your God. And the fear of Me is not in you. Jeremiah 2:19

By Solomon, the wise king:

As a dog returns to his own vomit, so a fool repeats his folly. Proverbs 26:11

By Bildad (Job's friend):

The same happens to all who forget God. The hopes of the godless evaporate. Their confidence hangs by a thread. They are leaning on a spider's web. They cling to their home for security, but it won't last. They try to hold it tight, but it will not endure. Job 8:13-15

By our dear Lord and Lover of our Souls, Jesus Christ:

No one, having put his hand to the plow, and looking back, is fit for the kingdom of God. Luke 9:62

By Apostle Peter:

For if, after they have escaped the pollutions of the world through the knowledge of the Lord and Savior Jesus Christ, they are again entangled in them and overcome, the latter end is worse for them than the beginning. For it would have been better for them not to have known the way of righteousness, than having known it, to turn from the holy commandment delivered to them. 2 Peter 2: 21-22

These are frightening passages to the heart, therefore, once we surrender, we must *stay* surrendered, and continue lying flat for that surgery to be completed, until that terrible yet great day of the coming of our Lord, Jesus Christ. We are in a process, a lifelong process. There is no timeline for the surgery. The only condition is to "abide." (John 15:4) The world will accept you back if you turn back, because the way is wide enough for all. but it will hate and not trust you for your instability. Besides, you will be drenched in blood, incoherent, and with the appearance of a madman, and no human will want to be around you, except to have a good laugh and mocking wonder. We can call this the *Demas Disorder.*[52]

> ***Writer's Note:** *Demas was a fellow worker with Paul and in Colossians 4:14, Paul wrote that Demas was sending his greetings to the Colossian church. Also, in the letter to Philemon, in 1:24, Paul referred to Demas as sending his greetings. All was well and good at these points. However, by 2 Timothy 4:10, Demas had deserted Paul because he fell in love with the world. So, I, the writer, have coined both terms, 'The Demas Disorder' and 'The John 666 Syndrome' [in reference to those who left Jesus after hearing His teachings in John 6:66] as a way of identifying backsliders or those who turn aside from the Faith i.e. backsliders. So, all those who were once in the light but have turned back into darkness are suffering from the Demas Disorder or have been struck with the John 666 Syndrome. May I, the writer, not be a victim of these hopeless diseases in the name of Jesus Christ. Amen.)*

Sir Thomas More, a man of rare and unmatched integrity, under King Henry VIII'S reign as British monarch, refused to sign the 1534 Oath of Succession. The Oath provided a repudiation of the Pope as the head of the Church of England, instead giving authority to the King as head of the Church. The Oath also annulled the King's marriage, allowing him to divorce his wife and legally marry a second wife. Refusal to swear to this oath was a treasonable offense, punishable by execution. Sir Thomas More, a man for *all* seasons, however, refused to back down from his refusal stance because his Christian faith directly contradicted the Oath. He was eventually beheaded for it.

In the days before his death, with his execution looming, his beloved daughter, Margaret, pleaded with him to at least say he accepted the Oath with his mouth, but to think differently in his head. His words to her were, 'When a man takes an oath, Meg, he's holding his own self in his own hands. Like water (he cups his hands) and if he opens his fingers then, he needn't hope to find himself again."[53]

This is why we must remain surrendered for ultimate perfection. To look back will be to lose hope of ever finding ourselves and reaching perfect completion. Even if we stray, imagine how the Doctor will feel when His beloved patient comes back to lie on that table for Him to finish the good work He started. In the face of severe pain, we very well may feel the need to rush off, but we must be patient and let the Lord do His work. There will be *some* evidence of His ongoing work for His glory and for our encouragement.

For we are the circumcision, which worship God in the Spirit, and rejoice in Christ

---

[52] 2 Timothy 4:10.
[53] Bolt, Robert. 1968. A man for all seasons: a play of Sir Thomas More.

Jesus, and have no confidence in the flesh. Philippians 3:3

This evidence is called Transformation - that which is *seen* by us and by the world. This is a metamorphosis from glory to glory here on earth, until ultimate and eternal Glory. It is not an external transformation which can be erased by a makeup wipe; it is not the transformation that the clothes are taken off at the end of the day, nor is it that transformation in which the money grows wings and flies away. No, it is a transformation which is the physical manifestation of an ongoing, internal, spiritual process in our hearts and in our minds. It is hard to miss because the transformation is a severe *lifestyle* overhaul. This transformation is, in fact, a radical, complete, uncomfortable, unrecognizable, unmissable, unbelievable, shocking, unwavering, egregious lifestyle change.

The clothes we will wear will be irremovable, never out of style, and they cannot be better off or worse off than the next person's attire. They are immune from competition and fashion trends, *unjudgeable* by any fashion police, and exempt from any best-dressed or worst-dressed lists. Our clothes will be above comment, law, or judgement, for we will be clothed in "compassion, kindness, humility, gentleness and patience and over all these... Love, which binds them all together in perfect unity." (Colossians 3: 12&14)

The need for man-made cosmetics will be futile; we will wear a natural, unremovable radiance, the effulgence of His glory upon our very selves; we will be smiling uncontrollably, even in the seclusion of our homes. When we are seen, like Jacob declared to Esau, it will be said, "For to see your face is like seeing the face of God" (Genesis 33:10), but we point them toward the Fact and make it clearly known that, "This is the LORD'S doing; it is marvelous in our eyes." (Psalm 118:23)

Personal results will include tenderness of heart; sensitivity to sin; carefulness of thought, word and deed; compassion for humanity; cautiousness of content viewed or listened to, and of places visited; accountability for time spent; willingness to fellowship and commune with fellow "patients;" a delicate enjoyment of the love of Jesus Christ, and an unsuppressed desire to share this Good News of Love, without shame nor palliation, with as many fellowmen as possible. Our life pledge will read "Sola Sciptura".

From old acquaintances, comments may sound along the lines of, "You are quite conservative," or, "I don't feel comfortable speaking to you anymore," or, "I miss the old you, this you is boring and unexciting," or, "Yes, we know you are a Christian, but does that mean you shouldn't care about your appearance? Please wear clothes that show off your figure," or, "There is something different about you," or, "I prefer your face when you used a lot of makeup," or, "I have an old bottle of wine to share with you, but I will not bring it out until you stop this 'thing' you are doing"…[54]

Our *personal brand* will then be: Personal Holiness, Personal Worship and Personal Penitence.

Personal Holiness: We constantly keep the big *"H"* in view, and we are ever aware of the two small *h's*. This means we realize that the **only** way to *Heaven* is *holiness,* otherwise its *hell,* because *"without holiness no man shall see the Lord."* (Hebrews 12:14) How dreadful would it be to finally *not* meet our Personal Physician on that Great Day to thank Him for His perfect work and successful surgery on us? So, we are careful in maintaining our *personal brand,* because we are eager to see Him, thank Him, behold His glory, worship Him face-to-face and reign with Him.

> **Oswald Chambers states**, *"Holiness means absolute purity of your walk before God, the words coming from your mouth, and every thought in your mind— placing every detail of your life under the scrutiny of God Himself. Holiness is not simply what God gives me, but what God has given me that is being exhibited in my life."*[55]

Apostle Paul says, **He died to make us holy.**[56]. If we are not working out holiness within and without, we are *yet* to accept the death of Jesus for our lives in its entirety.

Personal Worship: Our worship is not narcissistic anymore; it is heartfelt and filled with gratitude directly *to* God. When we begin to worship, the first song that comes to mind is not, *"Jesus you love me too much oh,"*[57] because that is not worship to God but self-centric amusement. We don't need to remind Him that He loves us. The Scripture in its entirety is simply Love, and that alone should weaken us with self-forgetful gratitude to Him. Nothing can ever separate us from His love, nothing. (Romans 8: 35-39)

Our heart's worship leads us to tears as we try to fathom how one Man could go through all He went through for all sinners; how all we need to do is believe in Him; how as ordinary men, we have direct access to the Almighty

---

[54] *Writer's note: These are all comments that have been said directly to me over a period since I got saved.

[55] Oswald Chambers, My Utmost for His Highest, Discovery House Publishers (2005).

[56] Colossians 1:22.

[57] Excess Love is a beautiful song written by Mercy Chinwo. She is a true worshipper and these can be felt from songs she had written. This analogy points to the fact that when as individuals we are worshipping and the first song is a song about God loving us rather than adoring Him in His glory and might.

God, the Creator of Heaven and earth. He is the God of Abraham, Isaac, and Jacob, the God Who answers by fire. He is the Righteous Judge coming back to judge the earth.

We think of heaven and the beauty and splendor of His Kingdom, and we are in awe with barely words to speak. Our worship is quiet, it is intimate, we feel the movement only in our hearts. The tears don't dance around our tear ducts. They flow freely.

Despite where we are, all we see, hear, and know is Jesus, the Most High God, higher than the highest. There is no shame, no covering up, because the veil has been torn from top, through the middle, to the bottom. We are completely exposed before Him and in awe of His Majesty. The heart's verisimilitude is without doubt. Hands are lifted. Knees are bent. It is intense, impassioned, and completely about *Him* and His glory. That is a *bit* of what Worship looks like. "Yet a time is coming and has now come when the true worshipers will worship the Father in the Spirit and in truth, for they are the kind of worshippers the Father seeks. God is spirit, and his worshipers must worship in the <u>Spirit</u> and in <u>truth</u>." (John 4:23-24)

Personal Penitence: As long as we are alive on earth, we know we are not immune to sin. Even after witnessing the glorious Transfiguration of Jesus, Apostle Peter still denied Him in the face of trial. When this happens however, like Apostle Peter, we remember the Cross and, "went outside and wept bitterly." (Luke22:62)

Historical records have it that Apostle Peter never truly recovered from the pain of his denial. Even after he received the Holy Spirit and became a powerful preacher, if a rooster ever crowed in the background when he was preaching in the Early Church, the sermon was cut short and he could go no further. However, when he was able to preach again, there would be such unction and warmth that his words satiated even the most broken of sinners in the congregation. Apostle Peter's was genuine repentance with genuine penitential tears.

To lack recognition of, or develop an indifference to sin, is treading a hazardous path to apostasy. This is a reprobate mind, i.e., somebody who "did not think it worthwhile to retain God in their knowledge" (Romans 1:28) and has been rejected by God.

Therefore, the Lord does not accept them He will remember their iniquity now, and punish their sins. Then the Lord said to me, 'Do not pray for this people, for their good. When they fast, I will not hear their cry; and when they offer burnt offering and grain offering, I will not accept them. But I will consume them by the sword, by the

39

famine, and by the pestilence.' Jeremiah 14:10-12

He is the same God of the Old Testament. He does not change. To know God once is *not* to know God all.

Daily, we must bring ourselves accountable to the Cross of Calvary, remembering that, to indulge sin and its appearances is "crucifying the Son of God all over again and subjecting him to public disgrace." (Hebrews 6:6 - should we add one more *6* to that?)

We might very well be mocked, scorned, shamed, doubted, or judged according to our *"pre-surgery"* days. They scoff and ask, *"Isn't this the carpenter's son? Isn't his mother's name Mary, and aren't his brothers James, Joseph, Simon and Judas? Aren't all his sisters with us? Where then did this man get all these things? And they took offense at him."* Matthew 13:55-57 Even Christians might be skeptical about our salvation; they say, *"Lord, I have heard from many about this man, how much harm he has done to Your saints in Jerusalem."* Acts 9:13

Then we recall, and bask in the soothing and forewarned Words of our Lord Jesus:

> *A prophet is NOT without honor EXCEPT in his own country and in his own house.* Matthew 11:57

So, we boldly declare these Words, for **"he who has ears, let him hear!"**[58]

> *My old self has been crucified with Christ. It is no longer I who live, but Christ lives in me. So I live in this earthly body by faith in the Son of God, who loved me and gave himself for me.* Galatians 2:20

> Then *shake the dust off your feet*[59] and move on without discouragement because *the harvest is plentiful but the laborers are few.* Matthew 9:37

The New Life

Now we are aware that we are in an ongoing, lifelong surgical process. The Great Physician's lights, which are far brighter than the sun's, are shining

---

[58] Matthew 11:15.
[59] Matthew 10:14.

directly upon on us, wherever we go. For His Eyes are light and He is ever looking upon us as He works in us. We are bloodied and helpless, yet still physically living and having to go about our daily lives. What must we do to stay perfectly still while the surgery is ongoing to avoid further complications in an already complicated situation?

(*Please read the following carefully, slowly, word-by-word and seriously):

17 With the Lord's authority I say this: Live no longer as the Gentiles do, for they are hopelessly confused.

18 Their minds are full of darkness; they wander far from the life God gives because they have closed their minds and hardened their hearts against him.

19 They have no sense of shame. They live for lustful pleasure and eagerly practice every kind of impurity.

20 But that isn't what you learned about Christ.

21 Since you have heard about Jesus and have learned the truth that comes from him,

22 THROW OFF your old sinful nature and your former way of life, which is corrupted by lust and deception.

23 Instead, let the Spirit renew your thoughts and attitudes.

24 Put on your new nature, created to be like God—truly righteous and holy.

25 So stop telling lies. Let us tell our neighbors the truth, for we are all parts of the same body.

26 And "don't sin by letting anger control you." Don't let the sun go down while you are still angry,

27 for anger gives a foothold to the devil.

28 If you are a thief, quit stealing. Instead, use your hands for good hard work, and then give generously to others in need.

29 Don't use foul or abusive language. Let everything you say be good and helpful, so that your words will be an encouragement to those who hear them.

30 And do not bring sorrow to God's Holy Spirit by the way you live. Remember, He has identified you as His own, guaranteeing that you will be saved on the day of redemption.

31 Get rid of all bitterness, rage, anger, harsh words, and slander, as well as all types of evil behavior.

32 Instead, be kind to each other, tenderhearted, forgiving one another, just as God through Christ has forgiven you

***

1 Imitate God, therefore, in everything you do, because you are his dear children.

2 Live a life filled with love, following the example of Christ. He loved us and offered himself as a sacrifice for us, a pleasing aroma to God.

3 Let there be no sexual immorality, impurity, or greed among you. Such sins have no place among God's people.

4 Obscene stories, foolish talk, and coarse jokes—these are not for you. Instead, let there be thankfulness to God.

5 You can be sure that no immoral, impure, or greedy person will inherit the. Kingdom of Christ and of God. For a greedy person is an idolater, worshiping the things of this world.

6 Don't be fooled by those who try to excuse these sins, for the anger of God will fall on all who disobey him.

7 Don't participate in the things these people do.

8 For once you were full of darkness, but now you have light from the Lord. So, live as people of light!

9 For this light within you produces only what is good and right and true.

10 CAREFULLY DETERMINE WHAT PLEASES THE LORD.

11 Take no part in the worthless deeds of evil and darkness; instead, expose them.

12 It is shameful even to talk about the things that ungodly people do in secret.

13 But their evil intentions will be exposed when the light shines on them,

14 for the light makes everything visible. This is why it is said, "Awake, O sleeper, rise up from the dead, and Christ will give you light."

Ephesians 4:17 – 5:14[60]

---

[60] A deep and personal meditation on the Book of Ephesians will be necessary.

Wow. This needs to be framed, recited, meditated upon, and lived daily. Heavy Words of Truth.

To summarize this in one word will be *light*; we are to live as light before the holiness of God's Light, within us and toward our fellow men.

To live as light is to live a *completely* transparent life. This cancels any preconceived notion of a personal right to "public and private life," but in the 21st Century, we have used our own hands to dissect our hearts into two or more parts, namely: "religious life" and "private life." Our protection comes not from the full amor of God, but from those four to six digits we fondly call "passcodes." "Jesus replied, 'Foxes have dens and birds have nests, but the Son of Man has no place to lay his head.'" (Luke 9:58)

Jesus knew that this world was not His home, therefore, He declared He had not even a place to lay His head. However, we are blessed to have roofs over our heads with multiple, sometimes unused room. Still, we hide, we still protect and privatize our lives. The bondage of protection has become a snare to us! This should not be the case for Christians at all. It should be clear to everyone around us that we are persuaded (except we're not) that we are **in** this world, but not **of** this world, "for our citizenship is in heaven." (Philippians 3:20) We are under no obligation to conform to any manmade trend.

For us, there is no church and there is no work. Church is work. Work is church. There's no "Christian life" and "private life." Private life *is* Christian; Christian life *is* private. "Since we are living by the Spirit, let us follow the Spirit's leading in every part of our lives" (Galatians 5:25 NLT). We must allow for the full permeation of the Holy Spirit in all parts of our lives as we adopt a nothing-to-hide before God and man type of life. There will be no getting caught unawares, no room for blackmail and blame, no room for guilt. Ours will be a life of integrity, of complete reliance, not on a passcode, but by putting on the whole armor of God for our protection.[61]

If King David had kept his sin private, or his confession private, and let them hold him down in shame, we would not have the Psalms we enjoy so much today. We might never have heard of David. At best, he would have been recorded as one of the failed kings of Israel. He declared; **my sin is always before me**.[62]

---

[61] Ephesians 6:10-17.
[62] Psalm 51:3.

Apostle Paul declared, "Christ Jesus came into the world to save sinners; of whom I am chief." (1 Timothy 1:15) That is complete transparency, freedom from the bondage of the shame of past sin, careful avoidance of future sin, outspokenness and rebuke of present sin by ourselves and others.

To be held in captivity by the bondage of the past is to be locked, inside-out, by your own doing. **If the Son makes you free, you shall be free indeed.**[63] It is cheerily singing "*Amazing Grace, how sweet the sound, that saved a wretch like me...*"

John Newton, the author of that classic hymn, was lost in a lifestyle of profanity, gambling and drinking before he came to Christ. He lived in the 18th Century when the slave trade was thriving heavily in England. Newton, however, as a white man who was self-described as an "infidel and libertine," was left as a slave in Sierra Leonne. The crew of his ship left him there because they could not stand his lewdness and churlish disposition. On one occasion aboard the ship, he was stripped to the waist and flogged with eight dozen lashes (96 stripes). So, this white British man, who was a slave trader himself, became a servant *of* slaves *to* Africans *in* West Africa! He was not rescued until three years after his father began a thorough search for him. Scorned by a life of disgrace and humiliation, he contemplated suicide.

After his rescue from slavery, during a four-week voyage back home from Sierra Leone, Newton found himself in a severe storm which was about to sink the ship on which he was traveling. This same man, who once had been described by the ship's captain as the most profane man he had ever met, began to plead for God's mercy not to let the ship sink. Our faithful God heard Newton and saved him. This event marked his journey to Christianity. According to him, after his initial conversion, he did not consider himself a full believer until a considerable time afterwards, because he was still actively involved in some unchristian practices. He ended up writing a public apology for his involvement in the slave trade, and eventually became a major ally and influence to Sir William Wilberforce who, also due to his conversion, ended up championing and persevering through the fight of the Abolition of Slave Trade Act 1807. That was a fight which lasted 25 years and finally passed into law a few months before the death of Sir John Newton.[64] What a transformation!

Saint Augustine's autobiography, *Confessions,* is a brutally honest account from his sinful youth to his new and unrecognizable life in Christ. His painful

---

[63] John 8:36.

[64] Newton John. Out of the Depths. Grand Rapids:Kregel(2003).

recollection tells how he was a sinful man of a depraved lifestyle who was under the siege of sexual indulgence. He committed theft, told lies, and was a follower of philosophy and astrology, rather than the *only* true Faith. He sugar-coated nothing, but boldly rebuked his former lifestyle. This adoringly honest, persuasive account of his life was an intentional, honest account on his part to show sinners the depths and riches of God's mercies, even to the worst of sinners. Sinner Augustine embraced his freedom in Christ and became Saint Augustine.

It is fair-minded to say that the conversion to genuine Christianity is not as treasured if you have not been a sinner, from the *lowest of lows,* before finding Christ. It *is* the same faith, but a *different* joy for that prodigal who is welcomed from afar with a great feast and open arms. The *"elder brothers"* might be bitter for it, or they might not. However, the great feast thrown by Jesus Himself cancels out the opinion and skeptical eyes of the elder brothers in the building! Jesus came for ALL sinners. We, the sick, hear, "I tell you that in the same way there will be more rejoicing in Heaven over one sinner who repents than over ninety-nine righteous persons who do not need to repent." (Luke 15:7)

That is why we declare the love of Christ Jesus passionately and unashamedly, for it can only be a divine, unstageable miracle of God's saving, impartial grace, to be lost and found, to be blind but seeing so clearly now. THANK YOU, JESUS!

Embrace the freedom found in Christ. The enlightenment and wisdom learned at His feet. Your victory is in your testimony of unrighteousness to righteousness in Christ Jesus! To back up from this is to stifle your progress to the Kingdom of Heaven. We were all conceived in sin. We were born into this world dead, and this was not without reason.

> *Then you shall know that I am the LORD, when I have opened your graves, O My people, and brought you up from your graves.* Ezekiel 37:13

All flesh and blood is sin. "All we like sheep have gone astray; We have turned, every one, to his own way; And the LORD has laid on Him the iniquity of us all" Isaiah 53:6, and because of our iniquities, which our perfect Lord Jesus Christ bore, our "iniquity has been pardoned; for she has received from the hand of the LORD double for all her sins." (Isaiah 40:2)

Christ, our Paschal Lamb, has been sacrificed for us…so celebrate with the unleavened bread of sincerity and truth! (1 Corinthians 5:7-8) **It is finished!**

To be ashamed of your inherent nature is to remain in bondage. To be *preaching the very faith you once tried to destroy,*[65] is a rare kind of victory. In this *picture-perfect-pretty-profile* 21st Century, it is a victory worth 10,000 shouts of joy from the heavens and earth! The masking and painting of a persona is the alluring, but biggest bondage that has tied down our generation. A faux cover-up! It is a Dummy Cake, prepared to *"perfection"* on the outside, with nothing edifying on the inside. It is an outside covered by money, followers, careers, *"experience,"* shoes, bags, perfumes, perfect bodies, earthly connections, and some travel. Who the Son sets free IS free *indeed!* Once lost, but now found means to rescue as many people as we can, *and more,* from the path of darkness into the way of everlasting life to the glory of the Almighty God.

The Charge

We have been set free from the bondage of sin and the cult of the flesh. What next? Is it time to wine and dine *"in moderation?"* Is it time to take pictures, post self-serving Bible verses, throw in a bit of Sunday service here and there, and acquire the latest of whatever is trending in the world? Is it time *to* pay our tithes and offerings, pray for miracles, declare that we are empowered to conquer our careers, and get to the top of the Rich List? Let's examine the message of Jesus to the church in Laodicea. Remember, these were members of a "saved" Church, *not Gentiles nor Jews* – as there is no such in Christ:[66]

> *You say, 'I am rich; I have acquired wealth and do not need a thing. But you do not realize that you are wretched, pitiful, poor, blind and naked.* Revelation 3:17

Meanwhile, to the Church in Smyrna, He said, "I know your affliction and your poverty— though you are rich!" (Revelation 2:8)

So, are we free when we have been set free? Unfortunately, the only answer for a Christian is, *no;* our freedom comes with a new "bondage." Nothing *really* goes for free.

> *But now having been set free from sin, and having become slaves of God, you have your fruit to holiness, and the end, everlasting life.* Romans 6:22

Is the new *bondage* to keep us bound? Or punish us for our sins? Is it for our

---

[65] Galatians 1:23.

[66] Galatians 3:28.

earthly suffering? Certainly not! Because we have already seen, as long as our souls our prospering, that God inspires us to prosper here on earth and be in good health. Besides, the wages paid to us by our old slave-master was death (Romans 6:23), but in our new role, the *free gift* we receive is unbelievable! What then is the essence of our new slavery?

So when the centurion and those with him, who were guarding Jesus, saw the earthquake and the things that had happened, they feared greatly, saying, "Truly this was the Son of God!" Matthew 27:54.

And because of my chains, most of the brothers and sisters have become confident in the Lord and dare all the more to proclaim the gospel without fear. Philippians 1:14

I am an ambassador in chains; that in it I may speak boldly, as I ought to speak. Ephesians 6:20.

First, our freedom releases us from the guilt and bondage of sin, enabling us to speak about the Good News freely. Second, our conviction and dedication even unto death, will build the faith of others, leading them to Christ.

In 2015, the Islamic militant group, Daesh, beheaded 20 Coptic (Egyptian) Orthodox Christians in Libya. A 21st victim, a Ghanaian man named Matthew Ayariga, when it was his turn for his head to be chopped off, was asked if he rejected Jesus as God. Matthew Ayariga, who prior to that moment was not a Christian, had seen the immense faith of his fellow Coptic Christian captives to die for Christ. He replied, "Their God is my God," and was likewise martyred.

They loved not their lives unto the death. Revelation 12:11

We should exercise the physical freedoms we enjoy in 2020, free speech, free movement, and human rights, as slaves for Christ. Lady Jane Grey, a 16-year-old *de facto* Queen of England, was charged with high treason in 1554 for assuming the title of Monarch, even though it had been rightly willed to her by the preceding King. At her trial, the evidence given against her was that she signed documents as "Jane the Quene" (sic), and this 16-year-old girl was beheaded, based on that single act.

Today, females even name themselves "King" or royalty on social media and in other public spaces, without having to face the consequence of what was, in history, seen as a capital offense. Our freedom in this sense should be used to God's glory. We can speak freely and share boldly about the Good News of Jesus.

The date of Lady Jane's execution was postponed by some days to give her

47

the opportunity, as advised by her chaplain, John Feckenham, to convert from her devout Protestant faith to Catholicism and thereby "save her soul." She did not accede to this offer. At the point of her death, she recited the *Miserere*, verbally forgave her executioner, and in the manner of Jesus Christ declared, "*Lord, into Thy hands, I commend my spirit!*" The "Nine Days Queen," as she is now memorably called, was known by an act which would easily be dismissed today as "youthful exuberance." Yet she was executed. More admirably, she loved not her life to death, and did not recant her faith to save herself.

Our dualistic nature of flesh and soul is still active, so while our surgery is in progress on one hand, simultaneously it is warfare on the other hand! As long as we abide with Him in spirit, however, we are still laid on that surgical table, secure and under the tender care of The Great Physician. He will never fight us. He is our Greatest Ally and has assured us that, "NOTHING can ever separate us from God's love. Neither death nor life, neither angels nor demons, neither our fears for today nor our worries about tomorrow—not even the powers of hell can separate us from God's love. No power in the sky above or in the earth below—indeed, nothing in all creation will ever be able to separate us from the love of God that is revealed in Christ Jesus our Lord." (Romans 8: 38-39)

With this surety, we can arise with all boldness and play our part in this *warfare*, because that is exactly what we are engaged in day and night. In **Daniel 10**, Daniel had been praying and fasting for three weeks, which he called "mourning," so we would understand the position of his heart. Finally, the Angel arrived and explained to him, since he *humbled himself* and *sought understanding* about his vision, that his request had been answered since day one. It was the demonic prince from the evil kingdom of Persia who blocked his way until Archangel Michael the Warrior came to deliver him. Our battle is spiritual! Our prayers assure us victory.

Warfare is neither easy, nor for the faint-hearted. The Kingdom of Heaven suffers violence; reaching the Kingdom is non-negotiable, therefore, the warfare is worth it! It is not easy, not enjoyable to our flesh, but it is worth it. It is Big "H" or nothing, Christ or nothing. Thus, Jesus tells us to count the cost. When we become Christians, we are saying a thousand things by that decision, but it sometimes remains unuttered. This verbal silence is the tragedy we witness amongst Christians who back out from the Faith. Nobody said being a Christian was going to be easy, or a smooth ride. As a matter of fact, the day, the very minute and millisecond, you make a decision to become a Christian, *is* the beginning of your problems! (***Writer's note:** *I promise you this very fact!*)

48

We are not entering the lottery by becoming a Christian. We are not in this battle for miracles, signs, and wonders, but for the **mercy** of God! We are not coming to seek the Hand of God, but the **face** of God! THE GOD ALMIGHTY, WHO CAN SEND SOULS TO HELL, IS NOT OUR SERVANT TO GIVE US WHAT WE ASK!

In His mercy, He can *if* He so desires. So how dare we, who are dust, dictate to God, "give me this, give me that?" Most of the things on our prayer request lists can be given to us by any human. Most times, what we really mean in our prayers is not "give me this" but "I want that person to help me – to offer me the job – to marry me -- to give me the promotion – to accept my application – to mark all my answers correctly – or even to die." These are weak prayers, weak *and* lame! If you really need all these, be bold and proactive enough to walk up to whoever has the answer to your little wish so they give it to you.

With a rude sense of entitlement, we demand "What is my purpose?" or, "I don't feel fulfilled," or, "What am I meant to do?" or, "Why am I on earth?" This trendy mind-set of self-fulfillment/self-realization is simply a never-ending, toxic self-destructing cycle; it is a cycle that will *never* end until we take our eyes *off* ourselves and look to the Cross of Calvary. Otherwise, it remains a total illusion, *even* as Christians, because we are *not* complete until Jesus' coming. "I am the bread of life. Whoever comes to me will never be hungry again. Whoever believes in me will never be thirsty." (John 6:35) Until this occurs, we will know no rest, no satisfaction, no contentment, nor security.

Besides, the answer to the 'broken-record' set of demands for self-fulfillment and self-purpose has been there from the beginning: "for Thou hast created all things, and for Thy pleasure they are and were created" Revelation 4:11, "and all things were created by Him, and FOR him." (Colossians 1:16)

SEEK YE **FIRST** THE KINGDOM OF GOD AND HIS RIGHTEOUS-NESS. How about, like Moses, we pray, "S*how me Your glory?*" That IS a prayer! What about, *"Jesus Christ, Son of David, have mercy on me?"* What about, *"I believe, Lord, help my unbelief?"* or *"Here I am, Lord. Send me."* What about, *"Forgive them Father, for they know not what they do?"* What about, *"Open thou my eyes O Lord that I may behold wondrous things out of thy Law?"* And more than ever in history and our generation, with its darkened enlightenment and man-made gods, where everyone drifts along with the latest buzz, how about we pray like the Great King Solomon, "Therefore give to Your servant an understanding heart to judge Your people, that I may discern between good and evil." (1 Kings 3:9). Guess what the Bible says about *that* prayer:

The Lord was pleased that Solomon had asked for this. So God said to him, "Since you have asked for this and not for long life or wealth for yourself, nor have you asked for the death of your enemies but for discernment in administering justice, I will do what you have asked. I will give you a wise and discerning heart, so that there will never have been anyone like you, nor will there ever be. Moreover, I will give you what you have not asked for—both wealth and honor—so that in your lifetime you will have no equal among kings. And if you walk in obedience to me and keep my decrees and commands as David your father did, I will give you a long life. 1 Kings 3:10-14.

We brood of vipers, tintinnabulating into the ear of *the* Sovereign God, the Owner of *all* silver and gold. We call Him, Abba, Father, yet we are rolling and forcing some salty liquid out of our eyes, because we don't have a mess of pottage when our birth-right is GUARANTEED! We insult and limit the Alpha and Omega, the Owner of time and seasons, Who turned a prisoner to a Prime Minister in less than 24 hours, and a shepherd boy to a mighty king in one day, to rules, regulations, deadlines, *"vision boards,"* and 5-, 10- or 50-year plans! Ludicrous! "You fool! This very night your soul is required of you and now who will own what you have prepared?" (Luke 12:20) *Please have mercy, Lord.*

David never prayed, "Dear Lord, will you be my Shepherd?" No, he *declared,* "The Lord IS my Shepherd!" In **Genesis 28: 13- 15**, God appeared to Jacob at Bethel, introduced Himself as the God of his ancestors *(Writer's note: which really was enough. Abraham's God needs no more to say)*, but in His mercy, He went on and gave Jacob specific promises for himself: That the land he was lying on belonged to him, that his descendants would be as numerous as the dust of the earth, and through him, ALL the families of the earth will be blessed. Finally, God promised him Divine protection until the very end. After that encounter, Jacob's vow to God was, if God indeed would protect him and give him food and clothing, then God would certainly be his God, and he'd give back 10% of every other thing God gave him. He didn't say, *if* God would truly give him all these descendants and this land, then he would give back to God. He asked for food, clothing, and God's protection.

And having food and clothing, with these we shall be content. 1 Timothy 6:8

Again, about 20 years after that encounter, Jacob had gathered an abundance of earthly wealth and he declared, "I have oxen, donkeys, flocks, and male and female servants." (Genesis 32:5) For gifts to his brother Esau, from his abundance, he selected 200 female goats, 20 male goats, 200 ewes, 20 rams, 30 female camels, with their young, 40 cows, 10 bulls, 20 female donkeys and 10 male donkeys… all these, just as gifts! Yet, he wrestled to the point of willingness to break his bones for God to *bless* him. Bless him? He had *all* the blessings… so we may think! But Jacob understood the insurmountable value of God's blessing.

God *indeed* blessed him, and the blessing was a name change. That will utterly be despised by the 21st Century Christian. Isn't it true that females don't necessarily change their names anymore when they get married? *Then a first name change?* We digress. Jacob knew that the blessings of God transcended what he could see, touch, gift and show-off.

Assume you were in a court of law, charged with an offense of which you were guilty beyond all reasonable doubt. Then the judge, for some reason, asks you to make a request which *will* be granted, regardless what you ask. Now, you are certainly guilty of the offense and you are probably facing life imprisonment without the possibility of parole, and the judge grants you this unbelievable opportunity to ask for *whatever*, and it will be given? Would you ask for some money to pay your legal fees or for your acquittal? I suppose the answer would be something which *only* the judge can grant you; anyone could pay legal fees. Besides, just that act of being free will afford you the opportunity to do many other things, such as get your life back on track, resolve to live a better life, get a job, and then have an income to pay your legal fees or repay the loan you used in paying them.

That is exactly what we do when we give God mediocre lists. We want "prosperity," influence and fulfilment. We want to pile up and pile up and pile up, forgetting that *sole* earthly prosperity is the Personal Brand, which is the distinguishing mark of the devil. Even he, the father of them who seek after such, declared that Jesus IS the Son of God! (Mark 3:11).

> *If my people, which are called by my name, shall humble themselves, and pray, and seek my face, and turn from their wicked ways; THEN will I hear from heaven, and will forgive their sin, and will heal their land.* 2 Chronicles 7:14

The heavenly mandate is, the soul prospers first, *then* whatever overflow comes from it; all glory be to God. We give it *back* to Him! We remember the poor and needy, *without* the *Judas Deceit*, "Now he said this, not because he was concerned about the poor" (John 12:6), because when we announce our acts and intentions of charity, that is exactly what we engage in – *the Judas Deceit*.

Any flicker of prosperity without the soul's prosperity is fiction. How could Job have lost *everything* he had, including his children, and declare in that state, "Naked I came from my mother's womb, and naked shall I return there. The Lord gave, and the Lord has taken away; Blessed be the name of the Lord" (Job 1:21)

Job's wife, on the other hand, was ready to curse God and die. Her prosperity was in what her hand could touch, and her eyes could see. What is Job's experience to a 21st Century Christian? God *must* be playing with fire! *Please have mercy*, Lord. The moment things begin to *visibly* seem not to be in our favor, the slave that we have made God in our heads must be cursed. Yet He is the One who created us for His pleasure. We must not be too quick to assess anyone as being prosperous.

Because the prosperity of our soul, i.e., heart, mind, will and emotions, is what determines prosperity, only each individual - on a personal, internal-reflective basis, will be able to declare whether or not they are prosperous. The downfall of many *great* men for the most unthinkable reasons will attest to this.

Charles Spurgeon said, *"Is not this a miracle of miracles, that 'God so loved the world that he gave his only begotten Son, that whosoever believeth in him might not perish?'[67] Surely that precious word, 'Whosoever will, let him come and take the water of life freely,'[68] and that solemn promise, 'Him that cometh unto me, I will in no wise cast out,'[69] are better than signs and wonders!"*

The Psalms are filled with an adoration of God and wonder at His person and Word. The longest chapter in the Bible is a whole chapter simply about the Word of God! The Word of God *IS* an unquestionable sign *and* wonder!

> *Nevertheless, do not rejoice in this, that the spirits are subject to you, but rather rejoice because your names are written in heaven.* Luke 10:20

We brood of vipers! Miracles, promotions, breakthroughs, signs and wonders are the "perks of the job," the freebies, the canapes, the advertisements, the by-products, the method by which He bears witness and backs up the Words of His servants, not the *essence* of the Kingdom! These are fleeting earthly needs that have no relevance in Heaven. Why are we disappointed and down-cast when we don't get all the items on our wish-list?

> *Though He slay me, yet will I trust Him.* Job 13:15.

> *Though the fig tree does not bud and no fruit is on the vines, though the olive crop fails and the fields produce no food, though the sheep are cut off from the fold and no cattle are in the stalls, 18 yet I will exult in the LORD; I will rejoice in the God of my salvation!* Habakkuk 3:17-18

---

[67] John 3:16.
[68] Revelation 22:17.
[69] John 6:37.

They absolutely must not and should not have any bearing on our faith or zeal for our pilgrimage. The One Who created the earth for His own pleasure owes us nothing. He is not a genie whom we call on to grant our wishes and then say, *"See you next time!"*

(***Writer's note:** *As providence will have it, as I wrote this text, I had just come across a post on Mass Media where a lady shared a "testimony" of the recent birth of a son after "a hard waiting period which nobody will understand if they have not been through [it]." I was quite happy for her because, according to her, she had received very hateful and shaming messages concerning her inability to bear a child and was going through a miscarriage during the period which those unkind messages were sent. She went on to share how, during her waiting period, she prayed to God and told God (or whatever god she prayed to, certainly not the God of Elijah) things like, "You are wicked. You give children to those who don't want it. We want it, yet you wouldn't give it to us." She added that God was silent and said nothing, so she cried to her slave-god and said, "Sebi you're deaf abi? You're doing as if you don't hear, right? Okay what do you have to say now?" [sic] [**I had serious dry heaves as I wrote this. Lord, please help me. **] Firstly, this ~~heretic~~ lady posed as a "religious influencer" and had used her platform to influence her adherents that it was okay to ask the sovereign God, Who makes the ear, whether He was deaf. She pointed out that she asked God a question and the God Who could not bear to look at His only Son on the cross of Calvary as He was murdered by this woman's hands, was not answering her. She went on to say further that the waiting period was very hard, and no one would ever understand it after she waited for TWO years after getting married to have a child. The God of Abraham to whom, at the age of 75 years, He gave a promise that he would be a father of nations, and had him wait another 25 years, yet kept this woman waiting for 2 years! Why did she deserve to wait? According to her, she and her husband had done the noblest thing by getting married as virgins so "there was absolutely no reason why we shouldn't have children when we wanted them." [**the dry heaves are increasing. Please help me, Lord. **] She finally rained insults and curses on her mockers and told them to come to her and ask for her forgiveness before she forgives them and says the same fate will befall them. Then she praised the name of her god and told those who might be in her situation that her god, "the God of Hannah," answers prayers. She went on to tell everybody to be kind, because we don't know what the next person might be passing through. I will reserve the very comments I would have said over this matter, but as John Calvin put it, "We should remember that Satan has his wonders, which, though they are juggling tricks rather than real miracles, are such as to delude the ignorant and inexperienced. Magicians and enchanters have always been famous for miracles; idolatry has been supported by astonishing miracles; and yet we admit them not as proofs of the superstition of magicians or idolaters.[70]" Another preacher said, "If Judas Iscariot's mother knew what her son will*

---

[70] Battles. Calvin: Institutes of the Christian Religion. Louisville, Ky: Westminster John Knox Press, 2001. Print.

become, she would have asked God not to have a child," and finally, "For behold, the days are coming when they will say, 'Blessed are the barren and the wombs that never bore and the breasts that never nursed!" [Luke 23:29])

We must stop these rather nonsensical prayers and get serious in our **warfare**! The end times are here, and we must be sensitive to the signs. Since the days in 2 Peter 3:4, we've been wondering when He is coming back, so for thousands of years we've been saying it. Well, in our generation, it's been 2,000 years since Jesus rose from the dead. Apostle Peter, not a man to mince words, tells us in 2 Peter 3:8 that a thousand years to us is but a day unto God. So, in essence, to God, it is barely two days and some hours since Jesus arose from the dead and ascended into Heaven. God is an eternal God. He has gone through whatever season is currently playing out in the land of the mortals. He is coming back very soon, in His mercy and for our awareness, to reject any plea of ignorance. The checklist for the end-times is listed in the Holy Bible. And when we compare that to what we live in today, we realize not a full stop, comma, or letter is out of place! It is a 100% accurate prediction:

1   *In the last days there will be very difficult times.*

2   *For people will love only themselves and their money. They will be boastful and proud, scoffing at God, disobedient to their parents, and ungrateful (Writer's note: to Jesus, to history!). They will consider nothing sacred.*

3   *They will be unloving and unforgiving; they will slander others and have no self-control. They will be cruel and hate what is good.*

4   *They will betray their friends, be reckless, be puffed up with pride, and love pleasure rather than God.*

5   *They will act religious, but they will reject the power that could make them godly. Stay away from people like that!*

9   *But they won't get away with this for long. Someday everyone will recognize what fools they are, just as with Jannes and Jambres.* (2 Timothy 3:1-5&9)

Standing ovation for the infallible Word of God! Christian, are we still in doubt? Where is the lie? **Hypocrites! You can discern the face of the sky and of the earth, but how is it you do not discern this time?**[71] The depraved, hedonism-addicted, corrupt, shameless society we live in, who are masked by that picture-perfect-pretty-profile, are forgetting that the demons

---

[71] Luke 12:56.

dress up as angels of light! Now it is make-up, nice cars, institutions attended, slaving away for a company, thriving businesses, fancy suits… and Christians look JUST like them! Are we submitting to everything that the *world* and *man-made trends* command us to do? Asked to introduce ourselves, we struggle with which of the titles we begin with, *BA, MSc, LLB, MPH, MBA, BL, MPA, Ph.D, FCIArb, M.IoD, fnimn, FCIA, FCPA, FICMC, FCTI, Commissioner for Home Affairs.*[72]

> *Adulterers and adulteresses! Do you not know that friendship with the world is enmity with God? Whoever therefore wants to be a friend of the world makes himself an enemy of God.* James 4:4

> *Therefore, beloved, looking forward to these things, be diligent to be found by Him in peace, without spot and blameless.* 2 Peter 3:14

To be forewarned is to be forearmed! The Lord is coming, and *every* eye **will** behold His coming. *Only* those who have lived just like Jesus lived will be confident to face Him when he comes (1 John 4:17). To fall into the Demas Disorder will result in shrinking back from Him in shame when He comes (1 John 2:28). Congratulations for living in, and experiencing first-hand, the events of the last days as they roll out *exactly* as foretold. We must be SOBER, VIGILANT *and* COUNT THE COST!

> *Jesus…said to him, "You still lack one thing. Sell all that you have…and come, follow Me." But when he heard this, he became very sorrowful, for he was very rich.* Luke 18:22-23

There's only one product of counting the cost and it lies in boldly declaring:

> *I consider my life worth nothing to me; my only aim is to finish the race and complete the task the Lord Jesus has given me--the task of testifying to the good news of God's grace.* Acts 20:24

If we need to preach a sermon or share a message even on our social media pages or Sunday best and there is an unwavering need to look a certain way, sound a certain way, have a certain background and lighting and will not do it any other way, unfortunately, we seriously deceive ourselves and are **yet** to count the COST! It costs us NOTHING! If our listeners are immediately thinking about who did our makeup, what a nice wrist watch, that weave is 'laid' – where is it from?, or they are thinking how cool we are because we have the latest release of some sneaker brand –selected in the rainbow edition

---

[72] This rather cumbersome list of titles was copied exactly as seen on the profile of one individual.

or whatever appearance that can for one millisecond take away the attention from the Message we are speaking (*or assume we are*), by an obvious and unnecessary display of vanity, unfortunately, we are preaching our gospel and not the gospel of Jesus Christ who died in shame for our sins. These days, we have preachers wearing shredded denim on stage to preach, then shamelessly backing it up with points about evolving, "new-school" freedom, and God's grace to do what they want. Yet, to visit the Queen, these same pastors wear their crispest shirts and best-fitting suits. Christianity does **not**, and will **never**, evolve! The same Gospel Jesus preached is the same St. Augustine, St. Benedict, Alfred The Great, John Calvin, Amy Carmichael, Pastor E.A. Adeboye, and Dr. Billy Graham preached! How dare we?

If we keep attempting to devalue and degrade the Gospel, what happens to the next generation? Will they be preaching in swimwear or be naked? Let us reflect with Oswald Chambers, "*This does not mean that I will not be saved, but it does mean that I cannot be entirely His.*"[73]

Yes! It is a *hard* journey on earth. A *true* Christian will, doubtless and from time to time, wonder, "*How much longer, Lord?*" Even Jesus wondered this while He was on earth (Matthew 17:17). If we profess ourselves to be Christian, and have never asked that question, we do *not* understand what we say we are. When all we want is long life, comfort, security and wealth here on earth, and have no groaning of Spirit for a foretaste of the future glory (Romans 8:23), unfortunately, it is not Jesus Christ's brand of Christianity we practice. We will be wise to quickly adjust before it gets too late. It *is* a hard journey on earth. So *how* exactly do *we* do this? We don't.

> For the grace of God has appeared that offers salvation to all people. It teaches us to say "No" to ungodliness and worldly passions, and to live self-controlled, upright and godly lives in this present age. Titus 2:11-12.

JESUS DOES! HIS GRACE DOES! That's what His grace is for. It is not to empower us to "*make it*" in life, nor is it a license for us to sin.

When the rich man, whom Jesus had told to sell his possessions and follow Him, developed the *Demas Disorder* due to his wealth, Jesus *affirmed* the hardship it takes to enter the Kingdom of God because of earthly wealth *and desires*. He said it will be easier for a camel to pass through the eye of needle![74]

Those with Him wondered, and rightly so, "<u>WHO</u> THEN CAN BE SAVED?" (Luke 18:26) "... All things which are impossible with men are

---

[73] Oswald Chambers, My Utmost for His Highest.
[74] Luke 18:22-25.

possible with God," Jesus encouraged. (Luke 18:27)

Imagine if we had to go through what the people went through before the Crucifixion to atone for our sins. The priests in the Old Testament could *not* sit down on the job. A chair was not even permitted in the tabernacle or temple (Hebrews 10:11). God wanted the people to know that when it came to their forgiveness, it was always *unfinished business;* so, day after day, every priest would stand and perform his religious duties. Again and again, he offered the same sacrifices, which could *never* take away sin; they only covered sin, year by year.

Now, what we have in Jesus is the permanent, effective, merciful intervention of God for forgiveness of our sins.

> But when this priest [Jesus] had offered for all time one sacrifice for sins, He sat down at the right hand of God. Hebrews 10:12

When Jesus had accomplished the all-encompassing take-away of our sins, He did what no priest could do in the Old Testament. He sat down, because all the work – for all time– was finished. *(Writer's note: If I were God, I would have kept the meaning of this sacrifice of Jesus Christ a secret until the day of judgement. We would all have had to continue working very hard for our salvation. Then, on that day, it would be,* 'Surprise! When Jesus died, you didn't have to do all of that again, enter into my rest." *At least, that would keep us on our toes, rather than the despicable way in which we all abuse GRACE today, but thank God, God is not man. Thank God, I am not God. We cannot and must stop continuing in sin for Grace to abound!)*

We need God and His mercies every day. That last day will certainly have a lot of weeping and regret. It really hurts to think about it, knowing, as long as we are alive, it is *never* too late to retrace our steps. Again, Christianity is an old-time religion, not a 21st Century phenomenon. These Liberal Theology, Progressive Christianity movements are man-made ideologies which spurn the unshakeable word of God. When we, *by ourselves,* reduce the Word of God and this ancient religion to motivational speeches, feel-good remedies, and empowerment sermons, leaving so many parts untouched, WE WILL BE JUDGED FOR IT. And we will be judged by *only* ONE   GOSPEL – "that which the Apostle Paul preached!" (Romans 2:16) If we are serious about reaching Heaven, eating from the Tree of Life, receiving the Crown of Life, holding fast to the old-time religion, and holding unto death, is a *sine qua non*; to be saved once is not to be saved all.

The Israelites were at the border of the Promised Land but failed to hold fast to their trust in God. It was their "evil heart of unbelief" that failed them. (Hebrews 3:6; 3:14; 10:23, Revelation 2:10). The way Apostles Paul, Peter,

John and all the other disciples who died a martyr's death, did it is the *only* way! Apostle Paul tells us in Philippians 3:17 to pattern our lives after his. (**Writer's Note*: Not one Christian can say this today! We brood of vipers! We are so quick to say we are just human and not perfect. Rubbish, stinking nonsense! Apostle Paul acknowledged that he was not perfect, but he was pressing on because he was determined to reach perfection in Christ. Yet to thwart the gospel and cover up for some disgusting sin and selfish ambition to which the devil has tied our souls, we plead imperfection. When caught red-handed in hideous atrocities, they dare plead imperfection. God have mercy on us. I wrote this with tears in my heart and eyes).*

Let no FLESH AND BLOOD deceive you! These obscene, anti-Christian demons very well dress up as angels of light, but they WILL be exposed SOON!

Adolf Hitler, whose mother (the only person he truly loved) was a devout Catholic, abhorred Christianity as did his father (with whom Adolf did not get along), who described it as a *"crutch for human weakness."* Adolf himself called it a weak, poor religion, declaring it as a, *"religion fit only for slaves because its teaching is a rebellion against the natural law of selection by struggle of the fittest."*[75] The Christians in his time *must* have been doing something right, because that is *exactly* the way Christians should be seen by people of the world: sober, slow to speak, slow to get angry, eager to forgive, peace-loving, helplessly generous, home-doors-flung-open, sharing, working diligently as unto the Lord not man, singing, praying *and hoping*! *That* is Christianity, not the 2020 Apostate religion of "tolerance," but calling sin exactly what it is, a *fleeing* from it and any appearance thereof. "Jesus dined with sinners?" If that is what your ground of defense is, be very well prepared to also fast in a wilderness for 40 days and 40 nights, then die for same sinners on a cross. Then you have a license to sin!

A.W Tozer wrote about what Christianity was becoming in his day, *"...that irresponsible, amusement-mad paganized pseudo-religion which passes today for the faith of Christ and which is being spread all over the world by unspiritual men employing unscriptural methods to achieve their unspiritual ends!"*[76]

Writer's Note: *Dear Sir, if only you could see what we live in now. I know you can. I know you weep for us. You have done your work, sir.*

Is it all bad news? Are we just here to slave away on earth, because a Man

---

[75] https://www.washingtonpost.com/history/2019/04/20/hitler-hated-judaism-he-loathed-christianity-too/

[76] https://www.gracegems.org/2016/06/That%20irresponsible,%20amusement-mad%20paganized%20pseudo-religion!.html

came to earth to die for us, even though we didn't ask Him to do so? Well, He never forced us to accept Him and He never will, for He is no taskmaster and expressly stated, "IF anyone will come after me" (Matthew 16:24) so if we have been wise enough to accept Him, there are principles that MUST be followed. From then on, it becomes, *"when ye pray," "when ye fast," "heal the sick," "raise the dead," "go and make disciples of all nations"*[77]

As soon as we take on His identity, there are standards, there are commands; Christianity is no weak religion. The end will make it all worth it, and if we could see the future glory, we would do it twice and even much harder again on earth, if we could. It *is* worth it. Take His Word for it. A mansion is being prepared for us; a crown is being customized to fit our heads *exactly*. There is no pain, no shame, in worshipping with Abraham and all the "cool kids" of our Faith. At last we will find the missing ones: Enoch, Moses and Elijah.

We will have a good laugh with Apostle Peter. We will give a "high five" to Apostle Paul, to thank him for his blunt letters that kicked us back on track when we attempted to derail. We finally see Apostle John and ask him the question we all want to ask: "So tell us, WHY didn't you just address yourself as John?" ***Writer's Note:** *if you don't understand that question, run and pick up your Bible and study the Book of John. If you do, awesome! Keep striving* Most important, we will see our darling, Lord Jesus, who made it ALL possible! IT IS WORTH IT! It is finished! Thank You, Jesus.)

So, it's not all bad news, *even* on earth. Jesus PROMISES us, "I assure you that everyone who has given up house or wife or brothers or parents or children, for the sake of the Kingdom of God, WILL BE REPAID MANY TIMES OVER IN THIS LIFE, and will have eternal life in the world to come." (Luke 18:29-30). Wait for it, it *will* surely come.

Now, therefore, to effectively face our warfare, Jesus warns us:

> *Watch and pray, that ye enter not into temptation: the spirit indeed is willing, but the flesh is weak.* Matthew 26:41

Apostle Peter advises us:

> *Be alert, be reflective, because your enemy Satan roars like a lion and is walking and seeking whom he may devour.* 1 Peter 5:8[78]

*Writers Note: *Phew! We've made it here! Awesome! Still willing to be a Christian?*

---

[77] Matthew 6:6; Matthew 6:16; Matthew 10:8; Matthew 28:19.
[78] Aramaic Bible in Plain English Version.

Then the following is for us.

Congratulations!

You have been enlisted as a Soldier under the Order of the Lord of Heaven's Armies!

COMMANDANT GENERAL: Jehovah Sabaoth

CAPTAIN GENERAL: Jesus Christ

MAJOR GENERAL: The Holy Spirit

BADGE: Christian

RANK: Soldier and Ambassador of Christ

COMBAT: The good fight of faith against *worldly desires that wage war against your very souls (1 Peter 2:11).*

DUTY STATION: Earth

UNIFORM: The whole armor of God

SOLDIER HANDBOOK: Sola Scriptura

DATE OF ENLISTMENT: Day of personal salvation

ANTHEM: To live is Christ and to die is gain. (Philippians 1:12)

PLEDGE: Deny myself, take up my cross daily and follow The Captain. (Matthew 16:24)

ENEMIES: Principalities, powers, rulers of the darkness of this age, spiritual hosts of wickedness in the heavenly places. (Ephesians 6:12)

STRATEGY: Pray without ceasing. (1 Thessalonians 5:17)

DAILY FIAT: We are more than conquerors through Him that loves us! (Romans 8:37)

WAGES: fruits of holiness

PENSION: Eternal life

RETIREMENT HOME: Heaven

What has it cost us? What have we denied ourselves? How do we take up His cross daily? Do we, like Mr. Keith Wheeler[79], who literally carries a 12-foot wooden cross round the world, do the same? Well, if we must follow Jesus, whatever radical, *violent*, or seemingly preposterous way we can, we must. The hymn-writer said, "My Jesus I love Thee…. For Thee **all** the pleasures of sin I resign."[80] Not just the sin, the pleasures which he would have enjoyed; what his flesh would have been thankful for; for that fleeting sensation of sinful satisfaction, he gave all of it up for **love.**

Have we denied ourselves the need to be "comfortable in your skin?" That is a buzz-phrase in our generation to promote vanity and lewdness. For the Christian, being comfortable in your own skin means accepting and loving the fact that you are created female or male. That is all that skin is about, because with God, there is no male or female. (Galatian 3:28) On earth, however, there is male or female, and we can never change that. We are to accept the gift of the earthly tent we're in and carry out our earthly gender roles as Jesus would have on earth. We are to cheerfully remain in that role, neither usurping nor abusing the other gender's role, or worse, physically changing from one sex to the other. (***Writer's note:** *What is it called? Transgender! Male, female, and transgender created He them? No.*)

Have we denied the need to feel heard because of our skin color? Or do we partake in the now rather awkward racial and gender equality movements and the like –initiatives which were originally founded strictly on the condition of peace, most of them inspired strongly by their founders' CHRISTIAN faith and conviction, which our generation, like *every* other thing we've received from our ancestors, has abused and attempted to destroy. We say equality. Our Role Model, Who, "being in very nature God, did not consider equality with God something to be used to his own advantage; rather, He made himself nothing by taking the very nature of a servant and was made in the likeness of men." (Philippians 2:6-7)

Black lives do not matter! White lives do not matter! These things account for nothing at the Gates of Heaven (Colossians 3:11). That heart. That soul. That mind. That will. That desire. Those works. *those* are what matter! "Let this mind be in you which was also in Christ Jesus." (Philippians 2:5)

---

[79] In 1982, Keith Wheeler committed his life to follow Jesus. In 1985, on Good Friday, in Tulsa, Oklahoma, USA, he began carrying a 12-foot, wooden cross. He has now walked over 25,000 miles, through more than 180 countries on all seven continents. (source: www.kw.org).
[80] William R. Featherston; *My Jesus, I love Thee* (1864).

Regardless what we profess, no matter how many pretty Bible verses we post on public spaces, no matter how well-known we are in church, no matter what size "Christian," "Child of God," "Lover of God" we put in the *bio* section of our profiles, yes, no matter how much we preach the gospel, or write Christian books: "Wherefore the Lord said, Forasmuch as this people draw near me with their mouth, and with their lips do honor me, BUT have removed their heart far from me, and their fear toward me is taught by the precept of men: Therefore, behold, I will proceed to do a marvelous work among this people, even a marvelous work and a wonder…" ***Writer's note:** *marvelous work and wonder? Wait for it*: "…for the wisdom of their wise men shall perish, and the understanding of their prudent men shall be hid. Woe unto them that seek deep to hide their counsel from the Lord, and their works are in the dark, and they say, Who seeth us? and who knoweth us?" (Isaiah 29:13-15)

What a terrific tragedy! As stated earlier, no one can teach anyone to fear God, or to do anything for God, unless each individual heart understands why. The true Christian, who understands God to an extent, will honestly want to remain in a cave and never come out, for fear of sin and worldly blemish. Not even the best preachers can teach anyone to fear God. Whatever premonition of fear or knowledge of God one may derive from regular church attendance or regular listening to sermons, will never stand as an immovable foundation for genuine fear of God. It will be evanescent in nature; before long, the individual will become weary and overburdened by the demands of the Christian faith.

To cheerfully deny oneself comes from *personal* understanding and knowledge of God. He cares nothing for our good works when our heart is stony, black, and dirty. The fact that He sees and knows all things we do, even in the dark, and the motives, even for the *seemingly* noblest of our actions is frightening enough.

There is a simple test for this: As long as we are *doing anything* or *not doing* anything to be noticed by humans, approved by humans, loved by humans, accepted by humans, or commended by humans, we are absolutely humanists; we are following the religion of humanism. We are not Christians following the religion of Christianity, regardless how similar those acts or non-acts might appear.

Absalom (2 Samuel 15:5-6), Herod (Mark 6:21-26), Felix (Acts 24:27) and even Apostle Peter (Galatians 2:11-14) - until he was publicly rebuked by Apostle Paul and repented - were all humanists, seeking the approval, praise, and acceptance of humans. Apostle Paul, on the other hand, made it clear,

"Obviously, I'm not trying to win the approval of people, but of God. If pleasing people were my goal, I would not be Christ's servant." (Galatians 1: 10) Joseph, in his privacy, said, "How then can I do this great wickedness and sin against God?" (Genesis 39:9) Also in His privacy, "Get out of here, Satan," Jesus told him. "For the Scriptures say, 'You must worship the Lord your God and serve only him.'" (Matthew 4:10) And He made it known, "I receive not honor from men." (John 5:41) As long as our heart's daily posture, in all our affairs, like the psalmist in Psalm 119:135 is, "smile on me, Lord," no sacrifice will be enough for Jesus Christ.

"IF anyone will come after me," Jesus said, "let him deny himself."

According to Merriam–Webster's definition, to "deny oneself" is *"to not allow oneself to enjoy things or to have the things one wants."*[81]

> *All things are lawful for me, but not all things are helpful; all things are lawful for me, but not all things edify.* 1 Corinthians 10:23

What have we denied? Fornication? Adultery? Smoking? Lying? Stealing? Drinking? Partying? Pornography? All moralistic. All legalistic. Even the cigarette companies will warn, **"Smokers are liable to die young."** So even if it is legal, they still warn you, knowing it is harmful to your health. Abstaining from evil, or doing what is morally or legally right, is nothing other than our human nature. Because we have been created in the likeness of a holy God, our consciences will naturally be affected by such unholy acts, *except for the reprobate.*

> *Indeed, when Gentiles, who do not have the law, do by nature what the law requires, they are a law to themselves, even though they do not have the law, since they show that the work of the Law is written on their hearts, their consciences also bearing witness, and their thoughts either accusing or defending them.* Romans 2:14-15

Moralism means not doing things for which you will feel guilty if you do them; that is not Christianity. Obeying all Ten Commandments (which no one perfectly can - *ask the Sanhedrin*) is nothing more than Biblical legalism, not Christianity. For instance, in Mormonism, a sect that identifies as Christian, their gospel of salvation teaches that, *"a god helps good people save themselves. They believe that their god was once a man who achieved godhood by obedience to the gospel plan. They believe they may do the same if they are obedient and participate in the right*

---

[81] https://www.merriam-webster.com/dictionary/deny%20one-self#:~:text=%3A%20to%20not%20allow%20oneself%20to,the%20simple%20pleasures%20in%20life.

ceremonies in their temples.'[82]

To think these acts will justify us before God signifies a fall from grace. That begs us to think what translation of the Holy Bible circulates in such a gathering: "Christ is become of no effect unto you, whosoever of you are justified by the law; ye are fallen from grace." (Galatians 5:4) Without the personal acceptance of Jesus Christ as your personal Lord and Savior, the journey still ends up in *small "h,"* hell. "But Lord, I have done all these things from birth." "Sell all you have, give the proceeds to the poor and follow me." The man departed sadly because he had great wealth…

All Jesus was asking the man to do was to deny himself. Yes, you have been an excellent moralist; yes, you have been the perfect legalist, *but* what have you denied as an expression of your love of Jesus? What do you love that you have given up, *because* you love, and not because you *have* to? Let's see this example: "God SO loved the world that He GAVE His ONLY begotten Son…" (John 3:16)

The "SO," adds emphasis to God's love. God hasn't merely loved us, He *SO* loved us. It was overwhelming. That can only be a heart thing. We say, "I love you, Jesus." We cry, "I love you, Jesus." Some decorate their bodies with graffiti which reads, "I love you, Jesus." Let's ask ourselves: Do we love Him, or do we *SO* love Him?

The "GAVE" is an expression of this enormous love He *gave* us. We say, "Thank You, Jesus, for what You did for me." Of course, thank You, Jesus, but this was a prerogative of a God Who *SO* loved us. This was an expression of His love – God's love, the same God whom some have called a moral monster *(have mercy Lord, for they know not what they do).* Our Jesus, whom we thank and love so much, was on the brink of asking for an alternative, even before His trial started. What Jesus did for us was obey the Father. The love was of the Father, and the Gift of Jesus was the personification of that love. Jesus did not come up with the idea of coming to die for us. God, who loved us, did so, and gave Jesus to us. So we say, "Thank You, Jesus for being a good and obedient Son. Thank You, God for loving us."

The "ONLY" aspect of this Gift means it was the *only* gift of its kind that existed. God, the Author of Love, knows very well that true love *will* cost something to the Giver, something which they must feel. He could not look at His own beloved Son, in Whom He was well pleased on that cross. The Omnipresent God who says, "never will I leave You, never will I forsake

---

[82] https://opc.org/new_horizons/NH04/07b.html

You" (Hebrews 13:5), for this split second, forsook His ONLY Son, and the ONLY Son said, *"Eloi, Eloi, lama sabachthani?"* (Mark 15:34) Some earthly parents comfort themselves when they see one of their children seeming to derail and say, "At least that is not our only child. We have more," but as God turned His face away from Jesus at that terrible hour, which other child could He look at? ***Writer's note:** *I was shuddering to think of the end of those who reject Jesus after this sacrifice of God. Please have mercy, Lord).* This was why Jesus resonated so much with the widow at the temple in Mark 12:42-44, whom He commended, 'For all they did cast in of their abundance; but she of her want did cast in all that she had, even all her living." and it was *her* gift which was counted worthy. Not the 10% from the abundance of the others.

Again, what have we denied? For every one of us, the *only* thing we have is our life; there is next to nothing else that cannot be replaced. Oh yes, there is nothing that cannot be replaced, added to, or embellished, apart from life. There is no other one of each of us on this earth. Each one of us has unique fingerprints. Therefore, to express the great love that some of us say we have for God, this will be the only and perfect gift we can *reasonably* give to Him (*but is it really a gift if, in the first place, it was given to us?*). To give our lives will not be to kill ourselves, but to do everything with our lives as a gift to God, whom we claim to love. This was also the only reason Abraham became who he was destined to be; it was his sacrificial act of *only*, his irreplaceable act of love. What have we denied ourselves as an expression of this love?

In our days, when we hear about Christians being persecuted and killed for their faith, our prayers go thus, "Lord, please save them. Remember Your children. Please Lord, deliver them." Deliver them? Deliver them to continue living? *On earth?* As opposed to going to Heaven as soon as possible to reign with our Creator and escape the sufferings of this present world?

To genuinely appreciate this faith we so quickly profess, we will need to go as far back and as deeply as possible into the available records history provides, from the early Church, to the early Christians, to the Apostles, and to our Lord Jesus, Himself.

The early Church in Rome lived under some of the most brutal leaders in history, specifically, Emperor Nero (37-68 AD) and Emperor Domitian (51-96 AD) who enjoyed the killing of Christians as leisure activities. These Roman Emperors saw themselves as gods. They then expected everyone under their rule to worship them as "lord" and "god," and executed every person, including members of their own family, who refused to do this, accusing them of atheism. Emperor Nero, within his 30 years on earth, managed to execute countless numbers of Christians. He also executed many others who did not swear allegiance to him alone, including his biological mother.

Identifying oneself as a Christian in this period was a capital offense. There were thousands of people, though, who took the name of Christ as all they had in this world and were eager to die for the faith. In his day, Ignatius, a Christian and Bishop of Antioch, prayed, *"I thank You, Lord, that You have thus honored me, like the Apostle Paul,"* shortly before he was dragged in chains to be devoured by lions in the Colosseum. That stadium-like building was filled with people who watched his gruesome death for their own gratification, because he refused to denounce Jesus Christ. His life's motto had been, *"The nearer the sword, the nearer God."*[83]

When tourists in the Medieval Age visited the Colosseum, they were told, *"Do you want martyr relics? Then take up the dust of the Colosseum – it is all the martyrs."* All the "sand" that filled the stadium grounds was the bodies of people who had been murdered, solely for being Christians. They had refused to denounce the faith after three lifelines were offered. The mass martyrdom of these believers served as a testimony to Christians and the Church. These martyrs' deaths led to the growth of the Church as the credibility of the faith was proven, becoming a Church *"worthy of God, worthy of honor and worthy of congratulations."*[84]

The Pauline Epistles, which today are a foundational source of many Christian doctrines, were mostly written by the Apostle Paul while he was imprisoned. Shortly before Apostle Paul embarked upon a journey to Jerusalem, where his fate of being imprisoned had been prophesied by Prophet Agabus, Apostle Paul declared thus as the people begged him not to go, **"**Why are you weeping and breaking my heart? I am ready not only to be bound, but also to die in Jerusalem for the name of the Lord Jesus." (Acts 21:13) He was ready to die, not just for the person of Jesus, but for the name of our Lord, Jesus Christ.

Perpetua (182-203 AD) was a 22-year-old widow and nursing mother. She was arrested under Emperor Septimius Severus of Carthage (*modern day Tunisia*) for being a Christian, and her pagan father pleaded with her to renounce her faith for the sake of her young child. While in her prison cell, Perpetua described it as becoming "a palace." On the day of her execution, she was given another opportunity by the Emperor to save herself for her child's sake by offering a sacrifice to the Emperor, but she refused. So, alongside four other Christians, she was taken to the local amphitheater, where they were

---

[83] Hanks G., 1992, 70 Great Christians, 1st edition, Evangel Publication.
[84] Ibis.

first savaged by wild beasts and then finally beheaded by sword.[85]

In Luke 14:26, Jesus warned, "IF anyone comes to me and does not hate father and mother, wife and children, brothers and sisters--yes, even their own life--such a person cannot be my disciple." Again, it is an *offer* and not a *summons*. We don't have to, but we may choose to. Nothing can be so dear that it is not worth giving up for Christ, and this is meant in its most literal terms. "Count the cost," He said.

Jochebed, the mother of Moses, took a risk by placing her three-month-old son in a basket and setting him adrift on the River Nile, leaving his fate up to God's will. Shortly after, she was given back her son to nurse him. This act of faith led her son to become the first great Israelite prophet. Moses was not only one of the greatest leaders of Israel, but it was he who led his people out of Egypt.

Abraham (Isaac), Hannah (Samuel), Elizabeth (John the Baptist), and the mother of Samson all gave up their children for God. He used them all mightily and all will never be forgotten in the sands of time. On the other hand, Eli refused to "hate" his children by disciplining them for God. He was a great prophet but came to a poor end.

> *He who loves his life will lose it, and he who hates his life in this world will keep it for eternal life.* John 12:25

There's a dear cost to self in following Jesus. There is no fast-track to Heaven. It is a life-long marathon, until our Commandant General blows the whistle to halt. There is no premium service to Heaven for the Soldier of Christ; it is the other way round. The more pain and suffering on earth, the greater we will be in the kingdom. The list of youngest Christian martyrs in history has boys and girls as young as ages six, seven, and eight, all killed because they stood for Jesus. We will never start living until we conquer the fear of death, despite our age, because we have the assurance that our Lord Jesus Christ has conquered death... *except we don't believe*. The fear of death is a paralyzing, lifetime bondage, and until we understand what Jesus has done for us, and abolish this fear by reason of this, we will *never* live as God intends us to (Hebrews 2:14-15)

The thought of death itself should bring some form of comfort and smiles to the faces of genuine Christians, because that is our stepping-stone into eternal glory. To die is better than to live. Paul knew this and in Philippians 1:23, he expressed his desire to be with Christ; he knew there was nothing

---

[85] Ibid.

better than for a Christian to be with Christ physically. King Solomon, in Ecclesiastes 7:1, declared, the day of death better than that of birth. Death is a good thing for a Christian, the devil himself becomes terrified of us, as there is nothing, he can do to us! Kill us, that's alright. ***It is finished!***

Ultimately, our greatest example is in our Lord Jesus, and the sacrifice He paid for us. Jesus could have, rightly and within His authority, done as He said, 'Do you think I cannot call on my Father, and he will at once put at my disposal more than twelve legions of angels?" (Matthew 26:52) Yet the price He paid for each and every one of us was by the most self-sacrificial statement in history, declared face-down, not once but twice, as recorded, by our Lord, Jesus Christ "nevertheless not as I will, but as Thou wilt." (Matthew 26: 39&42)

The Battle of Sense Over Soul

Our earthly bodies are weak, vile, and mortal (Philippians 3:21). Apostle Paul, with all the grace he had, said, "I cast a blow to my body and put it under subjection." We must each refuse to let our bodies and our senses, eyes, mouths, noses, ears, *and* touch/feel, render us castaways. Knowing these things, how would we let sense win over soul? Even if all five of our senses stopped working, our lives would not end with them. Even if our brains stopped working, life could go on; as for our heart, the gateway to our soul, the moment it stops working, it *is* over. Sense should not win over soul. Our senses are our slaves, not our taskmasters, otherwise, *"they condemn us to unceasing drudgery and reward us with pain, remorse and poverty,"*[86] "Use your sense," a phrase meant to connote acting wisely, is a farce! Our senses *will* fail us; wisdom comes from just one Source.

Apostle Paul's example of casting a blow to his body must be taken in its most literal sense. Flagellation, the process of flogging oneself for mortification of the flesh, was a trend in older centuries and as recently as Pope John Paul II's reign. Sarah Osborn, an American evangelist, undertook this process of regularly flogging herself *"to remind her of her continued sin, depravity, and vileness in the eyes of God,"*[87] Oh, the 21st Century Christian dare not; we say, "Jesus has died for me." Without holiness, no one is seeing God, so it might be

---

[86] KJV Dictionary Definition.
[87] Julius H. Rubin Religious Melancholy and Protestant Experience in America. Oxford University Press (1994).

necessary to put a good slap to our mouths from time to time. When we tell lies, we should pull our tongue out, twist it so hard, AND confess. "If you claim to be religious but don't control your tongue, you are fooling yourself and you religion is worthless." (James 1:27)

Ouch! Christians, we cannot use the same tongues to bless and curse. (James 3:7-12) It is not a "slip of tongue." Tame your *bloody* tongue! *Oops!* There you go. Proverbs also tells us it takes hands to build a home, but just words to destroy it. Men and women of God who engage in debates about God and His person should not be found among us. The danger of idleness, young widows being the context in which it was said, still applies to every human being:

> *And besides they learn to be idle, wandering about from house to house, and not only idle but also gossips and busybodies, saying things which they ought not.* 1 Timothy 5:13

Idleness has a ripple effect. The brain is stagnant and needs stimulation, so it urges the mouth to stimulate it by engaging in crass talk, but the Bible warns, "In the multitude of words sin is not lacking." (Proverbs 10:19) In their day, those idlers wandered from house to house, thus exercising their legs a bit. In our day, by contrast, we lay in the comfort of our homes, jumping from chat to chat, app to app, and gibbering, only to don our "passcode armor" to protect our privacy. We must work hard to restrain our tongues. This is arguably the hardest thing for humans to do and no, Christian, it is not the work of the Holy Spirit. We just need to shut up!

> *But Jesus made no reply, not even to a single charge--to the great amazement of the governor.* Matthew 27:14

Above all else:

> *But I tell you that men will give an account on the Day of Judgment for every careless word they have spoken. For by your words you will be acquitted, and by your words you will be condemned.* Matthew 12:36-37

Ears: We must be willing to put our hands over our ears and scream so loudly that we prevent the entrance of filthy information. We must be fiercely intentional about the music we listen to. Rap is your thing? There's Christian rap. Jazz? Got it. Classical? Check. There's Christian music in every genre. So, if there happens to be a genre in which Christian music isn't available, well, you just found your calling.

Listening to gossip and slander, whether directly or by mass media, we should completely avoid. Filtering the information that goes into our soul through the channel of our ears is vital. Once we realize that the thing is good, we ought to "be quick to listen." (James 1:19) The Bible tells us repeatedly to hear the word of God, for it is the only way to build faith.[88] When probing people who have fallen away from the Faith, in order to understand the reason, we will soon discover there was no conscientious, personal Bible study and meditation to begin with, or what had existed, was no longer. To stop hearing the Living Word of God is death to one's faith. There is absolutely no way to continue the race. (A rigorous study on this rather deep and delicate subject will be carried out in the next chapter.)

Eyes: In digital cell 2020, handcuffed by our little ~~demons~~ devices, our sight is the one sense about which we must be most radical! We must blindfold our eyes when we are seeing things that can corrupt our inner man, but not at injustice and cruelty. If our phones have become our gods, calling us to worship them first thing every morning and last thing before we go to bed, we should put the little demons in the bottom of our closets, only using them when we need them to work *for us*! "If your right eye causes you to sin, pluck it out and cast it from you; for it is more profitable for you that one of your members perish, than for your whole body to be cast into hell." (Matthew 5:29)

The first thought many may have about this verse is, "Jesus did not mean it literally," however, this text stands if we must do so to save our souls. If what we choose to look at has the possibility of destroying heart and soul, if we have become slaves to our eyes and what we must watch, we *will* need to pluck them out and rely on God to guide us. He promised:

> *I will bring the blind by a way they did not know; I will lead them in paths they have not known. I will make darkness light before them, and crooked places straight. These things I will do for them, and not forsake them.* Isaiah 42:16

In February 2018, then age 21, Kaylee Muthart ripped out both her eyeballs while she was high on methamphetamine. Although it was a drug-induced incident, in her words, "I had both my eyes, but they didn't help me notice how dangerous my life had become." Before tragically ripping out her eyes, Kaylee described herself as a straight-A student and a *religious* Christian. Two years later, this permanently blind young lady with prosthetic eyeballs to fill out her face, gave her testimony. She had rediscovered faith, accepted the Holy Spirit, and read her Braille Bible often. In her words, "God saved me. I might have lost my sight, but He saved me from death, because He knew, if I kept my sight, I'd be dead today...I'm happier blind than I ever was

---

[88] Romans 10:17.

sighted."[89]

Again, the sad story of Michal, the daughter of the failed King Saul and wife of King David, is an instructive example. Michal let her eyes fail her heart; "The light of the body is the eye: if therefore thine eye be single; thy whole body shall be full of light. But if thine eye be evil; thy whole body shall be full of darkness. If therefore the light that is in thee be darkness, how great is that darkness!" (Matthew 6:22-24) and let her heart fail her mouth; "...for out of the abundance of the heart, the mouth speaks." (Matthew 12:34) and let her mouth fail her ability to be fruitful and bear children. "So, Michal, the daughter of Saul, remained childless throughout her entire life." (2 Samuel 6:23)

Our eyes are the windows to our souls. We can choose to fill our souls with either darkness or light. Jesus made this statement over 2,000 years ago, but no generation has needed this as desperately as we do in the "Information Age." With easy access to anything and everything within seconds, we must be radical about what we use our eyes to view. If we ponder on *all that is in the world* listed in 1 John 2:16, i.e., the lust of the flesh, the lust of the eyes, and the pride of life, we will find that our little white eyeballs are the common factor in each of them.

Keep thy heart with all diligence; for out of it are the issues of life. Proverbs 4:23

"Anyone who looks at a woman lustfully has already committed adultery with her is his heart." (Matthew 5:28) *Who will deliver me from this body of death?*

Touch & Feel: "Touch no unclean thing;" (Isaiah 52:11) "Touch no unclean thing." (2 Corinthians 6:17) Oh, the sorrows that have come from a simple "touch." The pains, the regrets, the *"had-I-known's"* – all from a touch! We wanted to taste the drink, so we lifted it with our hands, took a sip with our mouths, and could barely remember anything the next day. We agreed to just touch, but now we are pondering how we will break the *"baby on the way"* news. We must possess, so with our hands, we steal.

The holy hands we lift up in prayer to God (1 Timothy 2:8), are the same hands with which we ask for anointing to heal the sick and raise the dead. They are the same hands with which we pray, "Bless the work of my hands." We use those same hands to invent evil. With those same hands, we write libel. In our digital cell 21st Century, our hands have become our mouths. We do not say it anymore, we type it. Not one of us can create a finger, much less hands, so we must honor this gift God has given to us and keep them

---

[89] https://www.wyff4.com/article/woman-who-gouged-her-own-eyes-out-rediscovers-faith-finds-new-vision/33610454

clean. God made man with His own hand and didn't speak us into existence like all His other creation. By our own hands, when we depart from the Faith, we pierce ourselves with sorrows, it is not the devil doing so (1 Timothy 6:10). The hand has the power to work wonders or to slog destruction

Mouth: Should our bellies and voracious appetites for food and carnal satisfaction become our gods? When our stomachs are rumbling, even when we are not fasting, we must be able to give it a physical blow and tell it to stop talking, lest it starve! Feed it with the Word of God and give joy and rejoicing to your heart (Jeremiah 15:16). "Food for the stomach and the stomach for food and God will destroy them both." (1 Corinthians 6:13) Feeding on the Word, which will never die, is much better than that which, in 48-hours, is into the pit of a septic tank.

We would, however, be misleading ourselves if we joined a trend of *Intermittent Fasting*, of which the sole purpose is to look a certain way, and then suppose this is us conquering our bellies. "…whatever you do, do it all for the glory of God." (1 Corinthians 10:31) Within the same time, or even less, it won't be a surprise to discover that the flesh will refuse to embark on a spiritual fast. The act of eating, or not eating, is not what matters, "food does not bring us near to God; we are no worse if we do not eat, and no better if we do." (1 Corinthians 8:8) What matters is our heart's posture and pleasure in sacrificing natural promptings out of love for God, or conquering the flesh and its desires to let the Spirit lead us.

NOSE: From Esau, basking in the savory smell of his brother's red pottage and giving up his birthright,[90] to the three Hebrew boys coming out of the fire without the smell of smoke, to the offering of the righteous being a sweet smell, a sacrifice acceptable well-pleasing to God,[91] we see the power of two tiny holes in our face called our nose.

How do we smell when we walk into a room? No matter what exotic, luxurious, limited-edition perfume we have applied to immerse ourselves, the malodorous, musty, putrid, funky smell of that salient but subtle *sin* will always overshadow its carrier: "I will not smell the savor of your sweet odours." (Leviticus 26:31) It is one of those foul smells that we know is coming from somewhere, but we can't place it. That is what the presence of sin does within us and to others around us. We look great, we have the best perfume on, yet we *know* we stink. We can't place that foul smell coming from within us, from our souls. We go to a place, even an outdoor public space where the air is so

---

[90] Genesis 25:29.
[91] Philippians 4:18.

72

fresh, the fragrance of the roses and lilies are blooming, yet something from us is overclouding the freshest air. Yet, everyone is repulsed by us, "instead of sweet smell there shall be stink." (Isaiah 3:24) That is that smell which is manufactured and sprayed only by the prince of the power of the air himself, CEO of Hades Corp., and founder of Pride™, leading a fast-track route to destruction.

We will be wise to smell this on ourselves first, and never bother to smell it on any other individual. We all have a smell. Almost-blind Isaac was only convinced to bless Jacob as Esau when he "caught the smell of his clothes." (Genesis 27:27) We will be wise to know the smell we carry, pleasant as Lebanon or vile as putrefaction. As long as we imagine we are able to point it out in another individual, we still just smell ourselves from within. "Rather, in humility value others above yourselves." (Philippians 2:3)

Remember, "I hate pride and arrogance" (Proverbs 8:13), and what is worse, "He is able to humble those who walk in pride" (Daniel 4:37), knowing that "It is a terrible thing to fall into the hands of the living God!" (Hebrews 10:31) *Please have mercy upon us, Lord.*

Thomas á Kempis stated:

> *A man makes the most progress and merits the most grace precisely in those matters wherein he gains the greatest victories over self and most mortifies his will. If there were nothing else to do but praise the Lord God with all your heart and voice, if you had never to eat, or drink, or sleep, but could praise God always and occupy yourself solely with spiritual pursuits, how much happier you would be than you are now, a slave to every necessity of the body! Would that there were no such needs, but only the spiritual refreshments of the soul which, sad to say, we taste too seldom!*[92]

The Kingdom of God suffers violence, *even from our earthly bodies/senses*, but our "violence," *and* the grace of God given to us, will take it by force. These things are neither childish nor extreme. These are proactive steps of guarding our hearts and saving our souls. Yes, **save *your* soul.** (James 1:21)

We must not underestimate the power of our "little members." Eyes? *Ask David.* Stomach? *Ask Esau.* Feelings? *Ask Cain.* Money? *Ask Ananias and Saphira.* Ego? *Ask Herod, Saul, Goliath, and most important, ask the little prince and ruler of this world, his royal, earthly, lowly worldliness, sir satan, lucifer, devil, founder and*

---

[92] Thomas A Kempis, Imitations of Christ.

CEO of Hades Corp., actively hiring members around the clock, every day.

Do we realize this, Christians? We are living in a world neither ruled, nor created by satan, whose government consists of stealing, killing, and destroying.[93] Have we met an angrier soul? The One and only Creator, Who created this world in which we live, has assured us that in this world of satan, we "shall have tribulation but be of good cheer, I have overcome the world." (John. 16:33) Two things are guaranteed from this statement: On one hand, there will be troubles, trials, temptations, and tribulation, and on the other, Jesus Christ *has* overcome the world. ***It is finished.***[94] Our King of glory, the Lord strong and mighty, mighty in battle,[95] has won the victory. He has shown us The Way by setting an example for us. Our King did not send us to the battlefield and stay back at home, lying in bed or strolling on the roof of His palace. As a Good Captain, He has led us by the hand and conquered every foe. So He urges us to fight with His assurance that, ***"I give you the authority to trample on serpents and scorpions, and over all the power of the enemy, and nothing shall by any means hurt you.***[96]***"*** Our enemies in their various forms have been defeated by our Redeemer: sin (*nailed to the cross!*[97]), death (*destroyed!*[98]), hell (*even if we tried, the great chasm bars us!*[99]), trials of fire (*not a smell of smoke!*[100]) storms of despair (*just cruising with God!*[101]), weapons (*doomed from start!*) [102]They might only try, but theirs is a lost battle, therefore, we should remain joyful and adore The One who has won it all for us.

As servants of Christ then, answering to Him every morning, afternoon and night, whether He calls us or not, whether we feel like it or not, but because we are His helpless servants, the antidote to the improper use of our senses will be: TASTE the Goodness of the Lord! SMELL the Fragrant Aroma of Christ! SEE the Finished Work of Jesus! HEAR the Spirit Bearing Witness! FEEL the Freedom of God's Grace.[103]

Our life's mission statement should be: "I want (need) to know Christ – yes, to know the power of His resurrection and participate in His sufferings,

---

[93] John 10:10.
[94] John 19:30.
[95] Psalm 24:8.
[96] Luke 10:19.
[97] Colossians 2:14.
[98] 2 Timothy 1:10.
[99] Luke 16:26.
[100] Daniel 3:27.
[101] Isaiah 43:7.
[102] Isaiah 54:7.
[103] Andrew Farley Bible' Plan, Awakening Your 5 Spiritual Senses to God's Grace, You Version Bible app.

becoming like Him in His death." (Philippians 3:10) In pursuit of this cause, denying ourselves is to win Christ. The only way to find Him is to seek Him with all our heart. (Jeremiah 29:13) The heroes of our Faith recorded in the Bible: Abel, Abraham, Moses, Joseph, the Apostles, and world-favorite, Rahab, amongst others; martyrs of ancient and modern history, Lady Jane Grey, Sophia and her three daughters, Faith, Hope and Charity; Magdalene of Nagasaki; Dietrich Bonhoeffer; Jim Eliot; "the man for all seasons," Sir Thomas More, and recently, the 2019 Sri Lankan martyrs, woke up every day and resolved in their hearts, "For to me, to live is Christ and to die is gain." (Philippians 1:21)

Amusingly, here's what is said about the celebrities of faith's *"Hall of Fame:"* "These were all commended for their faith, yet none of them received what had been promised." (Hebrews 11:39) They had not met Jesus Christ in their lifetime, yet they surrendered their lives to be ***tortured, refusing to turn from God in order to be set free. They placed their hope in a better life after the resurrection. Some were jeered at, and their backs were cut open with whips. Others were chained in prisons. Some died by stoning, some were sawed in half and others were killed with the sword. Some went about wearing skins of sheep and goats, destitute and oppressed and mistreated. They were too good for this world, wandering over deserts and mountains, hiding in caves and holes in the ground.***[104] They had no experience of resurrection, yet they believed. They had no direct access to God (before Jesus), yet they believed, to the extent that their mortal lives were offered as sacrifices unto God.

What about us? Blessed beyond deserving, with a wealth of people and encyclopedias of experiences as examples, mercifully provided us by God that we may learn:

> *Therefore, since we are surrounded by such a GREAT cloud of witnesses, let us throw off everything that hinders and the sin that so easily entangles. And let us run with perseverance the race marked out for us, fixing our eyes on Jesus, the Pioneer (author) and Perfecter (finisher) of faith. For the joy set before him he endured the cross, despised its shame, and is sat down at the right hand of the throne of God.* Hebrews 12:1-2

History gives us compendia of brothers and sisters, young and old, who resolved in their hearts and souls, ***that in nothing I shall be ashamed, but that with all boldness, as always, so now also Christ shall be magnified in my body, whether it be by life, or by death.***[105] Victoriously, they

---

[104] Hebrews 11: 35-38.
[105] Philippians 1:20.

sojourned this earthly pilgrimage right into the Kingdom of God. On the outside, they were *mere* flesh and blood, but the state of their hearts, the wealth of their souls, had a perfection we must strive to attain. How did the beautiful *Cinderella of the Bible*, Queen Esther, commoner to queen, put it? "If I die, I die." (Esther 4:16) Until we find a cause for Jesus Christ, to which we commit with the words, **If I perish, I perish,** we are simply Dummy Cakes, filling pews in a church, but not citizens of the Kingdom of Heaven.

We must choose to live internally. We must choose to live from the inside out. What a beautiful statement was made at the wedding of a friend, Mrs. Dolapo Alloh nee Faleti, when the brother of the groom made his Best Man Speech: *"Dolapo, the least beautiful thing about you is your beauty,"* and oh, Dolapo is very beautiful to the human eyes. However, the heart she carries? Goodness! That IS a heart! Christians, men and woman alike, such statements should be the slogan attached to our names. It is fruitless conformity to beautify/adorn ourselves the way the world does. Let God's own treasure, the cause of Christ, be the beauty we bear. No matter how clean and magnificent a cake we might appear to be on the outside, "Who can bring a clean thing out of an unclean thing? Not one." (Job 14:4) What an anti-climax!

> *You have already been pruned and purified by the message I have given you. Remain in me, and I will remain in you. For a branch cannot produce fruit if it is severed from the vine, and you cannot be fruitful unless you remain in me.* John 15:3-4

In beauty pageants every year, a beauty queen is crowned. The queen from the previous year has to stop whatever she is doing, fly from wherever she is in the world, attend the current pageantry, and with her own hands, take off her crown and title (which she received from someone else the previous year) and hand them over to "the next best thing." And the cycle continues. These terms and conditions are well-known, from the moment of signing up for the pageantry. I beg to question the essence in this rather "mess of pottage" exercise. At least, in a monarchy, as long as the reigning monarch is alive, the crown remains on their head, albeit, immediately after death knocks, their crown and throne are possessed by their heir apparent.

> *...They do it to get a crown that will not last (corruptible), but we do it to get a crown that will last forever (incorruptible). Therefore, I do not run like someone running aimlessly. I do not fight like a boxer beating the air.* 1 Corinthians 9:27-28

We must pass through life, and pass through it faithfully, to be fit for the Kingdom of Righteousness, Peace and Joy. We must present ourselves FIT for the Kingdom. Where are our scars of suffering in satan's world? Where is our proof of being hated for the sake of Jesus Christ? What story of rejection for the Cause do we have to tell? We must present ourselves FIT for the Kingdom by a testimony, *I have fought a good fight, I have finished my course, I have kept the faith,*[106] and then be told, *Well done, good and faithful servant... enter thou into the joy of your Lord.* [107] GLORY!

Where is our record of scars? Feel the pain, enjoy the pain, taste your tears. "When Jesus had tasted it, He said, "It is finished!' then He bowed His head and gave up His Spirit" (John 19:30) Christ rejected the offer of wine mixed with myrrh's soporific influence, which could have dulled the excruciating pain he went through (Mark 15:23). He needed no antidote to all that pain and suffering. No, if He was going to pay a price for us, He was going to pay it fully, without any shortcuts or easy ways-out. We, on the other hand, find it a task to simply say, "In Jesus' name," a meager "I-J-N," is what we offer to my Lord and personal Savior, Jesus Christ.

The second offer of wine, the sour wine which He drank, was given to keep Him conscious for as long as possible; the resulting effect of which was prolonged pain. (According to the Roman and Greek literature and as used in the old testament, Ruth 2:14, sour wine is a refreshing drink commonly used by laborers and soldiers because it relieved thirst more effectively than water.[108])

Why do we plead as hopeless people for the thorns in our flesh to cease? Apostle Paul pleaded with the Lord three times for his thorns - a messenger of satan to torment his flesh - to cease. However, this torment to his flesh – not his heart, soul nor spirit – was a gift to his soul to keep him from becoming conceited; this was to suppress the "superego," the pride of life that could have risen in his heart after being given "surpassingly great revelations." At the time of the torment, the pain to his flesh was severe, but Almighty God, Who hates the proud but gives grace to the humble, will chastise those He loves, assuring us that, "My grace is sufficient for you, for my power is made perfect in weakness." (2 Corinthians 12:9)

His testimony from this experience was, "Therefore I will boast all the more gladly about my weaknesses, so that Christ's power may rest on me... I delight in weaknesses, in insults, in hardships, in persecutions, in difficulties. For when I am weak, then I am strong." (2 Corinthians 12:10) The ruler of this world, and his principles, however, dictate the exact opposite of what the

---

[106] 2 Timothy 4:7.

[107] Matthew 25:21.

[108] https://www.desiringgod.org/articles/the-wine-jesus-drank

Lord will have us do. This strange land, where we temporarily lodge, expects our weaknesses to be hidden, masked under personal branding and image consultation, makeup, or careers, among other guises. Our anger problems, huge debts, poor character traits, addictions, immoralities, perversions, decadences, cycles of poor habits, and a variety of bitterness only each individual heart knows, (Proverbs 14:10) are suppressed. Thus, we fit into a world where we do not belong. By our own design, we render God's grace insufficient for us, because it is a grace invisible to the naked eye.

His power cannot work in our lives because there is a pre-condition for the perfection of His power to manifest. That non-negotiable pre-condition is weakness, unashamed weakness. It is proud weakness, boastful weakness, and hapless surrender. "He who covers sin will not prosper but whoever confesses and forsakes them will have mercy." Proverbs 28:13

The widow of the prophet who had died and left his family in debt, putting his sons at the risk of being sold into slavery,[109] thought to herself, *"How can I, a whole Prophet's wife beg for money? It is better for the boys to be sold to slavery. I can just tell people they have gone abroad as missionaries but never in a million years will I ever disgrace myself and my husband's reputation and ask for any help. My husband was a man who truly feared God so I am sure that God will send help because 'never have I seen the righteous nor forsaken nor his seed begging bread.'[110] "God will do His work."* No, dear friend, the Bible says **she cried out**[111] to Prophet Elisha for help.

From that helpless, transparent state of total surrender, she laid bare everything before the anointed man of God. She left nothing out, not even the seemingly insignificant small jar of olive oil, *the "little sin,"* as it was just "one time," or "a white lie," or "a long time ago," and therefore needed no acknowledgment. She laid it all out, and that small jar was the key to her complete breakthrough.

The instruction given to her was to gather as many empty jars as she could. As long as she brought empty vessels, there was sufficient oil for the filling. No record is given of how many empty vessels she provided, but if she brought 10,000,000,000,000,000,000,000,000,000,000,000,000 *empty* vessels, they *would* have been filled. (*We, on the other hand, have 10,000,000,000,000,000,000 selfies.*)

How can we be filled with God's grace, or allow for the perfect working of His power, if we have filled ourselves with so much of us? If our "significant

---

[109] 2 Kings 4:1-7.
[110] Psalm 37:25.
[111] 2 Kings 4:1.

others," careers, possessions, accolades, beauty, selfish and greedy ambitions, number of "followers," worldly pleasures, institutions we attended, number of countries we have visited, carnal plans, or *whatever idol fits each profile*, have filled us up, how exactly do we expect God's grace or abundance of mercy to work for us? No idol is a "small' jar." "A little yeast works through the whole batch of dough".[112] It will be an intellectual absurdity if we underestimate the power of these "little member(s) (because)... it is a fire, a world of evil among the parts of the body. It corrupts the whole body, sets the whole course of one's life on fire and is a fire that comes from the fire of hell itself." (James 3:5-6)

Like the Apostle Paul, we are to count everything, even the very best works of our hands, done in good faith, that could make us trust in ourselves, as garbage. (Philippians 3:8) We are to reject outright, every appearance of praise from people and point them toward God. Examine these scenarios:

Scenario A:

On the appointed day Herod, wearing his royal robes, sat on his throne and delivered a public address to the people. They shouted, "This is the voice of a god, not of a man." Immediately, because Herod did not give praise to God, an angel of the Lord struck him down, and he was eaten by worms and died. Acts 12:21-23

Scenario B:

Now while he was in Jerusalem at the Passover Festival, many people saw the signs he was performing and believed in his name. But Jesus would not entrust himself to them, for he knew all people. He did not need any testimony about mankind, for he knew what was in each person. John 2:23-25

Who, being in very nature God, did not consider equality with God something to be used to his own advantage; rather, he made himself nothing by taking the very nature of a servant, being made in human likeness. And being found in appearance as a man, he humbled himself by becoming obedient to death even death on a cross! Therefore, God exalted him to the highest place and gave him the name that is above every name, that at the name of Jesus every knee should bow, in heaven and on earth and under the earth, and every tongue acknowledge that Jesus Christ is Lord, to the glory of God the Father. Philippians 2:6-11

King Herod, by a mere speech he gave, let the praise of men cause his grisly death. Jesus, the Carpenter[113] from Nazareth, with the signs and wonders He

---

[112] Galatians 5:9.
[113] Mark 6:3.

performed, accepted no praise from men. He did not even think about it. Today, as He sits on His eternal throne, all men, from the *greatest* and *wisest* to the *smallest and most foolish,* call on His incomparable name to deliver us from any and every force. In these days of "having a voice," "being heard," *TedTalks,* and "influencer," we must rigorously deflect the praise and approval of humans; their mere appearance is all we can ever see and know.

Our self-emptying must *not* be partial; it must be absolute. Midway will *not* cut it. If we are to receive God's full grace to work in our weakness, there is no room for halfway, because **what harmony is there between Christ and belial? What agreement is there between the temple of God and idols?**[114] With emptiness in its entirety, out-and-out, we can be established in our resolve, that in the presence of all, whether friend or foe, the Almighty God, the Lifter of Men, He who works abundantly,[115] will so anoint our heads with oil that our cups will overflow. *But we **must** be empty.*

There is a pre-selection stage for partaking in this race; that is the genuine acceptance of Jesus Christ as our personal Lord and Savior. Until this act of faith is done, the individual remains doing tuck-jumps at the start line. At age 80 or age eight, if you have not received Jesus Christ as your personal Lord and Savior, you have been tuck-jumping your way through life, so know this: You have not started the race of life. It is illusory, because tuck-jumps, also a cardiovascular exercise just like running, will get the heart racing. The heart of somebody aged 80, who has been tuck-jumping away at the starting line of life, will be pumping very fast, producing *a lot* of sweat. Another individual, also aged 80, who has been running the race since accepting Jesus Christ at age 15, might outwardly look like their age-mate and also be sweating profusely. Yet when their 80-year-old hearts are examined, when questions are asked, as one of them begins to confabulate, it won't be long before discerning who has been jumping and who was been faithfully running. "I will judge between cattle and cattle." (Ezekiel 34:22)

Very likely, the faithful runner will be too exhausted to utter much chatter, as this race has been ongoing for 65 years and, *hopefully,* counting. Therefore, their views, experiences, trials, joys, highs, lows, adrenaline levels, dopamine levels, gains, denials, sacrifices, losses, tears, cheers, and a wealth of experience, will be much too overwhelming to utter all at once. It might take sharing an experience per day. The jumper, on the other hand, began confabulating and jumping on the same spot for 80 years with such a limited view; they see no finish line, but merely excite themselves at the *prospect* of running, not

---

[114114] 2 Corinthians 6:15-26).
[115] Titus 3:6.

actually running. It won't be long before one is discerned from the other; you can't miss it! *No fool like an old fool.*

How, then, do we accept Jesus? We lay aside every weight and the sin that so easily entangles us. We must examine what weights are, and jettison each and every one of them, if we are serious about this race:

The Weight That Hinders and The Sin That Entangles

Physical Weight:

These are the weights we see. As Christians, this simply means our appearance. It is very heart-breaking these days to see the way Christians appear. For goodness sake, where are the mirrors and front cameras of our phones? Why do we knowingly appear as circus clowns and claim the badge of Christian, even in the Tabernacle of God, the physical church? We have Jezebellian faces on the pulpit, causing a complete distraction from the Good News being preached. There are self-professed Christian women who boldly move about, with private, intimate parts of their bodies on full display.

For goodness sake, if cleavage were unique to an individual, if it were created by that individual *(we have doctors attempting to create it today)* by all means, put it all on display! You made it, show off your works! However, if the Creator of all things has given us these beautiful parts of our bodies, why don't we treasure them and keep the Temple of the Holy God sacred? That means keeping it exclusive, secure, clean, private, holy, and accessible only to the High Priest. Why don't we treat these bodies as the Holy of Holies, Christiana?[116]

Why does covering our hair become a source of debate and contempt within ourselves in the church, if the Church requests we do so? Whether or not it was a contextual issue when the Apostle Paul said so, is it such a big deal to cover our heads for a few hours before the God we love? Did we make our hair? *(These days, we seem to.)* Frankly, hats and head coverings are very elegant and add a Temple-worthy appearance to a woman. Why do we become embittered and enraged when the issue of covering our hair comes up? Where is the heart of love to Jesus? Where is the self-denial to flaunt the latest, silkiest, *sometimes hideous-looking* weaves? Why do we use ridiculous, clown-like colors, in the name of trends, freedom, and fashion? Where is modesty? Less

---

[116] This is the name the female Pilgrim is called in John Bunyan's 'The Pilgrim's Progress'.

has forever been, and always will be, more. The kingdom of God works with small…small everything.

Why do we "weighten" ourselves in our appearance? The shoes we wear are hard to walk in. The skirts and pants are too tight to sit in. *"Flaunting my figure,"* – unfortunately, the figure wasn't drawn by you. You are not your own! We must be grateful for whatever earthly tent Our Lord has given us, and treat it like the Lord's. Whatever appearance that will make us self-conscious, draw unnecessary attention to us, or even make us think twice about being appropriate if we stood before the Lord Jesus Christ, let us use that to test our physical presentation of self.

Why does our make-up have to conform to the dictates of the world's standards? Whatever the world loves, we must remember, God detests (Luke 16:15). God gave us nails, yet we prefer the world's talons so we look like those for whom our hearts truly pant. When we pay so much attention to our appearance, we have failed from the start. *All* the work we will ever need to do in this life is in our wicked hearts. That is where our full, undivided attention should be, but we have all neglected it so much that the trend in the world is immorality, depravation and shamelessness.

We hear of the piggish acts that some of the best-looking women engage in privately, and we are disappointed that our worldly heroes were not the angels of light they branded themselves to be. Why should there be any surprise when hearts have been dilapidated to the point of rottenness, sometimes, beyond redemption? We must never make our appearance our idol. We do not have to look a certain way for *any* reason. Who calls the shots for Servants of Christ? Our manual is the Holy Bible. It says modest, and modest we *will* be. To our discredit, Sister Christiana, I'll tell you who has set the standard in appearance for us: The Muslima[117] has set the standard for us.

Brother Christian,[118] this is more difficult for you, because the appearance of men is relatively more straight-forward than Christiana's. However, "some sins are clearly evident, preceding them to judgment, but those of some men follow later." (1 Timothy 5:24) Christiana's idol is the enemy we know and can easily tackle before judgement. What about those we can't see?

Regardless, some brothers in their appearance, even on the pulpit, can only cause wonder at whether it is the *same* gospel that the great men of our faith, both ancient and modern, have preached. Where is the simplicity? Why do we need to stir controversy over whether we are new school or old school?

---

[117] A female adherent of Islam
[118] Ibid. The male Pilgrim.

It is simply a personal test of which you love, for Jesus.

C.S Lewis stated,

A man who makes his golf or his motor-bicycle the center of his life, or a woman who devotes all her thoughts to clothes or bridge or her dog, is being just as 'intemperate' as someone who gets drunk every evening.[119]

It was said of the disciples in Acts 4:13, "and they took knowledge of them, that they had been with Jesus." The Jewish leaders recognized these men had been with Jesus. These days, with the way Christians appear, talk, walk and work, it's hard to tell if they've ever heard of church, not to mention Jesus Christ, who was beaten mercilessly and eventually died a lonely death on the Cross of Calvary. We will be shocked - *or not* - to discover they are pastors and pastoresses with *thriving* "ministries." We are not our appearances. We are our souls! Our names will be written in the Book of Life, not our passport photographs. What is attached to our names?

The world hated, rejected, and still rejects Christ, "But first must he suffer many things, and be rejected of this generation." (Luke 17:25) Why should they like us, accept us, approve us, feel comfortable around us? WHY should we *look* like the world? Our duty is to focus on loving every single person, without expecting reciprocation of such love. There is no better example of this act of giving, regardless of receiving love than, 'Father, forgive them, for they do not know what they do." (Luke 23:34) If we are so affected by any human being not loving us, our personal, emotional account in God's bound-less Bank of Love is in deficit. Fill it up.

Material Weight: "Narrow is the way," Jesus said in Matthew 7:14. As Christians, our options become more and more limited as we journey through earth. We begin to realize, if we must go through this pilgrimage in the most focused and pious manner, there are too many material things we will need to throw off. Jesus instructed His disciples, 'don't take any money in your money belts—no gold, silver, or even copper coins. Don't carry a traveler's bag with a change of clothes and sandals or even a walking stick." (Matthew 10:9-10)

The 21st Century Christian will shudder at this, but Francis of Assisi took this literally. He never wore shoes during his earthly sojourn. He was born to a wealthy cloth-merchant in Italy and, at first, lived a life of ease and luxury. Gambling, high-living with royalty and noblemen of his day, were common sport to Francis. When he became a Christian, his father called him a

---

[119] Lewis, C S. Mere Christianity. New York: Macmillan, 1960.

madman, and sued him in court when Francis used his money for religious purposes.

During the court hearing, in the cold winter months, given the option to deny his faith, Francis took off all his clothes before the onlookers, and gave them, as well as the money, back to his father, saying, *"I am resolved to serve God and from now on I will say, 'Our Father which art in heaven' and not 'my father Pietro Bernadone.'"*[120]

We must not wait until the storm before we realize the weight of our unnecessary possessions poses to us. In Jonah 1:4, the sailors in their desperation during the violent storm, began to throw their belongings into the sea. Again, in Acts 27:38, in the midst of a shipwreck, the sailors lightened the ship by throwing away their baggage. World-favorite Judas Iscariot, when he realized his soul was in a storm, "threw the money into the temple and left. Then he went away and hanged himself." (Matthew 27:5) This eventually was considered "blood money" buried, but did he just hang himself and die?

> *With the reward for his wickedness Judas bought a field; and there he fell headlong and burst open in the middle, and all his intestines spilled out.* Acts 1:18

> *What will it profit a man if he gains the whole world, yet forfeits his soul? Or what can a man give in exchange for his soul?* Matthew 16:26

We gather so much needless junk in our lives. What happens when our pilgrimage is up? We store up wealth for moths to eat, money, clothes, shoes, devices, jewelry, stuff, stuff, and more stuff. In the storm, which *will come*, these all will become burdensome. The things which we faithfully hoard could be forcefully taken from us, if we don't readjust our lives in due season; they will be eaten up by the materialism and consumerism, which are epidemics of our times. Less *is* always more.

Constantine the Great, notwithstanding his positive and historical contributions to Christianity, let his achievements go to his head. He built a new city for himself but didn't live long enough to enjoy it. He was baptized on his deathbed and swapped his imperial robes, adorned with sophisticated ornaments, and remained in his baptismal clothes until his eventual death, age 66.[121]

If the world's citizen travels with 10 suitcases of clothes and shoes for a two-week trip, we, as sojourners, simply cannot. Even in prison, Apostle Paul

---

[120] Hanks G., 1992, 70 Great Christians, 1st edition, Evangel Publication.
[121] G. Hanks, 70 Great Christians.

knew what his priorities were when he wrote to Timothy, asking for his belongings, emphasizing his books and parchment papers (2 Timothy 4:13). Our legacy should not rest in things that will run out of trend in an eye's blink. Jeremiah Burroughs describes Christian Contentment as a Rare Jewel.[122]

When do we realize enough is enough? When do we accept that Christ is enough? The illusion that there is more in this physical world is just that – an illusion. The theory of "the more we have the more we want" applies to all things: alcohol, drugs, immorality, money, and even spiritual experiences, but of the things of the world, we are told, nothing is new under the sun (Ecclesiastes 1:9). However, with the presence of God, when we are left longing for more, we have an assurance that there *is* more for, "No eye has seen, no ear has heard, no heart has imagined, what God has prepared for those who love Him." (1 Corinthians 2:9)

If we say and believe in our hearts, that we have been regenerated, our heart's focus should precisely be on things above, as directed in Colossians 3:1-2: "Since, then, you have been raised with Christ, set your hearts on things above, where Christ is, seated at the right hand of God. Set your minds on things above, not on earthly things." Our "Manual" tells us to lay up treasures in Heaven, where neither moth nor rust can corrupt them.

A story was told of a very earthly, rich woman, who burned suitcases of money she had kept in her home over a period, as they began to ooze an offensive smell. Our "Manual" tells us to be rich in faith and good works. Why? "For you died, and your life is now hidden with Christ in God. When Christ, who is your life, appears, then you also will appear with him in glory. (3-4) "

There is no such thing as "broke" for Christians. When we lay off unnecessary material weights, we realize the abundance with which we have been blessed:

But godliness with contentment is great gain.

For we brought nothing into the world, so we cannot carry anything out of it.

But if we have food and clothing, we will be content with these.

Those who want to be rich, however, fall into temptation and become ensnared by many foolish and harmful desires that plunge them into ruin and destruction.

---

[122] Burroughs J. 1981 'The Rare Jewel of Christian Contentment' Banner of Truth.

WHO?

For the love of money is the root of all kinds of evil, for which some have strayed from the faith in their greediness, and pierced themselves through with many sorrows.

1 Timothy 6:6-10

Lifestyle Weight: In digital age 21st Century, we have become subjects of the "Internet Constitution." We are commanded to be on all social media platforms and post something every day *(*Writer's Note: Day by day, as new manmade trends spring up, I'm more convinced about God. If we keep tracing back and tracing back to the very beginning, we will truly find that it was truly just The Word at the beginning. We are drifting along with the waves. Somebody says or does something, and then it becomes a trend. For instance, I remember when I started University in 2010, there was no social media as it has since become. Whichever ones were in existence were relatively new and were for good-natured banter. There was certainly none of the madness we live in today, empty, unintelligent, and distressing lives. I had a life in 2010. All was well and good [nothing is truly well or good without Jesus]. Now, I have to pledge my allegiance to the god of social media and social networking. I will not. I refuse. Who makes these rules!? I am older than these things! They work for me, I don't work for them. I delete them when I want, I pick them up when I want, and not as a pre-programmed obligation. "What's your 'handle?" Handle? My Handle? Is that DNA? I have to flaunt my professional and academic qualifications to determine my value? Now, it's a whole cult. It just makes everything clearer and clearer. The farther man drifts apart from God, the more glaring it is that God is everything His Word says He is, and more!)*

We are told by those who did not create marriage that we must have wedding hashtags for our weddings. We are told how we should even carry out our weddings, how many outfits we must wear, what make-up artist to use, what photographer to use, the style and theme of our own pictures, what designers we wear, what degrees we should pursue, how our profiles must be laid out…. When does it all end? When do we realize that we have our Life Manual, which "has given us everything we need for life and godliness through the knowledge of Him who called us by His own glory and excellence." (2 Peter 1:3)

On his wedding day, a pastor who was getting married and had never been a listener to non-gospel music, was made to dance to songs he knew nothing of; he was clearly uncomfortable about this with his bride. The bride had determined to dance to the world's trending songs, despite her pastor-husband's lifestyle *(unless she hadn't known him enough yet – as it's said we don't know who we get married to until we get married to them?).* And it was paramount to the bride to step into her wedding venue solely gyrating to music the world dictated to her, while her newlywed husband awkwardly walked into a ceremony with an atmosphere described as "Spirit-filled."

In the celebration of birthdays, as Christians, we must hear the hard truth. Every record of birthday celebration in the Bible was not by any of Christ's followers. As a matter of fact, John the Baptist, the forerunner of Christ, was beheaded as an amusement during the birthday party of King Herod (Matthew 14:1-12). The King had been pleased with his daughter's dance presentation and wanted to reward her for it. He promised her whatever she asked for, and her mother, who wanted revenge, took advantage of her little girl and made her request the head of John the Baptist. Now, if this king had not celebrated his birthday, this might not have happened.

It is by no means wrong to mark a birthday to thank God for adding a landmark year to one's life. The point being, we do not and should not, mark the day according to the dictated standards of a world we do not belong to (1 Corinthians 10:31). Our "Manual" tells us that when we are merry, we should sing psalms and make melody in our hearts to the Lord.

If we must own phones, we are under no obligation to use them every day; we are under no obligation to check our social media feeds or post something on media every day; We don't need to visit any app every day. These things work for us, not vice versa. The world will be without us one day; it will move on like we never existed. We must strive to be free from the need to do anything outside of our Faith.

We do not need to attend every event to which we are invited. Kill the desire to be seen, heard, appreciated, admired, and noticed. King Solomon said, "It is better to go to a house of mourning than to go to a house of feasting, because that is the end of every man, and the living takes it to heart." (Ecclesiastes 7:2) As Charles Spurgeon said of the counsel, "Solomon had tried both worldliness and holy fear: in the one he found vanity, in the other happiness. Let us not repeat his trial but abide by his verdict." [123]

We don't need to reply to everything said to us or about us. We are not the Omniscient God. Sometimes, "I don't know," is suitable; most times, silence is perfect. As servants of Christ, the only thing we are obligated to do is carry our cross daily.

It is of some value to write down plans, goals, and vision boards of our weekly, monthly, and yearly goals and present them to God. They fuel us to work hard and conquer physical feats. What's best is that every day, with every passing hour of each day, we think about our death and where we will

---

[123] C.H. Spurgeon Morning & Evening Devotional.

spend eternity (Ecclesiastes 7:4). With the "big H" in view, we have what is even better than happiness and have conquered physical feats. We have hope, we have peace.

King David said, *"As the deer pants for the water brooks, So, pants my soul for You, O God,"* (Psalm 42:1) and "My soul followeth hard after thee." (Psalm 63:8) No one can be taught to be desperate for God. When our soul follows *hard* after God, our flesh is completely dead. We have absolutely no time, desire, interest or pleasure in things and standards of the world. They can never coexist. It is one or the other. God or Belial. God or Mammon. God or Fame. God or Slay. God or Money. God or Possession. God or Net Worth. God or Career. God or Man. God or Spouse. God or Children. God or Lifestyle. Light or Darkness. Heaven or Hell. Life or Death. "Choose you this day whom you will serve," Joshua charged, "but as for me and my house we will serve the Lord." (Joshua 24:15)

Relational Weight: *They are the best and worst you've created…People, people, when you said you could heal me from anything, did You mean people, people…I don't know the damage or which one to blame it's just people, people, deliver me…*[124]

Dear Christian, Jesus had 12 disciples. Among his 12, He had his close three. Among the close three, He had one who is self-acclaimed as the one Jesus loved, and He had the one He asked, "Do you love me?" A crowd was sitting around Him, and they told Him, "Your mother and brothers are outside looking for you."

> *'Who are my mother and my brothers?' He asked. Then He looked at those seated in a circle around him and said, "Here are my mother and my brothers! Whoever does God's will is My brother and sister and mother.* Mark 3:33-35

Especially when we become Christians, this is the very first weight we must throw off. We have an obligation and command to love everyone as ourselves, but weights in the name of friendship, family, acquaintanceship, or history *will* hinder the race.

In every relationship, romantic, business or friendship, the personal standard should be *not unequally yoked.* Clay and iron cannot mix (Daniel 2:43), Light and darkness can have no communion (2 Corinthian 6:14) and most important, "Do not be deceived: evil communication corrupts good morals." (1 Corinthians 15:33)

Any relationship in which a Christian cannot freely speak about the Gospel

---

[124] McReynolds J. (2020) People. Entertainment One US LP.

of Jesus Christ (*unless during the initial stages of witnessing*) must be thrown off. We might witness to them, but the time comes when witnessing is enough, for **the harvest is plenty.** We must throw off that weight and pray for the Holy Spirit to do His work.

> *But when divers were hardened, and believed not, but spake evil of that way before the multitude, he departed from them, and separated the disciples.* Acts 19:9

Any relationship which will not lovingly encourage or boldly rebuke with the Word of God is an encumbrance to the Soldier of Christ. It starts with a compromise here and a compromise there, before we realize how far gone we are, and how we are unable to retrace our steps to where it all went wrong. Proverbs 22:25 warns us, "you may learn his ways and entangle yourself in a snare."

Personal relationships where Christ cannot joyfully, freely, and passionately be discussed and worshipped, and in which there is joint partaking in spiritual exercises, are ensnaring to a serious Christian; this is especially true when such a Christian has not built the spiritual stamina to resist some things. However, no Christian in flesh and blood, despite having spiritual "muscle and endurance," is absolved of the risk of being ensnared within relationships that are unequally yoked. It will take some convincing to show that one can have any form of inner peace, satisfaction, joy or contentment *even if* these busy schedules are religious events, when that person is so inundated with busy schedules, activities back-to-back, and one engagement or another over a sustained period, with little to no time for solitude, deep reflection, and communion with God. It also will require convincing to show that one who is ever away from "significant others," family, friends, and most important, those portable ~~demons~~ devices, over another period of time can achieve those aspects of their relationship with God. What if such an individual is a "religious influencer," who posts daily Bible verses in cute images that are the highlights of users' days, but has no time allowed for solitude, silence and quiet reflection?

"As often as I have been among men," said one writer, *"I have returned less a man."* If you've ever felt the emptiness that comes with taking part in long conversations without specific purpose or for a worthy cause, you will acknowledge the veracity of the weight and levels of truth in that simple, profound statement.

Solitude is fine, solitude is healthy, solitude is necessary, solitude is paramount, solitude is worthwhile. Without solitude, we will never know ourselves. Without solitude, we will *never* know God. It is even better to go into solitude without a mirror, in case God has given you matchless beauty, so you will not be deluded into thinking that is who you are. *It is still Dummy Cake.* Being alone with oneself and God is invaluable. "A single day in your courts is better than a thousand anywhere else." (Psalm 84:10) This was the one thing Jesus never failed to do. Despite crowds waiting for Him, His priority was to spend time alone, time with His Father.

Our relationship with God, the most important and only relationship we should wholeheartedly desire, must be heartfelt and intimate in the same way Adam "knew" Eve. That relationship should be Creator to maker, Potter to clay, Master to servant, Father to child, Lover to lover, Friend to friend, and should be dynamic, loving, and well flamed to keep the "spark" flying. We are forewarned in Matthew 24:12, "And because iniquity shall abound, the love of many shall wax cold but only the one who endures to the end will be saved." We must keep fanning our flames for Jesus Christ and ensure our "salt" does not lose its saltiness (Luke 14:34). To be saved once is not to be saved all.

It would be absurd, even to the point of comedy, if we imagine we know God because we are "blessed," comfortable, thriving in our careers, have happy homes, perform signs and wonders, have growing ministries, and feel all seems well and good.

> *For Jacob my servant's sake, and Israel mine elect, I have even called thee by thy name: I have surnamed thee, though thou hast not known me. I am the Lord, and there is none else, there is no God beside me: I girded thee, though thou hast not known me.* Isaiah 45:4-5

The gifts and calling of God are without repentance. Our well-being and seeming prosperity are of no effect to God. The fact that He is not as petty as man, to revoke the blessings and gifts He has bestowed upon us, is not a sign we know Him, we *still* know Him, or we are in right standing with Him. "He causes his sun to rise on the evil and the good and sends rain on the righteous and the unrighteous." (Matthew 5:45)

God knew Abraham, He knew Enoch, He knew Paul, He knew Jesus… Does He know you?

> *Many will say to Me on that day, 'Lord, Lord, did we not prophesy in Your name, and in Your name drive out demons and perform many miracles?' Then I will tell them plainly, 'I never knew you; depart from Me…'* Matthew 7:22-23

We must take heed, stay sober, and constantly seek knowledge of God *from* Him. Knowledge of God cannot be taught, it can only be personally

90

experienced. *To know God once is not to know God for all.*

Spiritual Weight: These are the things we can't see. They are not lifestyles; they are the weights of our hearts. Bondages such as fear, discouragement, doubt, unforgiveness, despair, anger, worry, anxiety, hopelessness, guilt, and shame, or *anything* that can harm the health of the heart should *not be thrown off;* we should lift these up to Jesus Christ. He alone can rid the heart of traps of the devil because a fearful heart can lead to blindness, dumbness, deafness and weakness. (Isaiah 35:3-8)

He invites:

> *Come to me, all you who are weary and burdened, and I will give you rest. Take my yoke upon you and learn from me, for I am gentle and humble in heart, and you will find rest for your souls. For my yoke is easy and my burden is light.* Matthew 11:28-30

Apostle Paul counsels:

> *Do not be anxious about anything, but in every situation, by prayer and petition, with thanksgiving, present your requests to God.* Philippians 4:6

There is one way to go about this, and that is through prevailing, ceaseless, importunate prayers to a merciful God, *not strict orders to our slave, nor sweet wishes to our genie.*

As we throw off these categories of enormous weights, we must renew our inner man with "holy contrition" as regularly as we breathe, and by meditating on "whatsoever things are true, whatsoever things are honest, whatsoever things are just, whatsoever things are pure, whatsoever things are lovely, whatsoever things are of good report; if there be any virtue, and if there be any praise, think on these things." (Philippians 4:8)

Sin That Easily Entangles Us: This snare is unique to every individual heart and varies by personality, sex, age, culture, exposure, status, and experience. Regardless, sin *is* sin. This is sin that easily snags us, aware or unaware, into its web of bondage. This is sin that produces shame, guilt, regret, defensiveness, and insecurity. We refer to all those effects as *"my weaknesses,"* which is almost synonymous with the worldly philosophical term, *"self-awareness."*

> *If we claim to have fellowship with Him and yet walk in the darkness, we lie and do not live out the truth. But if we walk in the light, as He is in the light, we have fellowship with one another, and the blood of Jesus, his Son, purifies us from all sin. If we claim to be without sin, we deceive ourselves and the truth is not in us. If we confess our sins, he is faithful and just and will forgive us our sins and purify us from all*

unrighteousness. If we claim we have not sinned, we make him out to be a liar and his word is not in us. 1 John 1:6-10

Only an honest heart will be quick to admit this personally, to others and to God, not as a weapon of defense but as a cry for help. It is, **O wretched man that I am, who will save me from this body of death?** It is coming into sincere fellowship with the Father of Lights, with whom there is no darkness, to expose that customized sin that battles our soul, and then surrendering ourselves for Him, to cleanse sin with the purifying blood of Jesus. And as that earnest heart's cry is made, a new awareness, albeit slowly *but* steadily, springs within us. This is called *"Christ-awareness."* The testimony of this is, *"I am not where I used to be, but not yet where I am going to be."* It is pressing forward, free from guilt, the past, insecurities, and shame, and despite what the mind or human voices might opine.

> *Therefore, if anyone is in Christ, he is a new creation; old things have passed away; behold, all things have become new…For He made Him who knew no sin to be sin for us, that we might become the righteousness of God in Him.* 2 Corinthians 5: 17&21

…It is becoming the righteousness of God.

"Therefore, since we are surrounded by such a huge crowd of witnesses to the life of faith, let us strip off every weight that slows us down especially the sin that so easily trips us up…"[125] This duty is ours by the help of the Holy Spirit, not the Holy Spirit's help while we relax and make lazy excuses.

Yes, it is by no means an easy combat, but the encouragement is that we are not alone, not the first and not the last. "Endure suffering along with me, as a good soldier of Christ Jesus." (2 Timothy 2:3)

This battle into which we've been enlisted is no mean march, so remember, it is an offer IF anyone would come after ME, Our Savior. Once accepted, there is absolutely no other means, despite what our evolving religion tells us. "A soldier refrains from entangling himself in civilian affairs, in order to please The One who enlisted him." (2 Timothy 2:4)

We confidently chant our daily fiat as we march on to combat, "We are more than conquerors through Him that loves us!"

---

[125] New Living Translation.

Run with Endurance/Patience/Perseverance...

...an athlete does not receive the Victor's crown except by competing according to the rules. 2 Timothy 2:5

General Instructions Before Beginning:

1. Begin with the end in mind.[126] We begin our Christian sojourn only because we know where we are heading. That is the "big H," Heaven. We do not deny ourselves and endure through life because we don't want to "enjoy" the pleasures the world offers. We take on this journey because, and only because, we know where we want our souls to retire. We realize that our lives on earth are mortal and *will* come to an end. We know that our souls are immortal and eternal. Every price we pay on earth adds to our Heavenly credit. This is why Jesus, "who for the joy that was set before Him endured the cross, despising the shame." (Hebrews 12:2) As the Apostle put it, we are not just shadow-boxing, that would be madness. We are not mad. A translation says, "I run with purpose in *every* step." Every step we take is toward Heaven, in thought, word and action, we keep the "big H" in view. Every minute is a step closer to Heaven, to rest, to eternal glory, to perfection, to *finally* meeting our Lord Jesus Christ (***Writer's Note:** *and to meet Apostle Paul.*)

2. Jesus and only Jesus is our coxswain in this race. He is The Author and Finisher of our faith, Our Beginning and Our Ending. Obeying any other voice *(not heard)* disqualifies us from the race. Your pastor is *not* the voice. Your spiritual mentor is *not* the voice. Your favorite preacher is *not* the voice. **Jesus Christ is the Voice.** Doubtless, there will be voices from the crowd, cheering us on, discouraging us, mocking us, or whatsoever those voices intend to do. Hearing these voices, however, does not disqualify us from the race; some of these voices may come from our own heads. Obeying/yielding to these voices will disqualify us from the race.

Now the Berean Jews were of more noble character than those in Thessalonica, for they received the message with great eagerness and examined the Scriptures every day to see

---

[126] Covey, Stephen R. The 7 Habits of Highly Effective People: Restoring The Character Ethic. 'Habit 2' Free Press, 2004. Print.

if what PAUL said was true. Acts 17:11

The devout Apostle Paul called, taught, and was trained directly by the Lord, yet by these wise Christians was received *but* examined. JESUS is our *only* voice in this race.

3. *No one, having put his hand to the plow, and looking back, is fit for the kingdom of God.* Luke 9:62

> This is the greatest struggle with many Christians today. It is simply the Demas Disorder. They started well, knew God, were devout, were dedicated, but the love of the world, the common trials of life, the desire to fit in and seem "new-school" or cool, caused them to turn back, regardless of the spiritual suicide they committed. This is why Jesus advises us to count the cost. We are warned in Peter's letter that it is better never to have seen the way of light and righteousness than to have seen it and turned back. It will be worse for those who turn back from the Faith than for those who never came to it. (2 Peter 2:20-22) Count the cost. Once we begin this sojourn, there is no turning back, there is only pressing on to higher ground and greater glory. It *is* worth it.

The Race

On Your Marks!   Get Set!   Go!

Our race has begun, but are we in a stadium, running a sprint on a track, or running a marathon? How do we know we will make it to Heaven after all these sacrifices? How do we know we will find peace? Dear Christian, it is the race of life. It is the marathon of our mortality and there is only one way to do this: By **keeping our eyes on Jesus.**

It still sounds spurious. How do we see Jesus? Where does He live? We do not. This religion we follow, this "Christian" badge we wear, is really "hearsay." None of us has seen Jesus, we only have records passed down to us, so all we do in this entire race is believe. The word is called **FAITH**.

Thomas the Disciple had it easy for Jesus Christ, he doubted. Thomas was not going to believe He had indeed conquered sin and death until he *saw* Jesus and the wounds in His hands. But it was not just that, it was not until Thomas pushed his hands into Jesus' wounds, which ordinarily would still have been sore, that he believed. *(*Writer's note: Is the heart of man desperately wicked or not? Thomas didn't just want to see, he wanted to prick the wounds).* Thomas' senses had won the battle over his soul. Eventually, and luckily for his eternity, he was fortunate enough to see Jesus, who then said to him, keeping us 21st *Centurians* in mind, "because you have seen Me, you have believed. Blessed are those who have not seen and yet have believed." (John 20:29) Brother and sister, when we believe, we are reflexively, directly blessed by Jesus!

However, this doubting Thomas, after he had seen and felt, and proclaimed, *"My Lord and my God!"* (John 20:28) became so convicted of his Jesus that he dedicated his life to preaching the gospel; he eventually died a martyr's death alone in India. That is exactly what will happen when we finally go to glory and see Jesus, knowing that this race was not a façade, as the "enlightened" of our generation would have us believe. We will declare, *"My Lord and my God!"* Glory! As a writer said, "It takes a lot of faith to be an atheist."

We must think very deeply about whether we really have faith, because faith is having a gun to our head and being told, "Deny Jesus or we kill you." And it is responding boldly, "Jesus is Lord. Jesus is the Son of God. JESUS IS GOD!" Faith is not giving away all the money in a bank account in hopes that we will receive it back one hundredfold. That is investment. In the former scenario, if we are unable to repeat those statements in the face of death, we have no faith; we deceive ourselves. Faith is going to the high streets of Saudi Arabia with a megaphone on a Friday afternoon at the end of their prayers, as they file out in thousands, and shouting, "Jesus Christ is Lord! I love You, Jesus. You are the only Way, Truth and Life." Yes, Faith IS foolish to the mortal brain.

Here's what the Bible says in Hebrews 11:6:

- ***But without faith it is impossible to please God.*** Impossible! Your good works are charity, your obedience is legalism, your kindness is humanity, but your race is *not* Christianity.

- ***for he that cometh to God must believe that He is.*** We must believe that everything we have heard about Him through the Word, our Holy Bible, our heroes of faith, and the historical records of tested and proven men and women of God, is true. We must believe what He said to Moses when He declared, ***"I am."*** We must believe that by Him, all things were created, and without Him nothing was made that was made. We must believe, verbatim, all the letters and punctuation marks laid down in the Holy Bible. We must believe that Jesus walked the same earthly ground on which we walk, was brutally beaten, and died a cursed death by being nailed to a cross. We must believe, after the third day, Jesus rose again and appeared to his disciples and over 500 men and women, all of whom saw Him at the same time. There was no *"Mandela Effect."* [the Mandela Effect occurs when a large group of people share false memories of the same event.] We must believe that the Holy Spirit came upon the disciples and Apostle Peter, who had previously denied Jesus, won 8,000 souls for the same Jesus within a matter of days. We must believe that He hates sin and will punish each and every person for their sins. We must believe He is coming back and He will reward each and every one of us according to our works. We must believe He has not yet come, because He is giving us time to repent.

- *and that he is a rewarder of them that diligently seek him.* We must believe all our inner groaning, our daily Bible Scripture, our importunities, our good works for His glory, our endurance of trials and temptations, our self-denials for His glory, and our waiting on Him, are not for nothing. We must believe our inner groaning, our importunities, are not unheard. We must believe "all things work together for those who love God and are called according to His purpose." We must believe nothing will ever separate us from His love. We must believe we *will* be rewarded for this life of holiness to which we have dedicated ourselves. We must believe, "Indeed, none of those who wait for You will be ashamed." (Psalm 25:3) We must believe God owes no man and we must "not be weary in well doing, for in due season, we shall reap, if we faint not." (Galatians 6:9) We must believe God *is* Faithful. Amen.

Then they said to Him, 'What shall we do, that we may work the works of God?' Jesus answered and said to them, 'This is the work of God, that you believe in Him whom He sent.' John 6:28-29

Our work is to believe, because without faith it is impossible to please God. Yet how hard is it to believe a God we can't see? The Bible tells us to take heed against the "evil heart of unbelief," (Hebrews 3:12) because to *not* believe is evil. The next verse of that Scripture tells us to warn each other about it **daily.** We must carefully and valiantly guard our hearts against fiery darts of doubt. It is evil to think the world and everything we see around us, the stars, seas, animals, trees, skies, moon, birds etc., came by magic.

It is not only evil, but moronic to believe a young man named Darwin, who came into a world which had existed long before he arrived, and continues to exist centuries after he returned to dust, devised a theory in 1859 that we came from monkeys. To not realize that the best scientists and thinkers have not and will never come up with a solution to death is evil. To think that when we die, which will be sooner or later, is the end of our lives is not only evil but tragic. It is evil to believe there is no God. To believe that Jesus is not the Son of God is not only evil, but useless. To believe that Jesus is not risen is not only evil, but ignorant; *some of the proven records we have of these events were not even recorded by Christians!* To believe Jesus is not coming back takes *a lot* of belief, and is not only evil but it is death, eternal death, i.e., dying, every day in hell, hades, fire, sheol.

This is the predominant danger in our world: People, even self-professed Christians, do not really believe that so much evil has bourgeoned and continues to multiply. We must guard our hearts with iron. *To know God once, is not to know God for all.* We don't accept and know there is more to everything we see around us. *Believe* in the One Whom He sent; that is our *daily* work, especially in Digital Age 2020. Blind, blind, blind, and blind, we must see, see, see, and see! *I believe in You, Jesus. Please help my unbelief.*

Subjecting Our Senses

Now we are running our race of life, keeping our eyes on Jesus, our coxswain, not by physically seeing Him, but *"that Christ may dwell in your hearts by Faith."* (Ephesians 3:17) We know, without it, no Kingdom transaction can take place, because the only currency God deals with is faith. What exactly is faith?

> *Faith is confidence in what we hope for and assurance about what we do not see.* Hebrews 11:1

In lay terms, faith is everything that goes directly against the promptings and natural inclinations of our senses.

We do not need a *wealth* of it. Is it as small as a mustard seed? Yes, so *it is* sufficient. What is the size of a mustard seed? 1 to 2 millimeters. How small is 1 to 2 millimeters?

*Graphic Warning! * If you pick a little booger from your nose with your index finger, it will be the size of the faith you need to come before The

97

Almighty God as a candidate.[127]

That is all the faith you need to fully enter and enjoy the insurmountable benefits of His Kingdom! Yes, in the Kingdom, what is "small" by our standards does magnanimous wonders! "Small" may be a negative amount, like a little bad yeast that permeates the whole dough, or it may be positive, like a tiny mustard seed that a man plants, grows into a tree, and even becomes a home to birds.

Our faith is for our own good and ours alone. "For what if some did not believe? Shall their unbelief make the faith of God without effect? God forbid." (Romans 3:3-4)

We must continually look to Jesus, *especially* in the times of the fiercest storms of life which will come. We must not look left, right, forward, or worse, backward. *I will lift UP my eyes to the Hills,[128]* the Psalmist said. In Matthew's account of the crucifixion, despite all the slander, abuse, beatings, lashings and accusations, the first thing Matthew wrote that Jesus said was, *Eloi, Eloi, lama sabachthani?[129]* This bitter cup that Jesus drank for all of us was completely vile, and even though His mother and disciples, who loved Him dearly, were present and arguably loved Him more than anyone on earth, He knew He could *trust* them, He didn't even ask them to pray for Him. At that point, in the hottest part of the fire of His cruel death, He faced His Father. As pilgrims, we must *never* look down, up, left, or right because, "Cursed is the man who trusts in man and makes flesh his strength, whose heart departs from the Lord." (Jeremiah 17:5)

In the regular trials, disappointments, losses, discouragements, pain, and suffering we will experience, we must, "consider Him who endured such hostility from sinners against Himself, lest you become weary and discouraged in your souls." (Hebrews 12:3) A practical way to do this is by regularly watching the movie, *The Passion of the Christ,[130]* as many times as possible in a year, not just once at Eastertime. This movie gives us a vivid representation of what Jesus went through on earth for us. Since we weren't there, it is a good supplement, alongside what we study in Scripture, for a visual representation of

---

[127] Only God has the authority to let anyone into His Kingdom. We can only hope through faith that we will enter His Kingdom. It will be an affront to His Holy Sovereignty for one man to promise another that they will enter into the Kingdom of The Righteous Judge for He is the Giver of the Crown of Righteousness we run to attain.

[128] Psalm 121:1.

[129] Matthew 27:46.

[130] Gibson, M., et al. (2004). The Passion of the Christ.

the propitiation of Christ in our hearts.

Also, Psalms 120 through 134, known as the "pilgrim Psalms, or songs of ascents," were sung by those who journeyed ("ascended") to the Temple for the annual festivals. Each Psalm represents a "step" along the journey. Psalm 120 begins the journey in a distant land, in hostile surroundings; Psalm 122 pictures the pilgrims arriving in Jerusalem. The rest of the psalms portray the pilgrims as they move toward the Temple, mentioning various characteristics of God. These psalms are given to us for our encouragement, edification, and meditation.

In subjecting our senses to our faith, Charles Spurgeon says, *"It is sight: 'Look unto me and be ye saved.' It is hearing: 'Hear, and your soul shall live.' Faith is smelling: 'All thy garments smell of myrrh, and aloes, and cassia;' Faith is spiritual touch. 'By this faith the woman came behind and touched the hem of Christ's garment,' and by this we handle the things of the good word of life. Faith is equally the spirit's taste. 'How sweet are thy words to my taste! yea, sweeter than honey to my lips. 'Except a man eat my flesh,' saith Christ, 'and drink my blood, there is no life in him.'"* [131]

Dear Modern-Day Christian, DARE to Be Different.

but the people that do know their God shall be strong,

and do exploits. Daniel 11:32

The verse above is yet another verse we declare for our amusement and personal gratification, forgetting that the young man to whom this mystery was revealed was famed for his earnest ability and self-will to stand out in a crowd filled with "belongers." He stood out by proposing in his **heart** not to defy himself with a portion of the *King's* meat, and he had like-minded friends. How many of us will be thrown into the fire for the Gospel's sake? Pray tell, how many of us will be willing to attend church when we wake up with a large zit on our faces?

First, the young man proposed in his heart, not on his vision board, his New Year's resolutions, or his affirmations list. He knew that all issues of life flow from the heart. He did not say it to his best friend, mentor, confidant, or post it on his social media page for "accountability." He proposed in the vessel of

---

[131] C.H Spurgeon Morning & Evening Devotional

life – his heart.

Second, he was not going to defy himself with the King's meat – not with meat. It was not because he didn't like meat, or that meat was a sin: "However, you may slaughter and eat meat within all your gates, whatever your heart desires, according to the blessing of the LORD your God which He has given you; the unclean and the clean may eat of it, of the gazelle and the deer alike." (Deuteronomy 12:15) God approves of meat. The reason for Daniel rejecting this meat was the *source* of the meat.

Usually, our first responses to these issues will be: "Is it wrong?" or, "Is it bad?" or, "Is it a sin?" We forget "that highly esteemed among men is abomination in the sight of God." (Luke 16:15) It is not a matter of right or wrong to be contended; it is the simple fact that if the world loves it, we cannot.

> *All things are lawful for me, but I will not be brought under the power of any.*
> 1 Corinthians 6:12

The challenge *is* to be different. In the Apostate culture of **"inclusivity"** that 21st Century mainstream screams, why should we not provoke ourselves to be different in a world we are in, but not of? The challenge lies not in being swept away by the waves, but in swimming against the ocean tide. In 1 Corinthians 5:1, Apostle Paul showed zero tolerance for inclusivity when he got a report of sexual immorality amongst Christians; rather than the Christians rebuking this act of spiritual suicide, they were proud of it. He immediately passed judgement on the persons involved and directed that they be removed from the church but our itchy hands refuse to turn to this part of the Word. We want to tolerate, include, and turn a blind eye to apparent wrong.

> *Draw nigh to God, and he will draw nigh to you. Cleanse your hands, ye sinners; and purify your hearts, ye double minded.* James 4:8

We want to be included, accepted, and liked by everyone. The perfect Jesus was not liked by everyone – to this day. Is it our careers that force us to be inclusive and join the bandwagon? Joseph of Arimathea was an earthly, wealthy man, and he was a respected member of the council of men who approved the death of Jesus. However, he, **"had not consented to their decision and action"**[132] of his colleagues and by himself approached Pilate for permission to take the responsibility of burying Jesus.

Despite our surroundings, we can be different. If our will power is too weak to choose differently, we must completely avoid such scenarios. This is

---

[132] Luke 23:50–56.

correct, avoiding rather than giving in to temptation that arises out of nothing but our own desires. Lot was a resident in a town filled with abominable acts of immorality, but he alone was delivered from destruction, because he was a righteous man who was distressed and tormented in his soul with the ungodly conduct of his people. (2 Peter 2:7-8)

We do not have to fit in for the sake of inclusion. As Kingdom Citizens, we are under a completely different government from what the world knows and understands. For instance, our government states, "Those who sin should be reprimanded in front of the whole church; this will serve as a strong warning to others" (1 Timothy 5:20); but the 21st Century "rights" obsessed Christian will sue the church and make libelous posts worthy of a mass media explosion, rather than appreciate this impeccable standard of high accountability. This standard is to keep us spotless for the Kingdom and true to our calling; even better, it is the standard for us to choose to live honorably, soberly and internally free, not from the *temptation* to sin, but from the bondage of *falling into* sin.

The Apostle became like a Jew to the Jews for the *sake of* the Gospel and ensured it was nothing that could displease God. The fact that it is popular opinion or culture is the glaring reason we must stand back. Darkness invites us further and more deeply; light pushes back. Light will initially push us back, exposing our sins and filth, but if we do not run away immediately from the initial sharp effect of the brightness of light, we get used to it. Then, we eventually see clearly, but darkness draws us in. Like blindfolded people, we stretch out our hands and keep going further, thinking there's "more" to be found until, boom! heads are knocked, excruciating pain is inflicted.

We lie if we say we have fellowship but live in darkness, when we are told by Jesus to **Let your light SO shine before men,**[133] knowing that when the Bible adds "so" to any statement, we are not called to a merely ordinary level. We are called to a simply extraordinary and unbelievable level of purity and shining in this dark world. Darkness covers, light exposes. Only God is the Light, the Source and Father of *all* lights. If what appears to us as light cannot stand in the face of God through His Word that exposes it, we must retrace our steps. He exposes our secret sins in the light of His countenance (Psalm 90:8). The ways of God will always be upside down to the human mind. God tells us the first will be last, and vice versa; He tells us the leader must be a servant; He tells us he that scatters, increases; He saves the best wine for last; He sets the needy among Kings. God *is* different.

---

[133] Matthew 5:16.

The fact is, the world itself expects us, who call ourselves Christian, to be different in appearance, conduct, speech, and lifestyle. Once we identify as Christian, they might not approve of our Faith, but they are consciously or *subconsciously* watching us. When we fail to be different, being tossed around like waves of the sea with every new trend, we weaken that which we profess. We weaken it first to those who do not believe, second to new believers, and most important, we weaken it to ourselves. Before God, our consciences must remain clear; before men, we must remain iron poles and unapologetic about our Faith. We must be unbending and unyielding for our Faith; when we do this, we provoke unbelievers to believe, we open room for questions of curiosity, and we have the opportunity to share the Gospel. We also help build the faith of new believers. (Philippians 1:13-14)

However, when we dilly-dally with our convictions, we weaken not the Gospel itself, of course, the Gospel is the strongest foundation, but by the words coming out of our own mouths, we will not be taken seriously, nor believed about anything we say. What will be said of us is, *"They said they are a Christian, yet they do this."*

> *That man should not expect to receive anything from the Lord.*
> *He is a double-minded man, unstable in all his ways.* James 1:7-8

When we continue dressing a certain way, keep going to certain places, keep ingesting certain things, and continue to "broaden" a way we know very well has been declared to be narrow, with few, strict and straight-forward options, we become false teachers, as seen in **Galatians 2.** When those who do not believe see no difference between us and themselves, there is neither justification, nor motivation on their part, to change. New believers fail to give up old lifestyles because they see us as their "role models," engaging in clearly anti-Christian activities, and continuing to appear in anti-Christian venues. "True religion is keeping unstained by the world." (James 1:27)

To accommodate our own lusts, we then begin to preach a new doctrine to ourselves and others, but that is in complete contradiction with the Word of God. His Word does not speak in parables when it comes to modesty, gentleness, throwing off weights, humility, abstinence from immorality, envy, wild parties, covetousness, abundance of possessions, and most important, pursuing peace and living in holiness, because without holiness we will **never** see God. "Be not deceived, God is not mocked." (Galatians 6:7)

We have turned the old-time Christian religion into a "cool movement," basically, the same, old personas with a slice of Jesus and a Bible verse, catwalking and trotting into Heaven. That uncomfortable, sacrificial, self-denying, completely radical concept of lifestyle change is extinct. Unfortunately, Christianity is NOT cool. Thankfully, we have records of history to learn from. This slant of Christianity as a trendy, fashionable movement, in the days of Constantine the Great, had an adverse effect on all the good he did. To join in the benefits afforded Christians, people began attending church, but only to become *nominal* members. There was a deviation from *personal* faith and conviction, so formalism in church services became a pattern. Congregations attended church to watch a performance with no experiential or transformative effect in their lives; this resulted in the decline of moral standards across England. It led, as well, to the increase of mere doctrine, rather than the lasting fruits produced when we have been broken by Jesus.

Immediately the believers in Acts 2: 41-47 were saved, they sold all their possessions to give the money to the poor, and found so much joy in these acts of love and community. Goodness! In our age, Christians have the best and latest of *everything*. It is a fact that the pair of sandals Jesus wore while He was on earth, as well as his robe, and supposedly even a drop of his tear from when He wept at Lazarus' death, are all relics that can be found on earth today. Therefore, if we are leaving *even* our tears behind *(i.e. just Christians who make heaven will not need their tears; briefcases and surplus storage of tears will be needed in hell)*, why do we burden ourselves with getting, acquiring, possessing, and surmounting *things*? (1 John 2:16-17)

Are we ready, for our soul's sake, to get serious in this generation? We do *not* have to go everywhere we are invited; we can and must restrain our feet. The Lord said of *His* people in Jeremiah 14:10 that they greatly loved to wander and, therefore, were rejected by Him. For the righteous, the only fear of missing out should be of the Wedding Feast of the Lamb (Hebrews 4:2). We must be terrified at the thought of ever hearing, 'depart from me ye workers of iniquity!' (Matthew 7:23), only to be told that when we did not feed the poor, we did not feed Jesus. How scary is that? Or how scary is it to be reminded that when we cannot control our tongues our religion is vain,[134] or knowing that life and death are in the power of the tongue, *or in our fingers for our techno-logical-chat-away generation*?

How long do we need to remain lost before we realize our need for salvation? If we refuse to pay this sacrifice, God Himself will separate the sheep from the goats. (Matthew 25:31-46) We are one or the other –hot or cold, wisdom or world, Heaven or hell, life or death, man or woman, there is no in-between. Jesus, the lover of our souls, tells us clearly that He will spit out those who

---

[134] James 1:26.

are neither hot nor cold; His desire is for us to *pick* a side (Revelation 3:16). There is absolutely no room for confusion or one leg-in, *Friday night* – out. We are either iced tea or hot chocolate. Never have we heard of warm coffee, for that *will* leave a nasty taste in our mouths, worth spitting out; and bank this, never will there be a warm coffee option. A lukewarm Christian is luke-warm coffee, and needs spitting out. At what point do we realize that all things the world offers us "are lies, vanity and things wherein there is NO profit?" (Jeremiah 16:19) We cannot love the creations of men more than the Creator of men, because we risk God's wrath. (Romans 1:25).

Jesus called us friends when He told us His secrets, but we are also told that friendship with the world is enmity with God, and friends of the world are called adulterers and adulteresses. You know what the Bible says about adul-terers and adulteresses? They have NO place in the Kingdom of God: no hut, no shed, no gatekeeper's lodge, and certainly no mansion. We need to decide whose friend we are. Hot or cold? What are our likes and dislikes? What default apps do we go to on our devices? What are the posts we find amusing on our social media pages? How do we feel towards sin?

If the world is so comfortable for us, if there is no situation in our lives we are "enduring" but for the assurance and hope of Jesus' coming, we must check ourselves for evidence of derailment (Matthew 24:12-13). In 1 Peter 4:1 we are given the singular test to know when we have conquered sin: **he that suffered in the flesh.** To be at peace, comfort and luxury in the world is to be far away from the Cross of Calvary. **Vodie Baucham** stated, *"The only way you are living your best life now is if you're going to hell."*

Why should we have it easy, smooth, and be acceptable by all? We have been told that anyone who wants to live for God *will* suffer persecution. (2 Timo-thy. 3:12) What must be non-negotiable for a Christian are conviction and genuine faith. If we are hated, rejected, or punished, it must be for the good of God, not for our bad doings or lack of integrity.

Archibald Brown laid out beautifully what our attitude as Christians should be towards the world: *"Strict separation and uncompromising hostility.* Pointing out that Jesus' *"demand for unworldliness was constant and emphatic. He sets forth in one short sentence, what He would have His disciples to be: 'You are the salt of the earth. Yes, the salt — not the sugar-candy! Something the world will be more inclined to spit out — than swallow with a smile. Something more calculated to bring water to the eye — than laughter to the lip.'"*[135]

As Jesus lit the torch, calling on His followers to be different, He assured us,

---

[135] https://www.gracegems.org/29/devils_mission_of_amusement.htm

"Blessed are you when men shall revile you, and persecute you, and shall say all manner of evil against you falsely, for My sake. Rejoice, and be exceedingly glad — for great is your reward in heaven! For so persecuted they the prophets who were before you." (Mathew 5:11) Here we see the Apostles continually carrying the torch, echoing the message of difference and separation amongst Christ-followers:

The charge in Romans is: "Be not conformed to this world, but be transformed." (12:2)

The rhetorical question in Corinthians is: "*What communion has light with darkness, and what concord has Christ with Belial?*" (2nd 6:15)

The character evidence in Galatians is: "Those who belong to Christ Jesus have crucified the flesh with its passions and desires." (5:24)

The clarion call in Ephesians is: "Do not be partakers with them. Have no fellowship with the unfruitful works of darkness, but rather reprove them." (5:11).

The advice in Philippians is: "That you may be blameless and pure, children of God who are faultless in a crooked and perverted generation, among whom you shine like stars in the world." (2:15)

The pronouncement in Colossians is: "Dead with Christ from the rudiments of the world." (2:20)

The command in Thessalonians is: "Abstain from all appearance of evil." (1st 5:22)

The condition in Timothy is: "If anyone purifies himself from these things, he will be a special instrument, set apart, useful to the Master, prepared for every good work." (2nd 2:21)

The cause for roistering in Hebrews is: "Let us then go to Him outside the camp, bearing His disgrace." (13:13)

The matter of fact in James is: "Friendship with the world is enmity with God; whoever, therefore, will be a friend of the world is the enemy of God." (4:4)

The parental reminder in Peter is: "As obedient children, do not be conformed to the desires of your former ignorance but, as the One who called you is holy, you also are to be holy in all your conduct; for it is written — Be holy, because I am holy." (1st 1:16)

The gist in the Johannine Epistles is: "Do not love the world or the things that belong to the world. If anyone loves the world, love for the Father is not in him. For everything that belongs to the world — the lust of the flesh, the lust of the eyes, and the pride in one's lifestyle — is not from the Father, but is from the world. And the world with its lust is passing away, but the one who does God's will remain forever." (1st 2:15-17)

The revelation in Revelation by our Commander Himself is: "Come out of her, my people, lest you share in her sins, and lest you receive of her plagues." (18:4)

Is there a reward for being different? Yes, there is. God Himself directly maintains and cares for us from His throne. The *glow* is different and cannot be wiped off or explained when Jehovah Nissi is the Source. "After 10 days, Daniel and his three friends looked healthier and better nourished than the young men who had been eating food assigned by the king." The testimony in Nehemiah 9:21 is "for forty years You sustained them in the wilderness and they lacked nothing, their clothes did not wear out and their feet did not swell." When God Himself, not the most exclusive and expensive, albeit consumable, cosmetic products, sustains, beautifies, and rests upon us, like Moses, the glow on us is cosmic and might just require a veil.

Dare to Be Called

Christianity is hard work for our flesh. It is not for the lazy, but it is for the disciplined, the diligent, the committed, and the humble. The basic truth is, even the unsaved have an idea of what a "saint" should look and act like, but when we try to run this race on our own, we become defensive when questions are raised, asking who anyone is to judge us.

Let's remember, the term, "Christian" was not self-derived by the group of people so-called. It was a mockery term. Many years ago, a group of seven young men who were students at the University of Oxford had a group called the *"Holy Club."* These youngsters dedicated their lives to a strict routine of meeting daily for prayer and study of the Word of God, and regular fasting. Their lives seemed to be so methodical, and their mates began to mock them, calling them, "Methodists." If you happen to be a member of the Methodist denomination today, that is the history of how your Church derived its name. The group, headed by brothers John and Charles Wesley, was so proud of this name that they named their ministry after this mocking term.

Our travel should be different, not to the latest tourist hotspot that the world commands us to visit. Jesus endorses our travel. He commands us to "go out into the world *to peach.*" Intentionality and purpose must be aligned with all our travel. There is absolutely no time for any of us to go to a location simply because we desire picturesque settings to get our mark of approval from the world. Are we travelling to share the Gospel? Are we travelling to places that will educate us more about the history of our Faith? Are we visiting relics and historic sites of our tradition that ultimately build and encourage our evidence-based Faith?

Are our budgets different? Is our charity expense costing us something to our satisfaction?

C.S Lewis exposits on this:

> *I am afraid the only safe rule is to give more than we can spare. In other words, if our expenditure on comforts, luxuries, amusements, etc., is up to the standard common among those with the same income as our own, we are probably giving away too little. If our charities do not at all pinch or hamper us, I should say they are too small...There ought to be things we should like to do and cannot do because our charities expenditure excludes them.[136]*

Like Jeremiah, can we boldly say to God, "I never joined the people in their merry feasts. I sat alone because your hand was on me. I was filled with indignation at their sins?" (Jeremiah 15:17) Could it be said of us, like the Christians in 3 John 2, "they received no help from pagans," that our needs are naught if the supply did not come from hands that glorified Christ?

To jump off the fast-moving ride of worldly conformity will bring us levels of joy we never thought possible. A time must come when we realize "that's enough." The world is constantly in competition between individuals trying to outdo each other, have a better profile layout, better personal branding, better dress sense, better family, better spouse, better wedding theme, better wedding look.... By default, everyone represents a subconscious competition with the next person. We can kill the need to "post" everything about our lives, creating an illusion of perfection, making ourselves mass-media zombies. We become like dummy cakes, choosing where to travel for whichever geotag and setting will make the best post. We choose where to eat to show that we have been to certain places. Our weddings are even planned by social media; we will only use a certain vendor to "tag" them. We have completely lost every form of control over our lives.

---

[136] Lewis, C S. Mere Christianity. New York: Macmillan, 1960.

We are prisoners in solitary confinement in the invisible jail of social acceptance; we are walking corpses. We must cease and desist from this satanic trend of self-glorification. No man must give glory to himself. What do we have which was not given to us? What did we come into this world with? *What* are we leaving with? How can we be so controlled by devices needing electricity and batteries to function when we have direct access to the Father of lights? Reject the likes of men. Hate the attention of men. Count achievements and earthly accomplishments as losses.

Our achievement and gathering of knowledge should terrify us, because God has promised to make the wisdom of the wise become foolish. Enjoy the company of ordinary and lowly men; the wisdom they ooze is raw, natural, and untainted with "exposure." Let us learn some shame. The average user on social media is simply shameless, with a dead beyond death conscience. We must cease to show off our religious pursuits. Self-righteousness does not inspire, it repels. The one and only area of our lives that should be private is our relationship with God. Where is our Secret Place? When you pray, do it **in secret,** as Jesus said and did.

When did coffee, flowers, and the double-edged sword of God become something for a "pretty post?" We must die daily. We must think nothing of ourselves. We are nothing. The lie that we are enough is the reason for depression because we are not enough. God and His Word are the only satisfaction. Jeremiah was known as the weeping prophet to men, but he stated that his true satisfaction and delight were in the Word of God (Jeremiah 15:16).

In our case, to men, we are perfect, prettily curated, and delightful, but we are weeping night after night in our closets. What a bunch of fungi-infested dummy cakes!

What are we outside of our money and the quest for it? How do we not loathe what money has become? How do we not detest it when we see flaunting by wicked hearts? How do we desperately desire the Number 1 god of this present world? We are Demas-adherents. Is all the money in the world worth our souls and shame? *What are we thinking?* As fast as we receive money, we must, in double-quick time, give it *all* away. Food + clothing = survival. That is all we need until we are called to our Kingdom. Lavish is loathsome. Meditate on death, not on the next show-off. Do we not learn lessons from history?

Jesus took absolutely no interest in the approval of men. The very acts He sought to keep private were the good acts He did. We would rather display our "nice" actions for the world to see, but hide our pain, imperfections, and insecurities, forgetting that the finest of us takes a smelly dump regularly. We have made ourselves angry, depressed, and dissatisfied with our lives by default, enrolling in the career of drama for which we never trained nor signed up for. We have that tummy-turning question of "how many likes," but when do we realize enough *is* enough? The world will move on from us as soon as the next best thing comes along. We will not trend forever. We *will* be forgotten and replaced in a wink, the moment we leave this earth, no matter what positions we occupied in our careers, our friendships, relationships, *and* families. We will never find satisfaction in anything done outside of *"to the glory of God."* Jesus knew men's hearts. His only duty and satisfaction were to do the will of His Father who sent Him. The best of earthly fathers will fail us; like the heart of any man, theirs is just as desperately wicked as the best of satan's best agents on earth, unless they are constantly broken by Christ.

The loving God who forgets sins, wipes away our tears, wraps us so tightly in His arms, and gives eternal joy, is the only firm foundation we can trust to never change. His love will cause our hearts to explode with love and compassion for our fellow humans, with no expectation of such love in return. His love will weaken our knees. His love will break our stony hearts. His love will rebuke us when we err but restore us to even better heights. He will *never* use our past against us. Our tears will move Him. His presence will forever be with the broken-hearted. He counts all His children worthy and will never forsake one for an imperfection. He will not expect that we stay in certain careers because He has given us certain talents, as long as we give Him returns and we do not sin. His gift to us is our talent, even if the return to Him comes by fixed deposit. He will find it acceptable and not command us to remain in certain places against our desire to serve Him. He will never call us names that will ring in our heads for years to come. He will never kill our spirits and desert us in permanent susceptibility to depression, because we are the black sheep of His flock which He wishes He never birthed. Rather, He will leave the 99 and chase after the wandering one. From afar, He will run to hug and throw a feast for the prodigal son who comes to repentance; He will not question whether His repentance is genuine. He will not question the brand of Bible we read, because the perfection He requires from us is not met. He will not use the Bible, of which He alone is the Author, to cast us out of our Faith. His correction will always make us better, and never break our spirits. He will never blame us for the death of another human being, because He knows that every man is appointed to die. He will never give us a reason to be suicidal. He will never revel in our tears; He will not mock us with regrets over good acts He has done for us, which we didn't deserve. His gifts and our calling are irrevocable. He will always take us to greater heights of glory and cause our hearts to dance with joy. Jesus is all the love, acceptance, and satisfaction we will ever need. That is what will *never* fail us!

Come out of them and be ye separate! is a command to fall in line[137] or move along. Our opinion on a holy writ is of no effect (1 Timothy 5:21). The standard and spirit for anyone who chooses to be called Christian is one: There are no concessions granted by age, culture, or location. Instead, there is unity beyond borders. Paul declared, "When I urged Titus to visit you and sent our other brother with him, did Titus take advantage of you? No! For we have the same spirit and walk in each other's steps, doing things the same way." (2 Corinthians 12:18) It was said of the Christians in Acts 4:32, "and the multitude of them that believed were of one heart and one soul."

Dear Modern-day Christian, can we dare to be holy? Can we dare to be called Christian?

Who?

The world directs us to self-identify by attaching titles to our name with gargantuan letters arranged after it, or by listing earthly accomplishments. On the other hand, to simply say we are Christian means we are called by the Lord and we believe in the Lord. It means we are guided by the Word; we are unashamed of the Word; we preach the Word; we live by the Word; we love the Word; we love our God, and we love every human with wide-open arms. It means we are salt, we are light, and we are fruitful. It means we hate sin, we speak truth, as our Father is the Founder of Truth. It means we work as unto God, we are not ruled by money, we pray, we are wise, we are content merely with food and clothing. It means we submit, we lead, we follow peace, we follow holiness, we are yes, we are no, we turn the other cheek, we go the extra mile, we are Christ-aware. It means we flee appearances of evil, we forget the past, we press on, we know God, we are strong, we engage in exploits, we are yoked equally in all our relationships. It means we keep, treat, and maintain our bodies as Temples of the Lord, we eschew weights, we pray, we are *in* this world but *not of* this world. Furthermore, we forgive, we weep at sin and immorality prevalent in our society, we repent, we confess, we pray, we fast, we self-deny, and we are not conformed. We are of integrity, we discern, we think good thoughts, we do not condemn, we isolate, we reflect,

---

[137] Pun rightly intended.

we wait, we encourage, we give, we help, we serve, we honor, we respect, we meditate, we pray, we focus on things above, we are at any time ready to die for the Cause of Jesus Christ. We were once dead in sin but are resurrected by grace. We are living our new lives through Christ, we pray, we are called out of darkness to show forth the praises of Him Who has called us into His marvelous light. We are Spirit-led, we pray, we are clean, we are renewed, we were blind but now we see. We are new, we are Heavenly, we are soldiers of Christ, we are ambassadors of Christ, we have the mind of Christ, we carry Christ, we pray, and we are partakers of the divine nature. We fight the good fight of faith, we are more than conquerors through Him who loves us, we are Kingdom Citizens, we are sealed by the Spirit, we endure, we think not highly of ourselves, we pray, we are constantly being worked on by our Potter, we are forever in the operation theatre, laying upon the Great Physician's table for our heart surgery. We will be perfected upon His coming, we pray, we persevere, we are hopeful, we are joyful, we are thankful, we are grateful, we are different, and we are free, **It is finished!**

Examine yourselves as to whether you are in the faith. Test yourselves. Do you not know yourselves, that Jesus Christ is in you? —unless indeed you are disqualified.' 2 Corinthians 13:5

Can we take this back to the beginning?

Hi! I am Eunice., *Eunice-Pauline*, sinner, saved by the grace of God and the blood of Jesus Christ. I am a Christian and I'm *very* pleased to meet you.

Who are you?

PART B

CHAPTER 2

KNOW!

For I desired mercy, and not sacrifice; the knowledge of God more than burnt offerings. **Hosea 6:6**

SoulTune: Ancient Words[138]

---

[138] Recorded by: Camille Aragones, Written by: Lyndd Deshazo, Album: Sweet Hour (2008) Camric Media.

*Writer's Note: *The chapter you are about to read is the most precious to me. The inspiration to put the words in this text, the foundation of this journey with God to the perfection of my inner man and true freedom, [not that which we deceive ourselves we have] came solely by studying the Word of God. James 1:23-25 describes God's Word as a mirror with the ability to set us free. As I sought God's face over the lockdown period of 2020 (Acts 17:27), I began to see myself clearly, and frankly, I felt ashamed and sad, convicted, and hopeful.*

I also began to worry for a lot of us Christians, because it is crystal clear that a lot of us do not study the Word of God, or we just refuse the power it has to transform us (2 Timothy 3:5). A verse here, a verse there, a Bible plan here, a Bible plan there, sporadic devotionals meant to be daily, yet we remain exactly the same as we have always been before we came to Jesus Christ. It is as if we have added just a sprinkle of church, then a splash of prayer, for God to supply our earthly needs.

It is alarming, distressing, and embittering to see the state of Christianity today. Christianity is no more than a casual routine to us, not a lifestyle or personality. For more people, it is a burden they consider dropping from time to time. At best, Christianity is what our church presents to us; our opinion of God goes as far as who our favorite preacher is and whatever they tell us.

We must understand this: we do not have to be Christian. In all frankness, consider why you have chosen to be a Christian. Is it something you grew up with? Has it become routine for you? Are there Christian influencers you admire? Take time to ponder this question: **Why am I a Christian**? *Did you need a miracle? Did you need a job? A spouse? Children? Did you need a house or more money? Are you a well-known and loved worker in the Church and it seems there is no way out? If it is any of the above options, or something close to them, please stop it today. Don't tie yourself up to this "sect" that you sometimes do enjoy, but other times you don't, and sometimes you even forget!*

If your answer is different however and for you, Christianity is first of all and mostly a deep desire to truly and personally know the King of this Kingdom, to swear your allegiance to the Cross of Calvary and to do everything to have a grand welcome into Heaven at the end of your life's journey, bearing gifts of gratitude with you i.e. the fruits you will produce – the souls you will win [because going anywhere empty handed is not biblical] to show how thankful you are for the honour and glory to reign eternally in a Kingdom so perfect, praising the King forever for delivering you from that near-miss of your soul's eternal damnation in that pit which burns forever with Sulphur and brimstone? Then welcome here.

Know this: There is a process to entering this Kingdom. There is a way, and the road is straight and narrow but open to all. There is also a Manual that tells us everything we **need** *to know about this Kingdom, what we can* **expect** *to encounter there, and some of*

114

the people we can assuredly meet (personally, after God and Jesus, I am heading straight to the Apostle Paul's mansion. Then we will stroll to Apostle Peter's, who will take us to meet all the martyrs from history to thank them personally – all those who sacrificed their lives for the Faith and fought a good fight on earth to ensure we enjoy all of the things we freely enjoy on earth today – the early Saints, the Reformers, the Revivalists, etc.) Most important, the Manual tells us how we can get there, how we can "endure" our time on earth, and it daily reminds us of the glory coming to us if we press on.

As stated earlier, studying the Word brought a lot of dry heaves and pain to my heart, over a number of things about me and our generation of Christians. The additional resources I used also put a lot of things in context. I could see how this Holy Manual came about, how we all have access to this Book of Wisdom and Life. I was seeing the sacrifices made and prices paid, not just by Jesus, but also by the lives of fellowmen, so that we freely have access to this Holy Bible we all enjoy today. I wept. Oh, I wept!

*According to **James 1:25**, the Good News is that this Word sets us free. Indeed, by God's grace, I found freedom from earthly bondage, freedom from the love of man. I found the satisfaction to my love language. I found "words of affirmation" meaning I can never run out of love as long as I remain on earth, due to the boundless supply of love letters found in the Word of God. This dynamic Word of Liberty has set me on a quest to stay free by the power of my Lord, Jesus Christ.*

*As you approach this chapter, **Know!** please note a few things:*

- *Opposing views on anything written therein could only be addressed by the Holy Spirit (1 John 2:27)*

- *Please approach this chapter with all quietness of mind and seriousness of heart as we step into Holy Ground….*

Open thou mine eyes, that I may behold wondrous things out of thy law. Psalm 119:18

"Holy words, long preserved, for our walk in this world, they resound with God's own heart…Ancient words ever true changing me and changing you, we have come with open hearts…Holy words of our Faith, handed down to this age, Came to us through sacrifice…"

The words above are excerpts from the SoulTune of this chapter, *Ancient Words*, a song we should listen to again and again until it drowns in our souls.

Let's play a game, *"Two Truths and One Lie,"* in the following sentence: *"Ancient Words ever true changing me and changing you."* What are the two truths and what is the one lie from that sentence?

Answer:

Truth 1: *The Words are ancient,* having been written thousands of years ago, yet they remain intact as they were initially said.

Truth 2: *Ever true.* The Words of God are true. They were true yesterday, they are true today, they will be true forever.

Lie: *Changing me and changing you.* Lie! The Words have no effect on the 21st Century Christian. The Word of God is not changing us. We are status quo. The reason for this is that we attempt to change the Words. We come with closed hearts and established, man-made views we have stuck in our heads about what life is and the way we should live. Rather than letting this Word have its proven transforming effect in our lives, we choose to twist it, mold it, and continue to tamper with it until it fits into our back pockets.

Why do we do this ungrateful act? These Words are rightly said and came to us through sacrifice of dreams, comfort, fortune, family *and* lives.

If you are an English reader of the Word of God, did you know that the first man who ever tried to translate the Holy Bible from its original text of Hebrew and Greek, rather than the Latin Vulgate, was strangled to death and then burned at the stake for this act of "heresy" his executors accused him of? Yes, his name was William Tyndale, not King James, and he was flesh and blood like any of us. He did not come from Heaven, nor was he conceived by the Holy Spirit.

He had parents and siblings, but because of the threat of religious authorities, who had recently burned seven people for teaching their children The Lord's Prayer, the Apostles Creed and the Ten Commandments in English, he had to flee from England. his home country, to Germany. He remained in hiding there while translating the Bible. During that time, he suffered a shipwreck and lost the manuscripts he had been working on. Not discouraged, he started again. Despite this effort, when he printed the copies he had completed of the New Testament and shipped them to England for the common man to be able to read, the Church leaders bought all the copies and burned them. Still, Tyndale was not discouraged; he borrowed money and printed more copies, all of which were bought and burned by the same Church leaders. He had begun a translation of the Old Testament and learned the Hebrew language for this single cause. He finished translating the Pentateuch, but at the age of 42, when he had begun 1 Chronicles, his life was cut short for trying to do what he referred to as his "purpose." He did this translation, not because he needed to understand the Bible, as he was an outstanding and decorated scholar who spoke over seven languages, but because he wanted you and me, laymen, to have access to the Word of God, not solely as the approved clergy of the Roman Catholic Church would have had it. His words to them were, *"I defy the Pope, and all his laws; and if God spares my life, ere many years, I will cause the boy that driveth the plow to know more of the Scriptures than thou dost!"* [139]

Indeed, he defied religious cults, was rejected by friends whose help he sought, and began his mission. At his death, his final words were, *"Lord! Open the King of England's eyes,"* and God being faithful indeed, opened the eyes of the King of England who approved the official translation of the Bible into the English language just a year after this noble man sacrificed his life for us.[140] Ninety percent of the Authorized Version (KJV) of the New Testament, and 75% of the Revised Standard Version we read today, remain as Tyndale translated them.

Common phrases we use today as laymen and as Christians, such as *"my brother's keeper,"* *"knock and it shall be opened unto you,"* *"a moment in time,"* *"seek and ye shall find,"* *"ask and it shall be given you,"* *"let there be light',"* *"the powers that be,"* *"the salt of the earth,"* *"the spirit is willing, but the flesh is weak,"* *"live, move and have our being,"* **and the world favorite**, *"judge not that ye be not judged,"* along with many others, were all coined by William Tyndale. No, not God. Yes, God's idea, but this man gave us those expressions. He was betrayed by a so-called Christian of the Church, then murdered for this *by* Christians! What was so special about this Word that a man was willing to give up friends, career, marriage, and his life for it?

Christiana, we are able to read the Bible freely today, and post pretty verses as we desire. But have we heard or known about Anne Askew?

Anne was a woman of intelligence and outstanding bravery who, at a time when reading the Bible was reserved for priests and exclusive men, went on to study her Bible. She studied it so much that she began to question and refute teaching in the Church by preachers who read the Bible in its original languages and taught something entirely different to their congregants. She became known as a "gospeller" in her day, i.e., someone who knew the Word by heart and could preach it. As someone from a high social class, this act by Anne would have attracted the unfavorable attention of the authorities. She

---

[139] G. Hanks, 70 Great Christians.

[140] Hamlin, Hannibal; Jones, Norman W. (2010), The King James Bible After Four Hundred Years: Literary, Linguistic, and Cultural Influences, Cambridge University Press.

was eventually tortured on the rack and burned to death at age 25, neither recanting her faith nor her stance on her interpretation of the Bible. She also refused to give up the names of her fellow Protestants, one of whom was Catherine, Queen of England at the time.[141]

With all this sacrifice handed down to us, and the surplus availability of the Holy Bible in practically every corner of the earth, why have we ungrateful, personal-branded 21st Centurians unrelentingly reduce the living Word of God to Chinese Whispers?[142] We read and hear the Word directly, then we become selective about what we hear and see and bring out whatever interpretation suits our lifestyles.

We discover that this trend of Chinese Whispers has been spreading since the days of Jesus when we examine these two scenarios:

SCENARIO A:

JEWISH LEADERS: *Is it lawful for us to pay taxes to Caesar or not?*

JESUS: *Give to Caesar what is Caesar's, and to God what is God's*

JEWISH LEADERS: *We found this fellow perverting the nation, and forbidding to pay taxes to Caesar, saying that He Himself is Christ, a King.*

Jesus: ......

(Luke 20:22&25; Luke 23:2)

SCENARIO B:

PETER: *Lord, what about him?*

JESUS: *If I want him to remain alive until I return, what is that to you? You must follow me.*

> *Because of this, the rumor spread among the believers that this disciple would not die. But Jesus did not say that he would not die; he only said, "If I want him to remain alive until I return, what is that to you?"* John 21:21-23

The rumor spread, not among laymen but among our very brothers and

---

[141] Ibid 139.

[142] Chinese Whispers is a game in which one person tells a story to the next person and so on; by the end of all the telling, the original story may be very different from the original

sisters. Jesus said one thing, they passed and passed and passed and passed it from one to the other, until it became something completely different from what He originally said. Could this be why the priests in the early Church reserved the Bible for only a select few to read in its original language and to interpret to the congregation in the way they deemed fit? The ubiquity of the Bible in our age exposes the Living Word of God to all manner of interpretation, disrespect, slander and heresy from even the most educated people, even some who started out correctly but have fallen from grace; they are either cognizant of this, or it is to their tragic oblivion.

We must know that the Holy Bible, which contains the Words of God Himself, cannot be read without the Holy Spirit's guidance for interpretation: "For what man knoweth the things of a man, save the spirit of man which is in him? even so the things of God knoweth no man, but the Spirit of God… But the natural man receiveth not the things of the Spirit of God: for they are foolishness unto him: neither can he know them, because they are spiritually discerned." (1 Corinthians 2:11&14)

A lady read 1 Timothy 2:9, "Likewise, I want the women to adorn themselves with respectable apparel, with modesty, and with self-control, not with braided hair or gold or pearls or expensive clothes." Right there and then she said, "Ladies must be modest when going *to church.*" This is exactly where the Chinese Whispers syndrome of the Word of God comes in. This is where we imagine we can dissect our lives into private and public, into church and secular. Nowhere in that verse is it stated that modesty is reserved only for church.

Again, a man once read, 'So he [Moses] was there with the LORD forty days and forty nights; he neither ate bread nor drank water" Exodus 34:28; and went on to say 40 days was figurative for "a long time" because the human body cannot survive that long without water.[143]

> *Seeing many things, but thou observest not; opening the ears, but he heareth not.* Isaiah 42:20

David, the psalmist, prayed for God to open his eyes to behold wondrous things from His Word (Psalm 119:18*).* We know for certain that David was not a blind man, his mere *sighting* of Bathsheba was what led to two of his legendary sins. However, when it came to the Word of God, that which only the Spirit of God can know, he prayed for his eyes to be open.

> *Knowing this first: that no prophecy of the scripture is of any private interpretation. For*

---

[143] These scenarios were picked from user public notes on verses from a Bible App.

the prophecy came not in old time by the will of man: but holy men of God spoke as they were moved by the Holy Ghost. 2 Peter 1:20-21

In the quote above, Apostle Peter was writing about the effect of the Apostles' first-hand experience of seeing Jesus die and rise again, which produced in them more confidence in the message of the Prophets of old. (It was not that they ever doubted Scripture but they were able to know for a surety that everything they read in Scripture was true [*the same way a big shock is coming to those who do not believe the exact words written in the Bible on the imminent coming of our Lord]*).

We are in no right standing, calling or position to ever *not* take the Word of God exactly as it is written. We have been given so much in this generation which has rendered us a collection of ingrates to the privileges we enjoy, having the Bible available in every nook and cranny.

What's worse, we subject God's Words to our own myopic, lustful, flesh-honoring interpretations. The Pauline Epistles are hard enough to understand as they've been written. Even Peter, who was a **"chiefest/super-Apostle"**[144] compared to Apostle Paul, admitted that in Paul's letters, **are some things hard to be understood,** and those who, according to their foolishness, interpret it do so **"unto their own destruction."** (2 Peter 3:16) Paul himself said of his own writings, "For I neither received it of man, neither was I taught it but by the revelation of Jesus Christ." (Galatians 1:12)

Paul warns those who are wise to remain steadfast, to hold fast to those things which were taught from the old days, otherwise, *as many already have today*, we fall into the **error of the wicked,**[145] "we" being the 21st Century apostates who would rather empower and amuse people with the Word than teach "iron-pole" truth; that is truth which can either be rested upon for comfort or hurt, or destroy when encountered, but will always stand firm! As for troublers of God's people by perversion/diversion and false interpretation of the Gospel of Jesus Christ, *even if* it is an angel, **let him be accursed** not once but twice, **let him be accursed.** (Galatians 1:7-9)

Some are quick to say some provisions of the Holy Bible are null and void, because it is "old testament." The Old and New Testaments are not separate. As a matter of fact, it was a man like us, a Christian scholar named Tertullian (155-240 AD), who gave this nomenclature, "Old" and "New" Testament. Of course, it is not of no effect, but God *never* said we should look at old/ new separately. We must rely on, pay close attention to, and

---

[144] 2 Corinthians 11:5.
[145] 2 Peter 3:17.

believe in every punctuation mark laid out in Scripture, because they are un-adulterated *Rhema* from Heaven and not expressions of its writer's intellect or fantasies.

Jeremiah: ***I, Ah, Lord God! behold, I cannot speak: for I am a child.***

Lord Almighty: ***Say not, I am a child: for thou shalt go to all that I shall send thee, and whatsoever I command thee thou shalt speak. Be not afraid of their faces: for I am with thee to deliver thee.*** (Then the Lord put forth his hand and touched my mouth).

Lord Almighty: "Behold, I have put my words in thy mouth." Jeremiah 1:6-9:

> *Help me Father, to hold these Ancient Words ever true. For by them, I have Light in darkness. By them, I have Christ, the Morning Star, shining in my heart, in Jesus' Name. Amen.*

If these Words resound God's very heart, why do we not crave the <u>sincere</u> Word, to which we have DIRECT access, and stop the Chinese Whispers for the sake of posterity? Do we not care? Should we, like the Apostle John, "have no greater joy than to hear that my children walk in truth?" (3 John 1:4) How much longer do we choose to remain ungrateful, ignorant thieves of history and sacrifice?

Respect

You see Christian, this Holy Bible which we possess -- *or not* -- is no ordinary being. Oh yes, the Bible is a living, breathing and Supreme Being; the Bible is Jesus Christ (John 1:1&14; 1 John 1). The Holy Bible is Jesus Christ on our shelves and tables and in our pockets.

A few years ago, a group of men was arrested by some religious leaders for disobeying their religious laws about preaching. They threw these men into a tightly secured prison until they were ready to bring them up for trial. The next day, when the imprisoners went to bring the men for trial, the men were nowhere to be found. Amazingly, however, the prison door locks were still securely fastened; it was a mystery to all.

Finally, the persecutors found the men in public, doing the same thing they had been warned not to do, and again brought them in for trial. At trial, they were asked why they had violated their orders and continued preaching in defiance of what had been ordered. These ordinary men boldly said to this powerful, educated, and highly placed group of leaders, that they were under no obligation to obey them; they were only to obey their own God. With such a disrespectful reply, these powerful men were, **cut to the heart.** *(Ouch! – the power of words)* and were determined to kill the men immediately.

However, as in any other sect, there will always be the "who" among the "who's who" hierarchy, i.e., that person whom even the most respected person respects. Within this group of religious leaders, it was no different. There was a man among them who was cool, calm, collected, full of wisdom, reputed, respected, and spoke few but powerful words,[146] whose name was Gamaliel. Respecting his position, he stood amidst the hubbub. Without doubt, his standing quieted the room. First things first, as a man of order and experience, he asked that these ordinary men who were on trial be taken out to give *a little space,* for men like himself don't speak in front of just anybody; their time costs a lot of money.

After these ordinary men were taken out, he aired his views on this matter which, in his own opinion, was not even worth their *touching.* He recalled two other men from the past who were similar to these ordinary men currently on trial. The first was called Theudas, who had come up, *boasting himself to be somebody,* alongside 400 men who followed him; in no time, however, this influencer, Theudas *was slain; and all, as many as obeyed him, were scattered and brought to nought.* (***Writer's Note:** *In these days, the followers run into tens of thousands and even millions, but the followship is done by clicking a button, not by physical presence, so one individual is deluded into thinking they are some kind of god, commonly called an "influencer." Then the others think they have found their messiah, following whatever this person recommends. But suddenly, the veil is torn, and these leaders plead for their followers not to look up to them as role models, because the pressure is too much and they are "only human." Oh!*)

The second influencer was called Judas,[147] *and drew away much people after him: he also perished; and all, even as many as obeyed him,* (like bees whose honeypot has been snatched) *dispersed (undoubtedly to look for the next trending thing to follow).*

So this wise man of nobility and experience went on to advise his colleagues, *refrain from these men and let them alone: for if this counselor work be of men it will come to nought but if it be of God you cannot*

---

[146] Proverbs 17:27.
[147] Of Galilee.

overthrow it—lest you even be found to fight against God; so the leaders saw that it was good, what the sagacious Gamaliel had counselled them. Therefore, they obeyed his counsel. However, their piqued hearts were still bleeding from that earlier cut, so they called these ordinary men back in, beat them, commanded that they should not speak in the name of **JESUS,** and let them go.[148] Not so long after:

So mightily grew the word of God and prevailed. Acts 19:20

Friend, these few years have been more than 2000 years and counting. The Word of God is not just on lips again, but on the hearts of *(some)* men, and has now been recorded, i.e., written down and translated, with the full Bible available in over 2,100 languages and counting. The New Testament alone has been translated into an additional 1,548 languages and counting. Biblical stories have been translated into 1,138 languages and counting, with at least some portions translated into 3,384 languages *and* counting.[149] These Words which, if they were not of God would have become extinct over 2,000 years ago, remain the best-selling book in all of history. As of 2015, according to *The Guinness Book of World Records,* the Bible has sold more than 5 billion copies, with annual hardcopy sales in the USA alone surpassing 20 million copies.[150]   In the year 2016 alone, The Gideon International distributed 59,460,000 Bibles worldwide, an average of more than 100 Bibles per minute.[151] In the English language alone, in which it was once forbidden to be translated (recall the martyrdom of William Tyndale), there are now over 2,013 English versions of the Holy Bible.[152]

We aren't done yet. In 2019, marking 11 years since its launch, the *YouVersion© Bible App* had been installed on more than 400 million unique devices, and downloaded in every country on earth, with availability in 1,343 languages, including 527 audio Bibles in 417 languages.[153] Hundreds of thousands of unique users have been recorded downloading the app every day, at an install rate of 1.3 seconds. On average, some 66,000 people have the Bible app open during any given second, and the figures climb much higher most times.[154] ***Writer's Note:** *At this point, it's important to note that if you have these*

---

[148] Account found in *Acts 5.*

[149] https://www.wycliffe.net/resources/scripture-access-statistics/

[150]https://brandongaille.com/27-good-bible-sales-statistics/#:~:text=20%20million.,year%20in%20the%20United%20States.

[151] Ibid

[152] https://www.youversion.com/share2019/

[153] Ibid

[154]https://www.nirandfar.com/the-app-of-god-getting-100-million-downloads-is-more-psychology-than-

Bible apps on your devices and you can carry them along with you to your debaucheries, nightclubs, and sinful reveling, you are committing a holy affront. It will be wise to respectfully delete them before engaging in your fleshly indulgences.)

Why is there this exponential and almost unbelievable growth of the words of ordinary men from over two thousand years ago? **TRUTH.**

When Jesus was on trial in John 18:38, Pilate demanded to know from Jesus, even though he did not wait for an answer, **What is truth?** A question everyone ought to ask. Indeed, many ask but are either asking the wrong way, asking the wrong source, or simply impatient, like Pilate, to receive an answer. A simple, "What is truth?" will provide an equally simple answer, found in John 17:17, "…Your Word is truth." Once that answer is received and accepted, a wonderful thing happens, "…the truth shall make you free." (John 8:32)

Yes, free from the default heartache and pain with which we are all born as a result of sin from failing to follow our Creator's instructions, which lead to a happy, productive and peaceful life, we are free to patiently endure this world with hope while we look forward to the world to come, The Kingdom of God which we really belong to; and that is the reason for the exponential spread of the Word of God. If rumors spread like wildfire, truth spreads double the speed of light, and the Word of God is that force that spreads faster than light's speed! The Bible *is* **TRUTH**. The Bible *is* Freedom!

This is the only Book that has never needed an updated version or correction of facts. The singular, most referenced source for art, literature, and motivational inspiration, there are billions of unique sermons preached from this Book daily and billions yet unfounded. God in His Word is the only Being which has outlived billions of generations, and will outlive billions to come, yet He has not aged a second. The Word is the most potent, powerful, dangerous weapon to ever exist. When all is said and done, when we all return to our dust, the Word is the only Thing that *will* remain, for it is the One which was here first, and the One which *will* be here last.

What an honor, what grace, what mercy to have access to this Holy Book of Knowledge, Wisdom, Life, Peace and Transformation. *(*Writer's Note: Oh Father! I am SO proud of You! Wow! I slowly fall on my knees at this moment, lift my hands above my head, and give a resounding ovation to the arrangement of ordinary letters into words which changed my life. The most powerful Being in heaven and earth — the*

---

miracles/#:~:text=The%20app%2C%20simply%20called%20%E2%80%9CBible,climbs%20much%20higher%20at%20times.

Living Word of God, through the most tempestuous storms of life. Peace like a river.)

   *This will be written for the generation to come, that a people yet to be created may praise
   the LORD.* Psalm 102:18

Yes, we, the beneficiaries of this Written Word, have been born, as accurately
prophesied by the Word which never lies. But are we praising God for it? Are
we not questioning, slandering, tossing, rejecting, debating, rationalizing, buf-
feting, and futilely trying to extinguish it?

On September 11, 2001, news outlets were buzzing with the news that two
planes had rammed into the Twin Towers, one had been used as a missile
against the Pentagon, and a third had crash into the ground near Shanksville,
Pennsylvania. There remains, however, a vital but unreported part of the
story by national media. The unreported part was written by Tom Lavis, a
correspondent for *The Tribune-Democrat*, a local paper which serves the community of Johnstown, Pennsylvania.

This report gave an accurate account, verified by multiple eyewitnesses, of
what the first responders saw upon their arrival at the crash site. Why, then,
did national media not report it? What piece of information in a historical
massacre was worth being left out of public knowledge? The first responders
found, unscathed among the smoldering wreckage, an open Bible. Terry
Shaffer, who was at the time the fire chief of the Shanksville fire department
said, *"The fumes of jet fuel burned my nostrils ...There were only two recognizable things
on the ground — a burning tire from the landing gear and the Bible laying open on the
ground with its pages as white as snow.... The leather cover on the Bible was singed, but
none of the pages was burned."*[155]

Are we still debating the supremacy of the immutable and infallible Word of
God, the Holy Loving God Almighty, who IS Jehovah El Shaddai, a Consuming Fire, yet honors this Word *above* the greatest, powerful, and most loving names we can ever call Him? (Psalm 138:2)

---

[155] https://www.christianpost.com/news/untold-story-of-unburnt-bible-at-9-11-crash-site-
is-a-message-from-god-opinion.html

Context

Quick, Powerful, Sharper than any Two-Edged Sword, Piercing, Discerning... profitable for doctrine, for reproof, for correction, for instruction in righteousness.

These are a range of characteristics and values of the Word of God, according to Hebrews 4:12 and 2 Timothy 3:16, respectively. We know that it is quick from its exponential growth due to its truth; we know it is a weapon of warfare on our lives and for our life battles.

As striking as the words in the official Bibles are, there is still so much information uncontained in them. Some of these, we have in books called "Apocrypha," meaning, "those that were hidden." In the Gospel of John, a lot of things Jesus did were left unrecorded, because all the space in the world would not be able to contain them. Also, Apostle John's letter to Elder Gaius in 3 John, verse 13 says, "I had many things to write, but I will not with ink and pen write unto thee." We know that God gives us the desire to will and to do (Philippians 2:13), so the fact that there were still many things John had to write to this Elder, but would not put on paper, were a result of God's unwillingness to have us know what those things were. Without doubt, if those things were meant to be in the Bible for us to know, John would have been inspired of God to write them down. The "little" that has been written for us was written with only one intention, "that you may believe that Jesus is the Christ, the Son of God, and that believing you may have life in His name." (John 20:31)

We must not take for granted this divine "inner-circle gist" we are privileged to read, for contempt or worse, subject them to our carnal interpretations. To come to the Word of God should be to come with awe-inspired reverence and hearts willing to undisputedly obey. Affirming this, Deuteronomy 29:29 says, "The secret things belong to the LORD our God, but those things which are revealed belong to us and to our children forever, that we may do all the words of this law."

Now, this Word had some diverse effects on those who heard or held it:

- *Jeremiah* said: *His Word was in mine heart as a burning fire.* (20:9)

- *Malachi* described it as the *burden of the Word of the Lord.* (1:11)

- Whenever King Herod spoke with John the Baptist, he *was greatly disturbed.* (Mark 6:20)

- In *Luke 24:32*, Cleopas and his companions had been talking to Jesus but their eyes had been shut from recognizing Him, however they said, *Did not our hearts burn within us, while he talked with us by the way?*

- In **Acts 2:37,** it was said of those who listened to Peter, whose words were uttered under the influence of the Holy Spirit:" *they were pricked in their hearts."*

- For Governor Felix and his wife Drusilla, who spoke with Apostle Paul the convict, *"As he reasoned with them about righteousness and self-control and the coming Day of Judgment, Felix became frightened. "Go away for now," he replied. "When it is more convenient, I'll call for you again.""* (Acts 24:25)

- In the days of the early Christians, there was a man called Marcion of Sinope, who studied the Bible and developed a gospel after his own name, which lasted for many centuries. His conclusion from the Word of God, on which he built his heretical doctrine, was that Yahweh of the Old Testament, the creator God, was different from the God who sent Jesus to die for us in the New Testament. Marcion stated the God of the Old Testament was belligerent. His actions were incompatible with the "God of Jesus." This doctrine might have been a fair point if God had not made it clear to us, *to people like Marcion,* several times, *I am, I change not, The Same yesterday, today and forever.* This rather lunatic effect on the Word is inevitable when it is not read through the lens of the Holy Spirit but through "wisdom" our scholarly hats have impressed on us.

- On the other hand, Bishop Ambrose of Milan, who studied the Word and sensed a call upon his life, started his ministry by disposing of the weights that his earthly wealth and property laid on him. For the rest of his life, Ambrose became a dutiful preacher of the true Word of God.

Irrespective of the vessel, God's Word will be *that* Truth with inconceivable effects. This is why Jesus said of the Pharisees in Matthew 23:2-3, that the things which they taught should be practiced and obeyed. Their examples, however, should *not* be followed, because they did not practice what they preached. *Truth.* On the other hand, this is why when God lays His Word on one's heart and there is a refusal and struggle not to say it, like Jeremiah, it will burn that heart so much, until you become worn out and weary trying to hold it in. You just cannot. ***Writer's Note:** *I couldn't help writing* The Untouched Part!

Why, then, is this same Word we know *not* without effect, rendered so ineffective in our generation? This same Word, which produced some radical effects in our ancestors, is having absolutely zilch effect on our generation. Surely, it is *not* the Word of the Consuming Fire we hear. Could it be that we are hardening our hearts when we hear It? (Hebrews 3:7-8) What a futile thing to do, because we can either fall on It to break us, or It falls on us and crushes us to irredeemable powder.

Have we deliberately chosen to accept the tone of Jesus in the Gospels, which was loving, warm, accepting, and inviting, but then ignore this *same* Jesus' tone? This is the same Jesus, Who had now paid the ultimate price for our sin in Revelation, which was uncoated, direct, sharp, rejecting of sin, uncompromising and judgmental. In the former, He was human and crucified in weakness, but that is all done, dusted and settled. Now He lives by the power of God (2 Corinthians 13:4); and is coming back to judge us. Are we choosing to not imagine how terrible it will be on that Last Day when He comes without notice to pass final verdict on our souls? This will be a time when He will directly "fight against (us) with the sword of (His) mouth." (Revelation 2:16) Oh yes, Jesus loves us, but He is no longer smiling on sin. He is no longer saying **neither do I condemn thee** when we choose to continue in sin for grace to abound. Grace will *not* abound. He commended some of the churches in Revelation for their zeal but told them **nevertheless I have somewhat against thee** for one thing or the other. Let us be fair to our souls.

Is it not true that we cherry pick the Word of God? The majority of believers will read parts of the Bible and attribute them to the "context of their culture, back in the day" as a way to nullify its provision, in order to excuse them from obedience. The "nicer" parts, however, they choose to keep as still relevant to them. Tithing is not relevant to us anymore, but "God so loved the world" is still relevant. We select the "nicer" parts and frame or post them, such as: **"I can do all Things through Christ who strengthens me,** failing to apply context to that tiny bit of a bigger work... a statement which was in context of the Apostle Paul affirming he had learned to be content in whatever situation he found himself, whether in plenty or in lack! He was able to do this *by* God's strengthening him. It was not that he was able to make heaps of money or get to the top of Forbes' list by God's strength.

We must study the Word of God in context, not in isolation. How many times do we find ourselves in situations where someone says we did or said something and we want to put it "in context" because they are completely missing the point, or picking one piece of a bigger picture and twisting or misunderstanding it? When that happens, we feel the frustration of knowing fully well that because that piece was ripped out of context, a completely different scenario is created out of the reality of things. We must take The

Word in its entirety, which is taking the whole of Jesus Christ. (Luke 24:27) When we separate or pick and choose within the Word, we are attempting to mutilate Jesus by picking out only His eyes, His fingernails, or any other specific part from His whole body. If we say and mean that we love Him, let us take Him, His word, as He is.

Another effect, when we claim a Bible verse, is that it seems nice and empowering for our personal gratification, when taken in isolation, or distorted from its original context and condition. In doing so, we deceive and frustrate no one but ourselves after we apply it to our lives and it accomplishes nothing for us. Some, then, go on to slander the Holy Word of God. **Let God be true and every man be a liar.** God's Word is infallible. It has existed for 2,000 years and counting; it is still the most used book in the world. If it does not work for a human being during their 120 years or fewer on earth, that *person* is the problem, *not* the Word of God. That person *will* pass away. His Word will not.

One the other hand, when the verse seems to empower our self-service, voices become so loud to invoke the "god of context." With the issue of women's hair covering, for instance, the default argument is that it was written by Paul to the Corinthian women and it was their tradition; from a cultural perspective, then, the rule will not apply to modern women.

Context is irrelevant when claiming, "my God shall supply all my needs according to His riches in glory," a verse from the same **Philippians 4** in which Paul was saying a prayer for people who had sacrificed their resources as a gift to him. (He didn't need the gifts but received them for God to bless those who gave the gifts.) Speaking again of context, it is interesting to think how disciples and even Jesus referred to their generation in the times they lived with such words as "depraved," "wicked" "crooked," "perverse," etc. If this were just contextual, surely the generation we live in now is but a slice of hell. Or is the Bible really alive throughout the ages?

We must learn to take the Word of God as it is. We were made to serve it, not the Word to serve our desires. It is an unchangeable constitution, a Divine Handbook. There is no review committee, no addenda, and no redundancy to any single part of God's Holy Word, which He honors above His greatest, strongest, and most powerful of Names. We must bow to it, not use our little, myopic, artificial brains to distort the long-preserved Holy Words of YHWH. "For we can do nothing against the truth, but for the truth." 2 Corinthians 13:8

The Word of God is a compass for redirection, a sun and a shield to hurt and heal, to rebuke and encourage, to refine and reveal. Grazing on It as if it were a buffet to control Its effects in our lives is a needless endeavor if we desire to produce lasting fruit. It is worthy of acceptance in its entirety. ALL Scripture IS God-breathed. The same breath that said, "I know the plans I have toward you," is the same that said, "for God so loved," and said, "all things work together for good." It is also the same breath which pronounced, "whom the Lord loves He chastises," "give and it shall be given unto you," and "follow peace with all men and holiness without which no man will see God." If we want to hear a certain part, but not another, we are better off purchasing motivational topics that cater to what our   itching ears crave. This Word of God stands without repentance on any punctuation mark.

Please, friend, come, let us reason together; we want to be human; we want to be nice and good people. After the sacrifices of these men and women like us who lived, is it fair to our sinless Lord Jesus, of whom the Bible tells us, **Consider Him**[156] and all He suffered for us at the hands of sinners, that we dishonor their sacrificial legacy? Is it fair to dishonor the legacy of those things for which they were killed, which we freely enjoy today? Is the least we can do to preserve their legacy, not to nit-pick their divine work? If this Word doesn't work for you, if by any means, one punctuation mark does not work for you, I beseech you, in view of God's mercies, drop the Holy Bible and write your personal life manual. The Gospel is simple, straightforward, narrow minded, clear, unapologetic, pure *and* the Truth! *Depart from It, ye worker of iniquity!*

Balance

Most of us know, or have even enjoyed, a seesaw ride at some point in our lives, whether as children or as kids trapped in adult bodies. We know it is no fun and it defeats the purpose when only one rider is seated. It is entirely useless then, because the presence of two riders is a requirement of the equipment (whose name is derived from a French word meaning "this-that") to carry out the back and forth motion for which a seesaw is constructed. As matter of fact, in the early 2000's, seesaws became banned in many areas of the United States due to safety concerns, because without coordination and cooperation by two riders, it posed a health hazard. When used appropriately, however, by two riders to provide balance, the seesaw ride provides a

---

[156] Hebrews 12:3.

phenomenal sensory experience to each.[157]

The same applies to the Word of God. The Holy Spirit in us is the fulcrum who gives us a balanced view of the Word. It is not solely Old Testament focused, in which some such as Marcion concluded it portrayed God as a belligerent or a "moralistic monster;" for some others, such as the Sanhedrin, it rendered them religious and legalistic, with nothing on the inside. On the other hand, solely based on the New Testament, it may portray Christianity as a lazy religion, in which all we need to do is "just believe." Then God's grace will cover us for all our sins and empower us with some faith and energy to reach the top of our careers, forgetting that the God of love is also a God of wrath and will never change.

We do not settle on either extreme spectra of the Word, but remain balanced and learning how the whole Bible comes together, as Jesus did with the Jewish leaders; He taught them how everything they had studied from the prophets pointed to Him. This balanced take on the Word produces the healthy fear and reverence for God which every Christian must have, being fully assured that the God of wrath and justice also provides comforting hope of salvation through our triumphant, loving Savior Jesus Christ, and through the Holy Spirit, an ever-present Help for our walk on earth.

Dear Teacher

Once upon a time, teachers of Scripture, in lieu of introducing themselves or providing letters of recommendation on their behalf, could freely say, "The only letter of recommendation we need is you yourselves. Your lives are a letter written in our hearts; everyone can read it and recognize our good work among you." (2 Corinthians 3:2) Their CV's and résumés attesting to their effectiveness and faithfulness of teaching God's Word in its truth, were the lives which their listeners led day-to-day.

Another time in Christianity, as the truth of God's Word was being taught, listeners in the audience would interrupt the teacher by shouting, **What must I do to be saved?** It happened in the days of Jesus (Luke 18:18), also in the days of the Apostles Peter (Acts 2:37) and Paul (Acts 16:30), and also in modern times, in the days of great revivalists such as Jonathan Edwards (1703-

---

[157] https://www.nytimes.com/2016/12/11/nyregion/the-downward-slide-of-the-see-saw.html

1758). His sermon, *"Sinners in the Hands of an Angry God"* (July 8, 1741) introduced a whole era of revival in history, The Great Awakening era (1730–1755)[158]. Since then, the accepted record of any notable form of mass revival in post-modern era is the Pyongyang Revival of Korea in 1907, more than a century ago, meaning that even the oldest of our generation is probably in such great slumber.

The 21st Century churches have become so excited. What exactly is so exciting about the Word of God on earth? Yes, it gives joy on earth, but the joy it gives is an inner joy, a silent and peaceable joy, which enables us to endure trials, cleave to Him, and hope in Him that we may walk our days on earth in a manner worthy of being fit for His Kingdom. How many serious preachers of past and present times do we see going about, laughing and jollying? As a matter of fact, these genuine teachers of the Word are the happiest, most fulfilled people on earth, but they maintain neutral countenances and let their hearts do the dancing, not their flesh. If we could get a view of their spirits, we would surely meet a feast, but never their flesh. They understand that absolutely nothing is exciting on this earth; their hearts have settled where their treasures are stored up - Heaven.

St. Benedictine laid out a practical guide to humility through 12 steps of a ladder ascending to Heaven, some of which included: "do not readily laugh," "do not speak until spoken to," "accept the meanest of tasks and hold oneself as a worthless workman."[159] Although some of these steps seem excessive, they are undoubtedly effective and trusted means of running this race. He understood that Christianity was a lifelong, sober walk with God, and most important, to be saved once is not to be saved all. A seemingly thriving and full-of-members-ministry is never a sign for the backing of God. Never.

Archibald Brown has a profound view on this scheme titled, *The Devils Mission of Amusement,* in which he succinctly expounds on how empowerment and amusement gospels are "contemptible failures," which in his interaction with thousands of recipients of this gospel, have produced zero converts. He states,

> *The mission of amusement is the devil's half-way house to the world! It is because of what I have seen that I feel deeply, and would sincerely write strongly. This thing is working rottenness in the Church of God, and blasting her service for the King. In the*

---

[158] Ostling, Richard (4 October 2003), "Theologian Still Relevant After 300 Years", Times Daily, Associated Press, retrieved 2020-23-09.

[159] https://christdesert.org/prayer/rule-of-st-benedict/chapter-7-humility/
https://d2y1pz2y630308.cloudfront.net/14273/documents/2018/8/Bene-dicts%2012%20steps%20to%20humility-3.pdf

guise of Christianity, it is accomplishing the devil's own work! Under the pretense of going out to reach the world — it is carrying our sons and daughters into the world with the plea of "Do not alienate the masses with your strictness," it is seducing the young disciples from the simplicity and the purity of the Gospel. Professing to win the world, it is turning the garden of the Lord into a public recreation ground! To fill the church with those who see no beauty in Christ — a grinning Dragon is put over the doorway!

For I desired mercy, and not sacrifice; and the knowledge of God more than burnt offerings. Hosea 6:6.

It is only during the past few years that "amusement" has become a recognized weapon of our warfare, and developed into a mission. [160]

The Apostle Paul advised us to work out our salvation with fear and trembling, to be sober, to walk circumspectly. So why are we so "uplifted?" We do not know the hour of Jesus' return and this should be a leveler of excessive emotions, whether good or bad. Why do we have so much noise and "Yes, pastor!" screams? What is the amusement about? Where are the burning hearts where "fear fell on them and the name of the Lord Jesus was magnified…Many who became believers confessed their sinful practices?" (Acts 19:17-18)

Where are the confessions today? Self-professing Christians today will jump up in aggravated self-defense at the prospect of anyone glancing, not to mention touching, their devices which hold the key to their true lives, protected by a set of numbers and letters to their "private lives." *Private?*

Gone are the days where Christians declared, *"But we have renounced the hidden things of shame"* (2 Corinthians 4:2) Those things which individual senses of "honor" or pride refuse to bring to light, leave their souls entangled in the bondage of sin, as the arrow of the accuser of the brethren remains pointed directly at their hearts. Christianity has become a *palooza* of the best cover-up. David declared his sin as being ever before him; Paul introduced himself as chief sinner and stated boldly those things which he did before he got saved. How often are our testimonies that God delivered us from the demonic family of liars? Do we testify that our immoral addictions have ceased? No, we want to show-off our man-made, earthly increases and parade them as God's miracles.

The mirrors we stand before demand us to be perfect. We paint our faces, wear the best clothes, take the worldly perfect pictures, and have the best

---

[160] https://www.gracegems.org/29/devils_mission_of_amusement.htm

careers, investments, and inventions. We do so as we stand before physical mirrors, under the best and brightest man-made lighting, looking clean. Our fleshly eyes send a signal to our dirty hearts, throwing them into the illusion that we white-washed sepulchers, as Jesus calls us, *are* clean.

> *Woe to you, scribes and Pharisees, you hypocrites! You clean the outside of the cup and dish, but inside they are full of greed and self-indulgence. Blind Pharisee! First clean the inside of the cup and dish, so that the outside may become clean as well.* Matthew 23:25-26

There is only one Light that exposes secret sin and that is the Light of God's countenance, i.e., His Person, His Word. (Psalm 90:8) There is only one Perfect Law of liberty which can set us free *indeed.* The same way we will not look at physical mirrors with one eye open – some having 360° mirrors to view even their backs and sides – we must not look into the Mirror of God's Word with one eye closed. We must cease and desist this disease of self and perfection that is eating us up; **every man at his best state is altogether vanity** (air, breath, empty, dust, balloon, Dummy Cake) (Psalm 39:5). When we appear dressed to the nines and imagine we are the best thing to exist, we must remember to congratulate ourselves with our real name, Vanity, and as we spiral into Vanity Fair, let us beware for, "when God with rebukes corrects man for iniquity, You make his beauty melt away like a moth" (Psalm 39:11) *Butterfly?* No, moth.

This could explain the highest rates of depression, suicide and drug-use in our generation today than in all of history, despite the presence of the most churches, missions, and Christian platforms that we have ever seen, thanks to technology. The Word has failed to pierce through hearts because ministries are more concerned about amusing their congregants, keeping attendance numbers high and benches warm, than about hearing cries of, *"What must we do to be saved?"* We are in a global snooze, a deep, deep slumber, and we call ourselves enlightened. *Are we all right?*

Some rationalize sin, they evolve sin, daring to say it matters no more in our day. *How frightening!* Sin *is* sin. Until we are ready to openly confess and renounce those seemingly little foxes, we can rest assured that eternal damnation is the end. If, however, we obstinately adhere to this warped view, we might as well go on to have a blast, feasting on the self-serve buffet of wide options of sin. It is denying yourself immense pleasure when you declare, "I didn't kill anybody," but you are bound by the chains of pornography. Immorality = drunkenness = disobedience = murder = lies = stealing = envy = strife = idolatry = gluttony = materialism = consumerism, an equal variety to pick from with the same result, Death.

In Numbers 27:3, a verse championed to justify the cursed movement of feminism, rather than the more alarming message therein, the bold daughters of Zelophehad, who came before Moses, Eleazar the Priest and the entire community, to claim property after their father had died said, *"Our father died in the wilderness, and he was not in the company of them that gathered themselves together against the Lord in the company of Korah; but died in his own sin… "*So, this man was exempt from the sin of rebellion against God but died in whatever buffet of sin options he chose to feast upon. Again, we might as well have a blast while we are at it if we choose to create a pecking order for sin. All have only one wage, Death. (Romans 6:23)

This is the standard Apostle Paul, who boldly told us to imitate him, laid out for teachers of the Word: "And how I kept back nothing that was profitable unto you, but have shewed you, and have taught you publicly, and from house to house… For I have not shunned to declare unto you all the counsel of God." (Acts 20:20&27)

He preached the **whole** Truth of God, because the consequence of anything otherwise would be murder; he exonerated himself by saying, "I am pure from the blood of all men." (Acts 20:26)

He finally warned *teachers*, "Take heed therefore unto yourselves, and to all the flock, over that which the Holy Ghost hath made you overseers, to feed the church of God, which he hath purchased with his own blood." (Acts 20:28) Do teachers of the Word and those in ministry positions see these parts of this same Bible we read? Your anti-Christ gospel of amusement is toying with the very blood of Jesus, with the souls of those for whom He paid the price.

Every teacher of the Gospel of Jesus Christ has been entrusted with divine, ageless, and immutable Truth; their duty is to keep that ministry Biblically sound as the salt of the earth, not pepper, not sugar candy. Even when it is uncomfortable, even when it might be too "salty," with all gentleness and humility, the minister will 'Preach the word! Be ready in season and out of season." (2 Timothy 4:2) A sound minister will be a "fool" for the Gospel and take the Word of God as it is, albeit as preposterous as it may appear to human reasoning, as long as it is done "out of love that comes from a pure heart, genuine faith and a clear conscience unto God." (1 Timothy 1:5)

We are failing God when we do not speak His Truth. We are abusing the trust given to us, and we will be held accountable. In *Luke 24*, after Jesus had risen and appeared to His disciples, He finally opened their eyes to understand all the parables He had been telling them about Himself from records of the Prophets; He then put "faith" in us to preach the Gospel. He gave these assignments to the Apostles who preserved and passed them on *intact* to us. Why do we break the causal chain by neglecting our duty to share it, as it is, to the itching hearts of impressionable followers? *"You had one job!"* The price has been paid; it is finished. Just tell the Truth as it is. One lie produces children, grandchildren, great-grandchildren and then generations, so tracing where such heretical doctrines started becomes almost impossible; it is just a matter of time before it fails. If teaching the right thing is impossible, it is okay to just read the Bible out loud and without exposition, and to pray for the Holy Spirit to teach the hearers. We barely hear Bible verses these days. One verse, and the next thing that comes is how we are empowered to conquer careers and "make it." *How weakening!*

'For I am not ashamed of the Gospel', Paul said, **'it has the power to bring salvation**[161].... Where is the Salvation!? The **evidence** of that **'salvation'** - *not pastors, not sermons, not church, not influencers* - which **teaches us to deny ungodliness and worldly lusts** but to live **soberly, righteously** and **godly in this present world!? (Titus 2:11-12).** Everyone walks around in shame, rather than basking in the freedom that comes from renouncing vice in its entirety, until there is no hidden dishonesty or craftiness in us *at all*, until we are transparent and child-like.

Is it the praise of men we desire? In Acts 14, Paul and Barnabas had performed a miracle of healing a crippled man before a crowd of people. These people were so amazed they were ready to offer sacrifices to them as the Greek gods, Hermes and Zeus, respectively. Alarmed at this barbaric act, the Apostles immediately tore their clothes and redirected the unwilling people back to the Almighty God, but without success. In that moment, some Jews who had previously been chasing Paul, trying to kill him, caught up with him. They immediately turned the hearts of this same crowd of people, who were just about to offer their range of sacrifices and crown these Apostles as their gods against them. The Jews beat Paul to death – or so they thought!

Listen, humans will be amused at whatever excites their senses at any given time. We barely see the miracles of the Bible in our time, which could justify the wonder and amazement of crowds in our time. A teacher of the Word, with a diverse CV and educational prowess, coupled with trendy shredded jeans or a fitted suit, will excite a crowd of impressionable sheep. However, when the next best thing comes their way, their loyalty will shift in the blink of an eye, even if it means killing the one whom they first exalted. The heart of man is desperately wicked and disloyal, even to itself. The only thing

---

[161] **Romans 1:16**

teachers of the Word can and should do is to preach Truth and suffer for it in honor before God. We *will* all suffer, but to be stoned and suffer for Jesus Christ is a worthy and acceptable price before God.

Paul said, "And my message and my preaching were very plain. Rather than using clever and persuasive speeches, I relied only on the power of the Holy Spirit." (1 Corinthians 2:4&5) Preaching becomes difficult or impossible when we try to be creative with it. Scripture is plain and simple; we cannot outdo it. The beauty of Scripture is its simple Truth, but when in the name of creativity, we turn God's Word into amusement for bored listeners, we put ourselves under our own lordship and suffer self-imposed pressure to outdo our last best thing; doing so, we eliminate the Holy Spirit from it and we derail in no time. Not that Apostle Paul's years of Harvard-like training, exposure and intellect were not something worth showing off through eloquence and gift of gab, but he knew better than to pitch himself, the channel, as a competitor against God on His own stage. However, when teachers stick to plain language in teaching God's Truth, as seemingly monotonous or repetitive as it sounds, even such teachers will be amused at the wondrous, varying, and unique effects their approach with personal simplicity, and a complete reliance on the Holy Spirit's empowerment, will produce in the hearts of its hearers; and they have to turn away their praises saying, "Sirs, why do ye these things? We also are men of like passions with you...." (Acts 14:15)

Charles Spurgeon and many great preachers commonly adopted a teaching approach called extemporaneous preaching, in which they did not prepare in advance for any specific sermon. Instead, they devoted their lifetimes to wholly learning the Word of God, and they relied on the Holy Spirit for delivery when the time came for any given sermon. To adopt this approach, however, is impossible for the indolent. As Spurgeon said, *'Only thoughtless persons think this to be easy; it is at once the most laborious and the most efficient mode of preaching.'*[162]

It is a painful display of incompetence when any teacher of the word cannot be called upon impromptu, to teach. **'In season and out of season'**, Paul directed. This is why a teacher of the Word's primary attention, should be adopted from the Apostles approach in **Acts 6:2-4**, who delegated weights that could hinder their sole focus on the Word rather than dabbling in social media affairs, reducing the work of God to a 'night-before-study- cram'

---

[162] Spurgeon, C.H. (1989). Lectures to my Students: Complete & Unabridged (New ed. containing selected lectures from series 1, 2 and 3. ed.). Grand Rapids, MI. Ministry Resources Library, Zondervan Publishing House. p. 142.

examination.

A testament to the value of Spurgeon's dedication is this writer's daily devotion to his works from more than a century after his life on earth. This writer's generation will read Spurgeon till the Lord returns. When the aim is to excite flesh, rather than pierce souls to produce true converts, that, like flesh, doesn't last. Like Theudas and Judas, once you die or while you yet live, your heresy goes back to dust with you. Like Paul Washer, Myles Munroe, C.S. Lewis, Oswald Chambers, Enoch Adeboye, Charles Stanley, Billy Graham, and so many faithful men and women teachers of the Word, nobody will read your books or listen to your lies 500 years later. Truth stands; lies will bow out with the grave. Determine where your hearts really lay. Heaven or earth? With God or with man? With Jesus or with mammon? In the fear of death or in the hope of the resurrection of the dead?

At the end of speaking Truth, if you are hated for it, so be it. Your hands are free from the blood of the dissenters, but be encouraged that, "He that despiseth these things despise not man but God." (1 Thessalonians 4:8) So be it! Saul, who rejected the Word of the Lord, was also rejected from being King (1 Samuel 15:23). Rejected for speaking God's Truth? So. Be. It.

Dear Individual

As the years roll by, as our days increase, as our time on earth decreases, as the Kingdom of God is at hand, many more interpretations, sects, ideologies, commentaries, and opinions on the Word of God are rising and thriving. There has never been a time in history like now, in which it is vital, pressing, and non-negotiable that every individual who identifies as Christian must know, not secondarily, not exhorted, not hearsay, not speculation, and not opined. Everyone who identifies as Christian must know **personally**, primarily, intricately, assuredly, and affirmatively, this Word of God. We have absolutely no excuse; we have audio Bibles, Bible apps, multiple versions, Bible reading plans, and we are beyond undeservedly ~~spoiled~~ blessed with resources. No generation has ever been so blessed, but the devil is also neither dead, nor sleeping; satan's corporation is growing, and he recruits staff by the millisecond to carry out his agenda of stealing, killing, and destroying; he will use the most unlikely and innocent looking things, jobs, or persons, even in the Church, to hinder us from personally knowing the Word of God.

This is why amusement in the Church is a major strategy for satan. The

138

adrenaline released when we leave Church feeling empowered, excited, and sometimes exhausted from screaming over amusing sermons, deceives us into thinking we have learned something; this is, however, a fleeting feeling of the flesh. The Word of God works in our hearts and should constantly keep us in reflective and meditative mode. The Word of God is very delicate and can rebuke, strike, and hurt, but it is also the greatest source of hope, comfort, and encouragement to any believer.

Please know the Word. Love the Word. The Bible is filled with funny stories, enjoyable to read and very enlightening. It is never the same lesson you learn, even if you chose the same portion every time. If you're privileged with the ability to read, you have NO excuse not to be versed in the Word. You're only failing yourself. A dear aunt of mine, Aunt Roselyn, who never went to school, and to this day is unable to read a word of English, knows the Scripture by heart, and is such a bundle of wisdom, that she serves as a classic example of the power of The Word.

Do not depend on anybody to know the Word of God for you. The human heart is naturally wicked, and even the most well-meaning people can misinterpret the Word of God. As a new believer, you will need people to guide you, but they do not assume the personal responsibility over your soul. Every individual is responsible for their own soul. Pastor Adeboye of The Redeemed Christian Church of God once shared how the very person who led him to Christ betrayed him in the same church. Once we have been led to Christ by someone, our faith must be placed in the One and Only Mediator between God and us, the Man, Christ Jesus. The Bible warns us to be careful about whom we call "Father," as we have direct access to Him through our Elder Brother, Jesus Christ.

The reason for this is for our conviction to be built upon unwavering and unshakeable faith in Christ, so that even if a "man/ woman of God," whom we hold in high esteem, falls as a result of their human nature, we remain unmoved; we continue to know that the One whose name is a Strong Tower, to which the righteous may run, will never fall. If Pastor Adeboye had not known the Word for himself, this person who led him to Christ would have caused him to turn away from the Faith after that betrayal. No matter what causes anyone to turn from the Faith, the Bible describes this act of leaving the body of Christ, the Church, as an anti-Christ. (1 John 2:18-19)

At the execution of Anne Askew (1521-15456), the *apostate* Nicholas Shaxton (1485-1556), former Bishop of Salisbury, who preached at her execution, was formerly meant to be executed alongside her. He, however, had recanted his faith to save his life. He tried to persuade Anne to do likewise, but she refused. The Word of God had sunk in and become so alive in her heart that even the persuasion of a bishop-turned-apostate had no effect on her faith. If Anne had relied on the bishop to know the Word, we would not be reading about her today. Females might have had to continually rely on whatever the preachers interpreted as God's Word. Anne, who had become versed in the Bible, had built her faith to the heavens, so much so that she knew her God; she had checked out of earth long before. In reality, she left those who killed her at her execution to kill someone who was already dead, dead to the world, but alive with her Lord at the young age of 25.

The Word will transform you. If the Word has not built our faith to a degree where we have died to the world and cannot be moved, shaken, nor frightened by anything... if we say we are Christian, but cannot die for the cause of Jesus Christ, well....

John Locke (1632-1704), the philosopher and "Father of Enlightenment" also abandoned the corpus of theological commentary that came with his exposure as a respected academic and researcher in favor of an "unprejudiced examination" of the Word of God alone. He heralded the idea that the essence of Christianity was a personal belief in Christ. From his personal study of the Word, he was able to form his ideologies based on equality of all humans, and his political and liberalist beliefs. In our days, however, people stand up for a cause with no foundation, no backing, and no understanding of what they attempt to fight for.

Never in history have true teachers of The Word been as powerful and popular in society as what we see in our generation; some are even celebrities. The Apostles were terribly hated in their society. They were treated as **the filth of the world** [163] and all of them were eventually murdered, as were the many other true men and women of God. Popularity and general acceptance/influence with the world is always a bad sign for a Christian. *Always.* Jesus says, **Woe unto you, when all men shall speak well of you!** (Luke 6:26) As a result of our self-imposed negligence, and because of the wicked nature of the human heart, teachers of the Word who perhaps started out well, have derailed and have begun teaching whatever their congregants wish to hear. These teachers capitalize on the laziness and failure of our generation to adopt personal pursuit of the knowledge of God. Our deliberate ignorance renders us susceptible to whatever anyone delivers to us, despite Truth and freedom being ubiquitously accessible to us all. There is no need to cry, **all we like sheep have gone astray** when we have that which redirects and sets the course of our lives. Charles Spurgeon asked, *"What is the mariner without*

---

[163] 1 Corinthians 4:13.

his compass (Google maps to our generation), *what is the Christian without the Bible?"*

What are we without our precious Life Manual and Recourse, a Lamp unto our wandering feet? We are only cheating our own souls, and that is a price we will pay dearly someday, if we do not discipline ourselves to perform our self-owed individual responsibilities.

Let the Word of God dwell in you richly, the Bible advises us in **Colossians 3:16**. "Dwell" means home. The Word of God should be Home in our hearts. To be home is to be at peace; to be home is to move about freely; to be home is to be comfortable; to be home is to be vulnerable; to be home is to be naked. This is how The Word of God should be in our hearts.

Desire the sincere Word and not "fables and commandments of men that turn from the Truth." (Titus 1:14) **Why?**

- **It is God's direct Gift to us**: God has been very kind to us in our generation, giving us the privilege to learn and live, rather than letting us experience the bitterness that could arise from living then learning. "For whatever things were written before were written for our learning, that we through the patience and comfort of the Scriptures might have hope" (Romans 15:4). Ignorance is no excuse. (Acts 17:30) Our so-called enlightenment will stand against us, because to whom much is given, much is expected, and all these records are magnanimous gifts which we do not deserve. In 1 Corinthians 10, while warning us why we should not test God, grumble, or complain, Paul recalls how the Israelites, God's own people, who, despite their mighty Exodus from slavery and divine sustenance in the wilderness, indulged in idolatry, feasting, drunkenness, revelry and incurred God's wrath. This led 23,000 of them to be destroyed by the Angel of Death in one day. Did God just want to kill his beloved people? No, He loved us so much and made His own people scapegoats for us, we 21st Century generation of ingrates. "Now all these things happened to them as examples, and they were written for our admonition, upon whom the ends of the ages have come." (1 Corinthians 10:11)

  In the Parable of the Rich Man and Lazarus, the rich man had enjoyed his earthly lavish life, gone to hell and the tables had turned for him and Lazarus. In his torment, the rich man pleaded for Lazarus to go back to the world to warn five of his family members, so they did not join him in hell; he was told that they had Moses and the prophets on earth to hear, and if they didn't hear them, a dead person rising up would not convince them (Luke 16:19-31). How much more, in our case? Christ is risen from the dead. We have bundles of records, relics, evidence, first-person accounts; if we will not learn for ourselves then live, still asking questions such as, *"What is truth? "What is the meaning of life?"* despite the Holy Bible's accessibility, we simply have no hope. "... So that through endurance and the encouragement of the Scriptures, we might have hope." (Romans 15:4)

- **It is a command:** In 2 Peter 3:16-18, we are commanded to grow in grace and in the knowledge of our Lord and Savior, unless, we fall into the **error of the wicked,** We have this warning that if we do not grow when we are saved, we **fall from our own steadfastness,** i.e., the *Demas Disorder,* aka the *John 666 Syndrome,* to our own destruction. Commandments do not cease until revoked by the Commander. Soldiers remain standing at attention until they hear, "at ease." This also is our command as soldiers of Christ: Grow in the knowledge of Our Lord! Soldier Paul, the hardest working Apostle who was directly called and taught by the Lord at the height of his own career, said, "That I may know him." (Philippians 3:10) How much more we sinners, saved by grace? There is no way to know God outside of His Word because He and His Word are one. (John 1:1)

There's a time to drink of the milk of the Word, but we must switch from milk to solid food after a while by applying a simple test: In earthly life, a mother is advised to exclusively breastfeed her baby for the first six months after birth. After six months, she may begin to introduce other delicate foods in reasonable quantities to the baby, but after two years, she must cease and desist from breastfeeding that child. She becomes an oddity after that.

This concept applies to our Pilgrimage. The first six months of being saved should exclusively be the basics of faith and repentance. (Hebrews 6:1) After six months, we may begin to introduce other parts of the warfare, pursuing holiness and living righteously, but after two years, if we are still dilly-dallying with what sin is, what right is, what wrong is and still depending on the 'Church' and pastors to do our feeding, we are an oddity. Unfit for the race. Oswald Chambers said,

"The greatest spiritual crisis comes when a person has to move a little farther on in his faith than the beliefs he has already accepted."[164]

We must desire to grow, but growth is not a pass to become too familiar with any part of the Word. Peter, at a time when his death was imminent, said he "will not be negligent to put you always in remembrance of these things, though ye know them." (2 Peter 1:12) He said that three times in that letter. His death had been revealed to him. He could have decided he had fulfilled his destiny and there was no need to keep preaching, but he refused to do so, likewise, the other Apostles, Paul (Philippians 3:1), John (1 John 2:21), and Jude (Jude 5). What part of Scripture do we think we know so well, or casually recite, that we do not need to read anymore?

We hear **Psalm 23** and don't bother to read it because we assume we know it. We hear **John 3:16** and don't bother to read it because we can recite it. That is a dangerous familiarity with a God so deep in knowledge and wisdom, whose judgments are unsearchable, whose ways are past finding out! (Romans 11:33) We can never be familiar with Jesus Christ whose riches are unsearchable and endless. (Ephesians 3:8) We must come in a very child-like state of mind when we come before the Word of God, and never fail to pray for the eyes of our understanding to be illuminated.

Thomas á Kempis stated, *"For the man who does not seek Jesus does himself much greater harm than the whole world and all his enemies could ever do. Keep on asking, and you will receive what you ask for. Keep on seeking, and you will find."*

- **It is our soul's DAILY manna:** In 1 Timothy 4:13, a version says, *be diligent in devouring the Word.* Our Bibles do not have to be neat; they should *not* be neat. Devour it with use, and when one has been devoured, there is an endless supply for refilling. Devour it. The Word does not die; it will be our loss if we do not. Our ancestors' Bibles were marked, over-used, and delicate. Our Generation of Technologist 's Bibles are clean, untouched, filled with dust, and will easily be sold as "brand new" at any given time. The Bible apps are the least visited on our devices. When we visit the app, it is to look for verses to tell us our purpose and encourage us that our earthly dreams will be fulfilled. Come on, people!

---

[164] Chambers. O., My Utmost for His Highest.

The Word of God is our soul's food and drink. In Matthew 4:4, Jesus recalled, in his own extreme state of physical famishment and dehydration, that we are not to live by bread alone, but by every Word that comes from the mouth of God. Those Words are in the Bible, Christian. Can our stomach survive on oxygen? Will we suck the air in a balloon to feed our stomachs? Will someone eat our daily meals on our behalf? If someone else will not eat or drink man-made meals on my behalf, no one will eat the Bread of Life or drink from the Cup of Living Water that does not run dry on my behalf. A day without the Word of God renders our souls starved, empty, unhealthy, skeletal, and sick!

That is why anyone can feel empty with an abundance of earthly wealth. That is why anyone can be looking for more. That "more" is the Word of God. It is the only way to true satisfaction, peace, and rest for our inner man. Stop killing yourself. Feed on every Word of God. Your soul, even as a Christian, is an empty hole, because you are reading and obeying the directive in Malachi 3:10, but not reading *or* reading and *not* obeying this advice, "Now therefore, it is already an utter failure for you that you go to law against one another. Why do you not rather accept wrong? Why do you not rather let yourselves be cheated?" (1 Corinthians 6:7) Instead, you will be street smart and not be taken advantage of because you are Christian. *Feed. On. Every. Word. Of.* God. The Eucharist is not the Word. Do this daily and you will find life, meaning, purpose, peace, fulfilment, freedom, and fullness of joy.

- **It is the only way to true success:** Career talks, seminars, and motivational speeches are all great for any individual, but these are without effect to any Christian without the Word of God. As Christians, we are beyond blessed; our destiny to earthly wealth is in our own hands, not God's: "This book of the law shall not depart out of thy mouth; but thou shalt meditate therein day and night...<u>for then thou shalt make thy way</u> prosperous, and then thou shalt have good success." (Joshua 1:8) A classic Christian song says, "Be a rich man, or a poor man, without Jesus, you can't be happy."

In Chapter 1, "*Who?*" we discovered, according to 3 John 2, that true prosperity for a Christian is that of soul first *then* earthly riches and health. "A little that a righteous man has is better than the riches of many wicked" (Psalm 37:16). Listen, Christian, the whole of **Psalm 37** is an encouragement for us, who are truly Christians but might not have an abundance of earthly wealth. It is a serious warning to those without Christ, who think they are rich and happy. First, we do not need wealth in a world where satan has his throne. Second, it is only a matter of time before those without Christ, who seem to be thriving on earth, will be begging for a drop of water as they roast in the torments of hell's eternal fire. Think about the Christians whom Jesus addressed in Revelation 2:9 and compare them to the Laodiceans at Revelation 3:17. There is an endless list of people who were earthly rich, but came to disastrous and embarrassing ends -- some now dead, some still alive with us, who still have hope for repentance. There is an ever-increasing Hall of Fame for that. To chase earthly wealth over righteousness is to pierce oneself through with *many* sorrows *and* regrets.

In 383 AD, Augustine, then a successful professor of rhetoric, on his way to becoming a provincial governor in Milan, once passed a beggar and was laughing; Augustine ruefully remarked, *"That poor wretch is happy and has what I cannot attain to."* Augustine, a self-described hedonist, had long battled unhappiness and an inner longing for peace, but rejected the Bible. Instead, he followed the Manichees (a persistent gnostic sect promising that knowing select spiritual truths would bring salvation) and the writings of the ancient philosophers Cicero and Plato. Jumping from one relationship to the next, he still did not attain the inner peace he desired, until providence prevailed. One day, a Christian friend persuaded Augustine to follow him to church. Slowly, Augustine began turning from philosophy to Scriptures, especially the Pauline epistles, to find his answers. As he read, he recognized *"how sordid, how full of spots and sores"* he was and wept bitterly. Within nine years, this marked the conversion of Augustine, the successful and ambitious sinner, to Bishop Augustine of Hippo, He gave up his promising career and lived a semi-monastic life devoted to reading and writing. His works, especially his daringly transparent autobiography, *Confessions,*[165] is still transforming lives, thousands of years later.

"He shall be like a tree planted by the rivers of water, that brings forth its fruit in its season, whose leaf also shall not wither; and whatever he does shall prosper." (Psalm 1:3) This is the promise of the God who cannot lie, His promise to the one who will meditate on

---

[165] Augustine, Saint, and Maria Boulding. *The Confessions.* New York: Vintage Books, 1998.

His Word day and night. Again, my dear Aunt Roselyn is an example that true prosperity lays not in earthly increase, but in the joy of the Lord. There is absolutely no peace for the wicked, "it shall be ill with him." (Isaiah 3:11) Time is *all* it needs.

If material wealth is still what you are after, if you want to build a sustainable, in-demand business, sell Bibles.

- **It is the only way to test the veracity of what we hear**: Jesus said in Revelation 2:2, "...thou hast tried them which say they are apostles and are not, and hast found them liars." Like the Berean Christians, if we do not search and know Scripture for ourselves, we will be tossed about and manipulated by the teaching of anyone who calls themselves preachers. We can only test the things we hear from any preacher, based on our personal knowledge of God's word. The heart of man is desperately wicked and the worldly-wise preachers will feast on the fact that many in this generation today are uninterested in knowing the Word for themselves; they will preach whatever the itching ears of their congregants want to hear. They might even perform *signs and wonders* as backing for their lies, but Jesus has warned us of all these beforehand in Matthew 24:23-25, so that our easily excited selves can take heed. We cannot run along with any teaching we hear and attribute it as Truth, whereas they really spring from the *depths of Satan* (Revelation 2:24), the father of all lies. We all have direct access to God's Word and have been gifted with the in-dwelling of the Holy Spirit to teach us God's mind, Himself.

Tertullian, the great writer and Christian apologist, despite the value of his literary contribution to the formation of Western Christian doctrine, was not without flaw; his writings on baptism being the way to regeneration and salvation, rather than faith in Christ, were possibly a misinterpretation of *1 Corinthians 15:29,* which led to the introduction of baptism of infants and even corpses as a means to salvation. He remained faithful as a defender of the Faith to the end, but if people had known Scripture for themselves, although they did not have access to Scripture during their time, this heretical doctrine would not have gained ground. Instead, it grew quickly and some individuals, such as the Mormons, still vicariously baptize infants and the dead today.

At Anne Askew's execution, when the apostate bishop preached the final sermon before her death alongside three other Christians, if he said anything she considered to be Truth in line with the Gospel, she

146

demonstrably expressed agreement, but when he said anything contrary to what Scripture stated, she spoke out, *"There he misseth, and speaketh without the Book."*[166] This was in the face of death. How much more, we freely wandering sheep? **'...rightly dividing the word of truth'** is the duty of every Christian workman. How do we rightly divide that which we do not know?

The book of **Jude** is a letter warning us about false teachers who are right there in the Church, eating and drinking with the brethren, but who are really on a lost mission to pervert the kingdom and satisfy their greedy desires at any cost. More than ever before, this is a time to know the Word of God, to avoid being tossed about by every new rising opinion about an ancient and settled Faith. (Galatians 1:6)

- **It is the trusted foundation for the impulsive seasons of life**: Life comes with vagaries and only one who is firmly rooted in the Word of God will be rooted to stand firm in the toughest seasons. Jesus is referred to as a Stone; (Psalm 118:22) a tried Stone; a precious Cornerstone, and a sure Foundation. (Isaiah 28:16) In Matthew 7:24, Jesus, who is one and the same as His Word, called His teachings a "Rock." This is why we mentioned earlier, if the Word of God is not working for any person, the person is the problem, not the Word; the Word has worked for generations over millennia, is working today, and will work until the end of the world. "Nevertheless, the solid foundation of God stands, having this seal: The Lord knows those who are His and, let everyone who names the name of Christ depart from iniquity." (2 Timothy 2:19) It is a never-ending, unsearchable, deep foundation, rich in wisdom and knowledge. That is why, every time hearts are open to learn, without an iota of familiarity, the Word can freely do its wondrous work of piercing parts of us we've never felt, and it will continue as long as we remain childlike.

His Word is iron-strong Truth, unaffected by its veracity. When we fall on this Stone, it breaks and remolds our lives beautifully. There is no answer anywhere else to the most complex questions anybody can ask about the past, present, future and life itself: "Lord, to whom shall we go? You have words of eternal life. And we have believed

---

[166] Foxe, John (1838). Cattley, Stephen Reed (ed.). The Acts and Monuments of John Foxe: A New and Complete Edition. **V**. London: R. B. Seeley and W. Burnside.

and have come to know that You are the Holy One of God." (John 6:68-69)

- **It is an education on Its own**: The Holy Bible is a lifelong education in Itself: "So now, brethren, I commend you to God and to the word of His grace, which is able to build you up…" (Acts 20: 32) Now, this is certainly not for those who are proud of their learning and scholarly accolades. It is first for those who fear God. (Proverbs 9:10) God has no business with those who consider themselves wise in their own intellect. He chooses the foolish and despised things of this world to shame those who pose as wise, so that no one will be able to boast outside of God. (1 Corinthians 1:27-29) He chooses those like my uneducated Aunt Roselyn, who has more wisdom than the most educated people I've ever come across. When we then come before Him, counting our achievements as garbage, we are told, "If any of you lack wisdom, let him ask of God, that giveth to all men liberally, and upbraideth not; and it shall be given him." (James 1:5) Without even asking God, He has given wisdom in abundance, in black and white pages with leather covers gathering dust; in our electronic devices, in our pockets! We know that King Solomon was gifted wisdom directly by God yet he claimed in Ecclesiastes 7:23-25, that he had searched everywhere for wisdom but it was hard to find and far from him, despite that, we, on the other hand, have access to all of Solomon's wisdom *and* have found that which he sought to but did not. What was this wisdom Solomon sought to find but could not? "Christ Jesus who became for us, wisdom from God," (1 Corinthians 1:30) and this Christ told us He and His Word are one, yet, we closed-minded generation of thankless folk remain ignorant of the "Holy Scriptures which are able to make thee wise unto salvation." (2 Timothy 3:15)

A five-year-old, with 5% of the Word of God sunk into their hearts, will be wiser than any 80-year-old with all the earthly recognition of achievement. C.S Lewis aptly stated, *"Anyone who is honestly trying to be a Christian will soon find his intelligence being sharpened: one of the reasons why it needs no special education to be a Christian is that Christianity is an education itself. That is why an uneducated believer like Bunyan was able to write a book that has astonished the whole world.*[167]*"* In **Hosea 4:6** God laments, **"my people are destroyed for lack of knowledge!"**

---

[167] C.S. Lewis Mere Christianity.

- **It is the solution to EVERY problem**: Whatever problem we face, the solution is in the Holy Bible. In our generation, our default approach to solving problems is to enact modern world wars through keyboards and screens. This unfruitful, man-made, weak approach of the worldly is against the provision of God's Word. The Word of God is that weapon which we must use to fight every battle - personal, cultural, political, academic, and spiritual. Jesus famously set this example for our learning and imitation. In an extreme state of starvation and deprivation after 40 days of fasting, the devil came to tempt Him, and on all three occasions, His preceding defense each time was, "It is written." (Matthew 4:1-11)

If we do not know the Word of God, we will be defeated on the day of battle. It will not work for *any* Christian, because we have been given the Sword of the Spirit. No soldier picks up his weapon on the day of battle. The soldier has practiced with their sword so much and has become expert at applying it on any day, especially the day of battle. Like serious warriors, we must adopt this approach and have the Word at hand to avoid defeat.

"He isn't here! He is risen from the dead! Remember what He told you back in Galilee…Then they remembered that he had said this." (Luke 24:6&8) The Holy Spirit's work is to remind and teach us. Not to read for us. Christianity is not a lazy walk. Study (*work hard*) to show thyself approved as a Christian.

If we had Christians in leadership positions and in government, who rigorously and blindly, albeit foolishly to the ordinary man, followed the Bible as a Manual to guide their office, we would be perfect beings in an imperfect world. Yes, the Bible makes the one who follows it daily to be as perfect as Jesus was on earth each day. (2 Timothy 3:17) This approach of Scripture as the ruling authority was the method by which Alfred The Great, the only King of England to ever be accorded the titled, "The Great," ruled his kingdom. His laws were first based on the Ten Commandments and the Golden Rule of Jesus.

Over the building of a great kingdom for himself, King Alfred's ambition, as a Christian before as a King, was to devote himself wholly to the welfare of the people of his kingdom. He encouraged all his subjects to live according to the precepts of the Bible, setting a leadership-by-example pattern of love and mercy, over justice and punishment, for wrongdoers. Because of this Christian king and many other Christians, the United Kingdom and indeed, modern Western Culture in its entirety, will always be indebted for the solid role Christianity played in its formation, delivering them from blue-eyed barbarian worship.

It was this same approach of Biblically grounded leadership which Constantine The Great adopted during his reign as Roman Emperor; he made multiple Scriptures available, appointed members of the clergy to important state positions, and made Christianity fashionable, which, of course, led to the influx of wolves among sheep in the Church.

So-called Christians join the masses to curse, insult, shame and throw slander at those in authority when Scripture directs us to pray for them and submit to their rule (1 Timothy 2:2; Titus 3:1). People like William Wilberforce, William Crawford, John Newton, and Martin Luther King Jr., who in their various capacities fought for the abolition of slave trade and equality for all men, did so with strong Biblical backing. Never, for once, was violence or insult applied as a means for defense and this was what enabled them to persevere until the end, despite strong torrents of opposition from the earthly great and mighty. They all saw in the Word of God that all men were made in God's image and of one blood (Acts 17:26); and fought a good cause in the most peaceable way, using words from the Bible, evidence and reason, persevering until they won, and some even dying before their dreams were accomplished. Whatever oppression we assume we are going through by men on earth, the ridiculous and outright embarrassing approach adopted for fighting them causes more damage than salvage.

Where there is no Scriptural backing, where there is no reason, where there is no reliance on the Word of God, we have a bunch of angry, entitled, destructively opinionated, bunch of individuals who will apply any soul-losing means to find solutions to an ultimately, temporal cause for the carnal satisfaction of adding something to the world.

Our battle is never with flesh and blood, especially not *white or male* flesh and blood (Ephesians 6:12). The Sword with which we should fight every battle – injustice, social and gender inequality, corruption, racial segregation, plural moralism, poor healthcare, unemployment, and every good fight IS the Word of God. If God's Word could create the Heavens, earth and all therein, will It not regulate its affairs? (Daniel 4:17)

150

Our duty is to search Scripture and know it; we are to arm ourselves fully with His word, not merely take a glance, not read a verse, not do a Bible plan. We are to search with our eyes, hands, and hearts. When we have any question at all, the answer *will* be found in Genesis to Revelation; it has been right before our eyes all the while. We have been looking too far away or not looking into it hard enough.

Pastor Adeboye, who holds a doctorate in mathematics, told of how he was able to solve a worldwide, unsolved mathematical problem when he read the story of the Israelites at the Red Sea. Again, it certainly was not the first time he had heard or read that story, but he approached it with an open heart and not with the dangerous and contemptuous stance of familiarity.

The people of old did not have scriptures to refer to, so the highly esteemed rabbis came to Jesus to ask Him some hard questions, *good teacher, tell us....* they would say to Him, Who in turn deflected their pretentious "good,"[168] but answered their questions. How blessed are we? All the answers for which the rabbis had to come off their high horses to ask Jesus, we have in our pockets and shelves, gathering dust. Then we book appointments with equally confused, self-prescribed psychologists, positivity enthusiasts, and counsellors to give us answers to questions on problems and dissatisfaction about our lives. Yet '*HIS name shall be called ...COUNSELLOR...*' (Isaiah 9:6). We look to flesh and blood, so-called influencers to give us "lifestyle tips." This is nonsense! We want a step-by-step guide to finding purpose, and when we are given that, in no time, we find ourselves in an even deeper bondage and state of confusion than when we began.

We then lament with embarrassment how we miss the simpler and "good old days," when Ecclesiastes 7:10 tells us, "Don't long for 'the good old days.' This is not wise"; when Apostle Paul said, "but this one thing I do, forgetting those things which are behind",[169]and forgetting not just the bad, but also the good, even his great accomplishments, for he said, "whatever was gain to me I count as loss for the sake of Christ...I count all things as loss compared to the surpassing excellence of knowing Christ Jesus my Lord, for whom I have lost all things. I consider them rubbish that I may gain Christ".[170]

---

[168] Luke 18:18-19.
[169] Philippians 3:13.
[170] Philippians 3:8.

And it is rightly so, because after Saul met Christ, he changed his name to Paul, which means "little."

However, some will rather have their past successes and feats as the shackles on their feet, the weight which hinders them from success-fully completing the race they once started well. *Acts 2:17* says when God pours out his spirit on all flesh, *old men will dream dreams,* but rather than let His Spirit inspire us to dream bigger as we age, our reminiscing on the done and dusted has become a favorite pastime. Above all, Jesus said, *No one who puts his hand to the plow and then looks back is fit for the kingdom of God.[171]*

Christian, the Bible is the solution to every problem in the world, NOT Christians. Any depraved pagan living daily by the Bible for its divine wisdom will lead a better life than a Biblically-ignorant Pope. Our ignorance, coupled with laziness, is our only problem.

- **It builds our PERSONAL faith**: We hear more sermons being preached on faith than on preaching the actual Word of God. Faith is a personal virtue, not a collective one. We can all attend church and hear sermons screamed at us to "have faith," which is unfortu-nate, because faith comes by hearing the Word, not by being com-manded to "have faith." The one who has personally known the Word of God might have built faith that can move mountains and not know what to call it. Some say they have faith, but when it is time to show the evidence of faith, there is no faith to be found. The essence of knowing and the particular emphasis of personal knowledge is the production of a thing called **Conviction** (2 Timo-thy 1:12), from which we are able to say, even though we're chained in prison, "I am not ashamed of the Gospel," and continue to preach it. Without personal conviction, all we do is act and copy whichever spiritual figure is pleasing to us at any season. Then, the earthly de-mands of the Kingdom will be seen as burdensome and unnecessary restrictions to freedom, rather than as self-sacrificial acts done out of love for Christ.

Even in the instance of our best Christian figures falling from the faith, we remain unmoved, because conviction produces a *personal* virtue, independent of man's weakness rising from inner desires. "Then we will no longer be infants, tossed back and forth by the waves, and blown here and there by every wind of teaching and by

---

[171] Luke 9:62.

the cunning and craftiness of people in their deceitful scheming." (Ephesians 4:14)

Paul encouraged young Timothy not to be wavered by men and women of God he heard doing such and such things, clearly against the faith, which was only going to get worse by their deceit, and the deceit of the vulnerable by them. He said to him, "continue thou in the things which thou hast learned and been assured of" (2 Timothy 3:13-14). The things he had learned were God's Truth and the assurance which produced personal conviction. At the time this letter was written to Timothy, there was no Bible. How privileged we are to have it on demand. To honor rather than cheapen the "Old Book" should be our utmost desire.

Christianity is a religion somewhat based on hearsay, which is why many devote their time to proving or failing to disprove the existence of God. None of us in the past few thousand years ever saw any of what is claimed to have happened. We can only believe it did, and if we are not taking the trouble to know this for ourselves, like that life built on sand, we will crumble in the storm. Nobody can build faith on behalf of anybody. Yes, someone can lead us to the Faith, but after we have received Christ, it becomes our personal duty to perseveringly "work out your salvation with fear and trembling." (Philippians 1:12)

- **It aids us in praying effectively:** In the writer's note at the beginning of this chapter, each reader was asked to consider why they are Christian. This is a serious question which every individual must ponder. Is it to lead a moral life on earth? Is it to build faith? Is it to have the Word of God to help us in the time of trials? Is it for finding purpose? Is someone we admire a Christian? Were we born into Christian homes? Do we love worship songs? Do we desperately need prayers answered? Healing? Marriage? Children? Really, Christian, why have you taken up this burdensome path, which in truth marks the beginning of your problems on earth? The Bible has a Word of encouragement for you.

If in this life only we have hope in Christ, we are of all men most miserable. 1 Corinthians 15:19

You are a miserable individual. No, *the most miserable* individual in the world, who needs a lot of pity *(not I, says so, the Word)*. As someone

153

else said, if our hope in Christ is for this life alone, we are pretty hopeless.

Christianity is that religion with which we must begin and which we must follow through, with the end in mind. *"Who for the joy set before Him, endured..."* Why do we think those who follow the heretical doctrine of baptizing the dead as a means to salvation do this? Are they crazy individuals who have lost the ability to reason? Like the rich man did from hell, they are trying to save the souls of those dead ones, despite that it is too late and is a fruitless endeavor. Their reasoning will probably be along the lines of, "Maybe God will have mercy on this desperate effort of ours and let this soul into heaven."

When a serious athlete is running a race, the first thought in their mind isn't, "Where is water? Where is glucose? Where is a towel to wipe off my sweat?" No, the athlete is focused on winning that gold medal. It is the duty of the runner's coach to provide whatever correct supplement they need for their well-being. Even the rules of the race, it is not the athlete's duty to seek it out. It is the duty of the coach to provide it for the athlete whose duty is to obey that which has been provided to him so he does not make a foul move, disqualifying him from the race. A coach who does not perform these requisite duties will be an irresponsible coach, who sets up the athlete for defeat. Consider car racing contests and all the help the racer gets once he stops for a break. The racer does nothing but focus on his race. He does not need to ask for water or a change of tires. Those are already done. His only desire, and that of his team, is to win the race.

Christian, you are in a race! Asking for water is a distraction to your victory. Your Coach, Who placed you on this earth; Who, for fun, dresses the lilies of the field much better than Solomon in all his splendor ever looked; Who feeds the lazy fowls of the air as a hobby; Who clothes the useless grasses of the field because He can; your Heavenly Father knows you need such things and as many more as desired to enable you to successfully complete your race. Therefore, "seek ye first the kingdom of God and His righteousness." (Matthew 6:33)

Can you imagine how frustrating it will be for the coach if his athlete stopped running every time, they wanted to request things already taken care of? First, it would be an insult to that coach, because the athlete is, in effect, saying, "I don't trust that you remembered to bring water and all the other things I need; I don't think you are smart enough or farsighted enough to have anticipated that I will need those things." An angry coach would resign from coaching that athlete, but the God whose gifts are without repentance will never turn His back on us, despite our multiple affronts to Him. Asking Him, who claims to be a God of love, why there are problems and troubles in this temporal world and why He can't save us like our mentor, the sinner on the cross, who asked Jesus to save him to continue leaving in a suffering world, as if, had Jesus actually saved Him, He will never have died again.

Christian, when our prayers are forever about our earthly needs, we have veered off course. We are insulting our Coach. What will it profit us to gain the world but lose our souls? The most important prayers we can pray are prayers for our souls and prayers about the way we live on earth to make us fit for Heaven; without peace with all men and holiness, we will never see God. Mercy, like that of the wise sinner on the cross, is what our hearts and carnal inclinations need.

There is nothing like having a wise mother, and one of the wisest mothers we can learn from in the Bible is Mrs. Zebedee. In the somewhat amusing, but thought-provoking account recorded in Matthew 20:20-28, Mrs. Zebedee came to Jesus, Who was at this time seriously warning His disciples of the Passion that was about to befall Him in Jerusalem. She came to Jesus with her two sons, James and John, knelt before Him in worship, and prayed an audacious prayer, "Grant that these two sons of mine may sit, one on Your right hand and the other on the left, in Your Kingdom."

First, this woman, a mother of sacrifice, was not even asking for herself, she was asking on behalf of her sons, who were already in Jesus' inner circle, were His closest friends, and one of whom He particularly loved. The same sacrificial love Moses had for the Israelites when he entreated God, "Yet now, if You will forgive their sin—but if not, I pray, blot me out of Your book which You have written." (Exodus 32:32)

Second, Jesus asked if they were able to drink from the bitter cup of suffering from which He was about to drink, and the sons affirmed that they were able. This shows that the sons were not being forced into this prayer their mother prayed. They might have been the ones

155

who asked her to make this bold request to Jesus on their behalf, knowing that Jesus honored, cared for, and respected mothers, so He would probably have granted their mother's request.

Third, despite the fact Jesus affirmed they were indeed going to suffer for His sake, He told them it was not His duty, but His Father's, to decide who got what position in Heaven. This just shows, despite what we go through on earth for Jesus, despite our sacrifices for the Kingdom, despite our endurance, that it is still God's prerogative to decide who enters and gets what place in His Kingdom.

Fourth, the 10 other disciples were very angry about this request by James and John, for they all wanted that special place in Heaven. Although Jesus reproved the others for their indignation and taught them that whoever wants to be the greatest must be the least and whoever wants to be master must be servant, it showed that their treasures and their hearts were set on Heaven. Judas, of course, was solely set on how he was going to spend his blood-money, 30 pieces of silver. He certainly was not concerned with any Kingdom talk.

We must consider how many of us will be angry at someone praying they got a better place than us in Heaven. Most likely, we'd be unbothered, but some might say, as long as we get there, that is all that matters. On the other hand, if someone prayed to be promoted over us in a job, to have better children, to have a better spouse, to have more blessings and miracles, that will wake up sleeping, fiery beasts in our souls.

Christian, where do our treasures lie? Earthly thrills and social elevation should not be the focal point of our prayers. The best of everything on earth reaches a climax, then we deal with the falling action. This is true of every single thing, even *that* which we do for God. There is a retirement age with the best career; there is a reality after the fairy tale of a wedding ceremony and honeymoon; there are wrinkles after the best skin; there is adulthood after childhood; the most delicious meals go down the sewer; the party comes to an end; the movie ends; the tears dry; the laughter fades, and the storms settle. All in all, death sweeps us away. So, when we get it all, when we have it all, what next? Jesus is the only gift that keeps giving. Only the ~~nominal~~ Christian has resurrection after death unto everlasting life. Only the Christian's race reaches a climax at the end and has no falling action, because it loads us with an ***eternal weight of glory.*** (2 Corinthians 4:17)

156

The most important prayer anyone can pray is that they are not rendered a castaway from Heaven's Gates and that our dear *"Jesus, You love me too much,"* will not deny us and say, *"Depart from me! I do not know you."* Does the thought of this not frighten us, Christian?

Ponder on the hourly risk on his life Paul went through for the Faith:

For I swear, dear brothers and sisters, that I face death daily. This is as certain as my pride in what Christ Jesus our Lord has done in you. And what value was there in fighting wild beasts—those people of Ephesus —if there will be no resurrection from the dead? And if there is no resurrection, "Let's feast and drink, for tomorrow we die!" Don't be fooled by those who say such things, for "bad company corrupts good character." Think carefully about what is right, and stop sinning. For to your shame I say that some of you don't know God at all.
1 Corinthians 15:31-34

Enough of these misplaced prayers, Christian. Everything will pass away, yet we hope to be raised with Christ on that Last Day and to avoid eternal damnation. A translation of the Bible[172] tells us to think straight and awaken to the holiness of life, because ignorance is a luxury we cannot afford in our times. Unbiblical Christians who are on this journey for any form of earthly gain or satisfaction, are unnecessarily mortifying themselves and are described as a shame to the body of Christ who have no knowledge of God. This is why there must be no room for spiritual pride in any one of us, so *let him who thinks he stands take heed lest he fall.* [173] Furthermore, we must be poor in spirit and remain so till the end if we desire to inherit Kingdom of God. (Matthew 5:3)

Again, it isn't all bad news. We are not prohibited from praying for what we desire. It is a matter of priorities and what is capable of shaking us up or invoking our anger, over which will we say, "I have great heaviness and continual sorrow in my heart" (Romans 9:2) Sin or earthly blessings? For the Apostle Paul, it was the sin of his Jewish brothers and sisters, God's own children, who wanted to voluntarily render themselves bastards by their legalistic lifestyle of works and refusal for their faith to fall on Jesus, The Rock that breaks. What makes our hearts heavy? What causes us continual sorrow? What are we willing to sacrifice for it? Paul was ready to lose his salvation and

---

[172] The Message Translation.
[173] 1 Corinthians 10:14.

be cut off from Christ, for whom he lived, if it would save his people. (Romans 9:3)

We are to follow the correct order laid out by Jesus for the Christian in *John* **15:7**, which states first and of utmost importance:

1. *If you abide in Me*

2. *My words abide in you.*

He then assures us:

3. You *will ask what you desire*

4. *And it shall be done for you.*

Selah.

Please, Christian, He is not a God of disorder, God's Kingdom and righteousness come first, our needs after.

- **It saves us from shame when we call ourselves Christians:** "A workman that need not be ashamed...' (2 Timothy 2:15). Shame to such a Christian who does not know the Word of God! Shame! As an ambassador of Christ, the Christian must be familiar with His Master so in every situation, "What would Jesus do?" is a no-brainer. We must be so versed in His Word that we begin to speak like Him, respond like Him, imitate Him, and pattern the way in which we carry ourselves after Him. The charge given to us is to "be ready always to give an answer to every man that asketh you a reason of the hope that is in you with meekness and fear." (1 Peter 3:15)

First, we are to be ready *always*, in season and out of season. Even when we do not feel like talking, while the question is, "Why are you a Christian?" our command is to be ready to answer. To *not* answer is disobedience...witchcraft=sin=death! There is no room for "come back, later." Are you a Christian? Do you call on the name of Jesus as your Lord and Savior? Do you pray in the name of Jesus to God, the Father? Then, ye Soldiers of Christ, anytime you are asked *any* question about your faith, you are commanded to speak or die!

Now, since we are under this compulsion, will it not be to our shame and shame to the Cross of Christ, if we have no answer or are rambling? This is the reason Christianity suffers a lot of slander. Those who have taken up this name do not know what they are saying. Unfortunately, there is no option for "semi-Christian," or "aspiring Christian" which might have been better, but since there is none, as long as we choose to remain Christian, we must know and grow in knowledge!

Why are we to **always** answer this question about faith to enquirers? "If God perhaps will grant them repentance, so that they may know the truth, and that they may come to their senses and escape the snare of the devil, having been taken captive by him to do his will." (2 Timothy 2:25-26) Yes, you self-righteous children of Jonah, that will be the downside of Christianity for you, because Christianity is for those who will genuinely turn from their wicked ways and turn to Christ. We serve a just and merciful God "who desires all men to be saved and to come to the knowledge of the truth." (1 Timothy 2:4) Any fair-minded person will find this the most humbling fact about Christianity: that this saving grace is free for all and the God who saved us, the worst of sinners, will save just anybody whom His sovereign mercy will save; that the freedom we found in the Gospel has also freed so many people and will set free as many people as will come to Its knowledge. For "God so loved the world that He gave His only begotten son that WHOSOEVER believes in Him will not perish but have eternal life." (John 3:16) *Thank You, God! Thank You, sweet Jesus!*

So, we must put away selfishness and this temptingly greedy approach to our faith; we must joyfully share to all who enquire, the same way Jesus Himself did, even late at night to society big man, Nicodemus.[174] ***Writer's Note:** *As for ye, inaccessible celebrity pastors, I shudder to think of where your 'busyness' will end you up.*

Second, we are to do this with meekness and fear. Listen Christian, however you got saved is unique to you; please *stay* saved. Ultimately, Christianity is based on faith which produces hope. None of us has seen Christ in Whom we believe, and as some said about their Faith, *"I believe because it is absurd."* For whatever reason we believe, we also were once lost in darkness, with dead consciences, until Christ raised us into life. Despite this, to be saved once is not to be saved all. In an age of reason and logic, if we are not patient in answering people who just cannot believe, if we are not kind in telling them, we will only send souls away from God, and the one who turns a sinner from the "error of his way shall save a soul from death." (James 5:20)

What we would have done would have been to kill a soul. There's a point at which we discern that we have done all we can in our human capacity and leave the Holy Spirit to do His work in their lives, but we must do everything

---

[174] John 3:1-21.

we can to answer in love and meekness. Romans 14:1 tells us to "accept him whose faith is weak, without passing judgment on his opinions." If Apostle Paul could say, "to the weak I became as weak, that I might win the weak" (1 Corinthians 9:22), then who are we? A Christian who becomes aggressive when asked about the Faith is an ignorant individual whose defense is merely a means of covering up for their lack of knowledge and their shame. The one who knows the Word of God, and meditates on it morning and evening, is bold and courageous, with no reason to show fear masked with aggression. (Joshua 1:8-9)

- **It brings unity and love:** Racial segregation, white supremacy, black subordination, and all other causes which underlie the fact that one individual is better than the other due to race, are injustices which many still cannot comprehend today, because they acknowledge that no one should be treated differently from another due to their skin color or race. This is rightly an incomprehensible state of mind, but this incomprehension was a secret ordained by Someone who makes all things work together for good, and who had a plan in this 'unnecessary' mystery: "This mystery is that through the gospel the Gentiles are heirs together with Israel, members together of one body, and sharers together in the promise in Christ Jesus." (Ephesians 3:6) Nor is this without reason, because the unquestionable God did this so that He, through the Church, could show-off His wisdom. (Ephesians 3:10)

Until we come into the Light which Jesus was made for our sakes,[175] we will continue to remain in self-imposed darkness. It is like remaining in a prison cell which the jailer has unlocked and gone his way but we sit still, expecting him to carry us out. There was a mystery behind God separating nations in times past, distinguishing Jews from every other person who was not a Jew, aka a Gentile. He had a plan and if we did not go through that pain, dissatisfaction, and unworthiness that came with not being Jewish, we would never have appreciated the value of the immense and permanent freedom the simplicity of the Gospel of Jesus Christ has given to us, in which He broke the **wall of hostility** separating nations and made us **one new man.** (Ephesians 2: 14-15) This was and is the freedom by which He commands us, "go out into the world..." (Mark 16:15)

A fair-minded individual would understand the fact that this was something we could **never** achieve with our human efforts, and which all movements for such causes founded outside the Gospel will fail in no time. How can we ever repay Jesus for this gift? Apostle Paul, once a chief discriminator in the

---

[175] Isaiah 49:6.

class of the "societal supremes," showed us, "For this reason I kneel before the Father" (Ephesians 3:14) after which he prayed for the people. We can only kneel and thank God for His immeasurable love, then embrace our divine and physical freedom.

There is unmatched power in unity, and God acquiesced to this fact during the construction of the Tower of Babel.[176] The people's unity of tongue for an evil cause caught God's attention and He caused them to babble in different languages, rendering their mission redundant for confusion's sake. The language of everything in the world is babbling. No one is speaking the same tongue, and this is why the world and those of it try to outdo themselves; try to be better than the last; try to set and beat the standard; try to win the award. Two brands, inventors, CEOs, presidents, artists, movie stars, social media influencers, designers, etc., will meet and may barely acknowledge each other. Husband and wife, or even siblings living in the same household and eating from the same pot, will barely acknowledge each other.

Only the **true** Gospel of Jesus Christ has been in unity over the ages. Irrespective of age, class, race, gender, status, finances, and superfluous doctrine, the Gospel always promotes itself. This is the reason that **true** carriers of the **genuine** word of God, one from Jupiter, the other from Saturn will meet on Mars for the first time, fully embrace each other, and declare, "my brother, my sister," with unfeigned rejoicing and genuine gladness of heart.

Until this fact is accepted, there are only two categories of people in this world: Those who have come into the light, freedom, and unity of the Gospel of Jesus Christ by faith, and those locked in darkness from the inside out, divided by race but united in death. These are the wheat and the tares, the sheep and the goats. ***Writer's Note:** Do we notice how sheep and wheat are ordinarily not pluralized? God is perfect!

Those who claim they are in the first category should examine themselves thus: "Whoever says he is in the light and hates his brother is still in darkness." (1 John 2:9)

- **It restores the essence of the Church:** The Church, the gathering of believers in a physical structure, for as many times in a week as scheduled, has different functions for two categories of people: The self–professing Christian, and the unbeliever. The average 21st Century Christian is as strong as the last empowering sermon they listened to, and as weak as their unanswered prayers. We need to correct this erroneous thinking

---

[176] Genesis 11:1-8.

that the Church is the place for learning and growing as Christians. Studying the Word is an expectation of God for every believer for whom there will be no ground for appeal on the Day of Judgment. (Acts 17:30) The people of old had Moses and the prophets, so they could have argued that they wanted their only authority to be God, not flesh and blood, which was why they scorned Moses and the prophets. We have Jesus in our pockets. What is our excuse? We are to cast our burdens on Jesus, not the Church. We expect way too much from a church, and we leave God completely out of everything. There is some extent of encouragement and prayer which a church will provide, but that is the best you will ever get out of any church, not peace, not hope, not faith.

Paul even forbade women from speaking in the church if they had any questions about what was taught. That just shows the church is never the primary place of growing; that place is in our privacy. We have our own "secret place" duty of studying the Word for ourselves and being taught by the Holy Spirit. When we carry out this duty faithfully, the purpose of the physical church as an open celebration and fellowship of mutual secret place love is restored. We can go into the church with hearts of gladness and joy, without expecting any minister to solve our problems.

We might receive miracles, healing, or something we were expecting in the church, but that is only God backing up His servant's word, or a demon performing signs and wonders. In terms of growth, it will never happen; we will never know God —*especially not inside the 21st Century church* -and grow in our knowledge of Him. We will constantly depend on flesh and blood, the best of which will die one day.

When people gather for a wedding ceremony between a man and a woman, they are not expecting them to begin a courtship on the same day as their wedding. They are coming to openly witness a celebration of what has been brewing behind the scenes. Present for the ceremony are those who might be familiar with the couple, and there are those attending the wedding who were probably invited by friends but do not know the couple. Now, if this couple did not really know each other and had just recently met, if their families had never met or had just barely met a few days prior to the wedding, the day of that wedding would be very awkward. The members of the family and their close friends might try to mask the awkwardness, but a discerning guest would sense that the wedding is a strange one, and any display of love between the couple is cosmetic and forced.

"Therefore, if the whole church comes together in one place, and all speak with tongues, and there come in those who are uninformed or unbelievers, will they not say that you

are out of your mind?"

On the other hand, if this couple had gone through a period of solid, Christ-honoring courtship, built true love behind the scenes and are finally getting joined together in Holy Matrimony, those who are familiar with the couple and those who have been married before or gone through this Holy Matrimonial process themselves, might just smile and affirm their love, appreciating the display because they understand the joy but will not necessarily be as blown away as a guest, who never believed in love or marriage but is now witnessing this genuine, heart-felt display of love and is moved with so much emotion that a tear or 2 or a flood runs down their face and they wonder if they will ever experience such love.

But if an unbeliever or uninstructed person comes in while everyone is prophesying, he will be convicted and called to account by all, and the secrets of his heart will be made known. So he will fall facedown and worship God, proclaiming, "God is truly among you!" 1 Corinthians 14:23-25

The couple is every individual Christian as the bride and Christ as the Groom (2 Corinthians 11:2). You say you have been a Christian (this is using the milk to solid food test); for the first six months, you are learning about faith and repentance, growing steadily and the Church is fully responsible for you.

Between six months of being born again and two years, you are still learning the basics of faith and repentance, building faith by dedicatedly studying the word of God and repenting from sins that easily entangled you but you are also learning other parts of the Christian life in part, while the church is still responsible for nurturing and building you up. However, if you have been saved for more than 2 years, you are very well expected to be a person of solid knowledge of God where you do not need to be spoon fed by anyone. You might make mistakes here and there but your heart is grieved when you sin. You have your Pastor/Shepherd to encourage you in your journey but not to do your learning for you. You understand that your Savior is Jesus and Jesus, alone and coming into the presence of God is to celebrate that which other believers like you carry out in private.

If this "secret place" duty of intimacy with our Lover is not done mutually by all believers in a church, or is done only by a few people, or by none at all, that church will be weak. What we will have is confusion. How can we want to only meet in public, someone we claim to intimately love? If any person calls themselves Christian, but will not study their Bible personally, on what ground can they really be called Christian? Such a person is engaging in nothing but wishful thinking. Please stop telling lies and embarrassing the body of Christ! For such people, Christianity means they go to church to fill their soul's holes, and maybe not look for it in parties, relationships, drugs, or drink, but they are still as empty as anyone seeking for that inner fulfilment outside the Word of God. They are still strangers to Christ, *"what is Nahum?"* They give their abominable offerings and feel entitled to the church, doing their spiritual growth for themselves. When they do not get that which no church can ever give, they slander true men and women of God and like antichrists, they leave the church.

On the other hand, the church is pressured to keep up with the demands of goats by implementing artificial, superficial, mundane thrills to fill up the holes which only personal communion with the Holy Spirit floods. We use petroleum to do what olive oil should do; we engage in empowerment, concerts, career counselling, business seminars, and such other activities that bring the world into the church. How dare we? Are we to turn the Father's House into a den of robbers? Jesus told us to learn from the people of the world, for they are wiser than the so-called children of light (Luke 16:8). If it were to be empowerment seminars and career tips, they would do a better job than anyone in the church could ever do. That is their expertise.

Any message that is not bringing the undiluted Gospel of Christ has no place in the House of God, for that is the mandate laid out by the Owner of the Church. Imagine Apostle Peter, the rock on whom the Church was built, walking into the Church and asking us what we are talking about? Suppose we respond, "We are having a business and purpose empowerment seminar to be shining lights in our workplace." I dare say, but for Jesus, we would have our ears struck off! We cannot bring the world into the Church. The world has enough of the world. We do not need more of the world in the Church. Our churches must be kept holy and completely centered on the Gospel of Jesus Christ. We take the Gospel out of the Church into the world, not the other way around. That, the Good News of Life, the world needs an abundance of.

An unbeliever who comes into our midst can come in and leave with such slanderous comments about the Church. They wonder what the difference would be if they went to church and if they did not. They come in, sit in the midst of strangers of Christ, who have no knowledge of Him, to express genuine love to Him, but they are equally as confused as the unbeliever. The believers are dressed exactly like them, the so-called believers pay no attention to the new people in their midst, because the believers themselves are searching for the exact thing the unbelievers sought when they walked into their midst. They come in, scoff, and wonder why they ever came in at all. They feel awkward, uncared for, and unnoticed; they imagine that this is what

Jesus is about. Oh dear! "And whoever welcomes a little child like this in My name welcomes Me. But if anyone causes one of these little ones who believe in Me to stumble, it would be better for him to have a large millstone hung around his neck and to be drowned in the depths of the sea." (Matthew 18:5-6)

Any unbeliever who walks into the midst of believers is a babe in Christ and if they are left feeling awkward rather than enamored by the display of love between each believer and Christ and out of which same love is shown to them, where they can declare, *'God is in this place'*, be convicted of sin and desperate to have such feeling in his soul, we have failed! The self-centered, world-competing, world-adapting, world-envying, world-inspired, 21st century Church has blatantly failed! What an embarrassment!

What then is the pastor to do? "Their responsibility is to equip God's people to do his work and build up the church, the Body of Christ. This will continue until we all come to such unity in our faith and knowledge of God's Son that we will be mature in the Lord, measuring up to the full and complete standard of Christ. Then we will no longer be immature like children." (Ephesians 4:12-13)

The pastor is to equip us and not use the equipment on our behalf. He is to encourage us and cheer us on in our race for a certain period, namely, the milk and solid food test. He is to oversee the church and, most important, he is to carry out his "secret place" duty with utmost diligence, lest he fall into the mouths of his wolves and be eaten up. He is to stand firm and eliminate those who try to infiltrate the Body of Christ with their bile. He is to ponder on these words from Archibald Brown:

> *Renounce all the worldly policy of the age. Trample upon Saul's armour. Grasp the Book of God. Trust the Spirit who wrote its pages. Fight with this weapon — only and always. Cease to amuse — and seek to arouse with the preaching of the Word. Shun the clap of a delighted audience, and listen for the sobs of a convicted one. Give up trying to "please" men who have only the thickness of the ribs between their souls and hell! Warn, and plead, and entreat — as those who see the fires of eternity about to devour the lost! Let the Church again confront the world — testify against it — and meet it only behind the cross! And, like her Lord, she shall overcome, and with Him share the victory!*[177]

Let the Church retrace her steps to the days of old, and welcome back her first Love into her midst. Let sinners come into her midst and be convicted, rather than affirmed. Bring back open celebration of "secret place"

---

[177] https://www.gracegems.org/29/devils_mission_of_amusement.htm

communion. Christian, pray for your church leader(s). You cannot imagine the load on them. They bleed blood like you and are not and will never be God. A true leader of God was chosen by God, not the other way around. Many of them have had times they wanted to give up. The demands placed on these people for that which only God can do, is disheartening. The Bible they read has no supernatural letters different from the Bible in your pocket. The God to whom they pray is the same One to whom you have access. Their hours in a day are the same as ours. They sleep, eat, cry, and have families too. They have earthly needs too.

Know the Word, restore the Church!

Practical Tips for Studying the Holy Bible

There are people who genuinely want to study the Word of God, but find themselves struggling, not knowing where to start. Some confess they find it boring. There are also Christians who know the Bible just as head knowledge, as recitations with no in-depth grip of It or of the characters who make it alive in their hearts.

First, the Bible is God's Word. Only the Spirit of God can tell anyone what such and such means. Second, the Bible is a Living Being; the Bible is Jesus. Imagine if you came to someone you love, stared at them, and left. How would that person feel? You will need to pause between staring and let them speak to you. Don't read the Bible as a set of creeds. No, please. The Bible is very much alive and will speak to you if you allow Him to, rather than staring and walking away.

Here are some tips I, the writer, have found helpful. I hope they can help you too:

i.   Pray for understanding and discernment. Only God knows what He means in His Word. "Then he opened their minds to understand the Scriptures." (Luke 24:45) In 2 Samuel 16:23, undiscerning Absalom concluded that Ahithophel's wicked advice was like God's. This is what happens when anybody with a load of followers on social media spews their insubstantial opinion on any given matter, and is taken by undiscerning followers to be truth; the followers are unmindful of the "opinion" being words that could only have come from satan.

166

ii.   Approach studying with an open heart. Be ready to be rebuked, corrected, and encouraged. This is why you should learn the Word in the secret place, so that its effects can flow freely. You may cry, dance, laugh, weep, dry heave, or get a runny nose – the effects are boundless, but the results will be known to all. Most important, do not come from a questioning standpoint, come with reverence and submission to obey whatever the Word says. The foundation of God stands firm. Be a blind follower of the Word, *especially* when it hurts the flesh and natural desires. It will *never* fail you.

The devil knows the Word and is an expert at misinterpreting it. If our reliance is on our head knowledge, we are doomed from the start. We must open the Word of God helplessly and with the emptiest state of mind and heart to be filled. We are honored to be fed manna straight from Heaven when we come before His Word. If the heart's posture is to look for points for debates or points to question, that heart is doomed from the start and should not expect to receive anything. (James 4:11)

We should realize that we are using the same eyes to view and digest evil, as to read the Holy Precepts of a God who does not behold evil and will turn His face away from sin. If there are, and there will be, areas which we don't understand, in reverent silence we must let our hearts plead for revelation. Mark Twain remarked: *"It is not the things which I do not understand in the Bible which trouble me, but the things which I do understand."* [178] What are we doing with those parts which are clear?

iii.   I lean toward a school of thought that suggests new believers start with the book of Galatians before any of the Gospels. Some believe John, some believe Mark, but I recommend   Galatians. Whichever the Holy Spirit wills you to do after praying is fine. *Do not start with Revelation… or maybe.*

iv.   With the Pauline letters, understand the common themes for each church or individual to whom that letter was originally addressed. Understand why he wrote to the Corinthian church, why their letters were the longest, and why he wrote to them twice. What were the peculiarities of the Philippian, Galatian and Roman churches? Were all his letters written from prison? What was

---

[178] https://quoteinvestigator.com/2017/09/22/bible/

the difference between the need of the Colossian church and of the Thessalonian? Why did he write to Timothy and Philemon? This makes for easy reference when we need to refer to a particular theme. We know where to search about immorality, forgiveness and restoration, youthful zeal, and the difference between the old and the new life in Christ. Read them as if you were a member of each church.

v.   Use the Bible app to compare up to four versions of a text, especially if the King James is not your preferred version. I have discovered some incorrect interpretations to a text when I solely relied on one version, only to discover that up to six other versions said something completely different. A number of versions do not have Matthew 17:21 in them. They skip from verse 20 to verse 22. Some versions also leave out *"and fasting"* from Mark 9:21. Other times, it is good to start with a simpler version of a passage to get the gist of what is being said, then read that same passage in the more formal versions. The *Message* version uses a translation style called "dynamic equivalence," which means it gives you a sense of what is being said, but not what was really said. This translation is excellent to use with another formal translation but gravely insufficient to be solely used. I generally have a primary version I use each year, but I use other versions alongside for reference. At the beginning of a new year, I select a new version. There's a variety, so knock yourself out!

vi.   Technology has enormously contributed to our Christian walk by enabling easy access to the Word. It will, however, be inadequate and lazy, if our study of the Word is limited to an electronic device, powered by man-made electricity, and subject to the ability of a battery to function. The Holy Bible IS Holy. It must be given that honor. Every Christian should have a personal hard copy of the Holy Bible, bought for themselves, as a precious gift to themselves, and to read for and by themselves. And yes, we need a copy of the King James Version and as many more versions as we choose; this is mandatory if we are serious about our growth. An app should be a supplement, but never the sole source of the Word. It is not the same. The benefits are innumerable. Could it be that the transforming effects which the Word of God had on people of the old religion was because they had been with the Word, i.e. their physical hard copy Bible, which allowed it to dwell and settle in their hearts as a direct contrast to switching between apps, while studying the Word in our day?

Our Bibles should be the most cherished inheritance we pass on to our seed when we depart from earth. If all we have is an app, how is this achieved? The children of the late Dr. Martin Luther King, Jr. have a case in court, as at the time of this writing, for a dispute over their father's Bible. The older sons would like to auction it to the highest bidder, but the last born of the family, clearly the wisest, has vowed that it is one legacy that will never be commercialized. That child is willing to fight to the end. As at the time of writing this, Dr. King's Bible is currently in the custody of a judge. That is a legacy, a precious legacy. Fashion will change, trends will change, the value of money will change, but we must choose to leave a legacy of our personal ownership of that which will never change; it will be incomplete if our personal notes are missing. It's not just about having a copy of the Bible; it's leaving a legacy that shares our experience and walk with the Word of God for our children and children's children.

If anything, a physical Bible saves our eyes from *all that* screen-time. There is barely any time allowing it sink in when we read on the screen. We pick a pretty verse, highlight it, make an image and maybe post it, then we run to the next thing. This ought not to be. The Bible is our closest link to God. We cannot pray effectively if we do not know it. It is holy ground. Honor It.

vii.   Use a hard copy Bible to read only the Words of Jesus in red. As Soldiers of Christ, we must be knowledgeable (*not pridefully familiar*) with everything He said, so that in every situation, we can think, "What would Jesus do/say in this?" before acting. Get that sense of "WWJD/S."

viii.   A study Bible is essential. It provides commentaries, cross-references, maps, extra notes on the characters, timelines of events… it makes your study experience come alive.

ix.   Notes. Making notes is important, because what a verse might speak to you at a particular reading, isn't what it will speak to you during a subsequent reading. Over the years, as you grow in your knowledge of God, you will also see how your thinking has evolved. Past notes will throw more insight or make you realize that a particular verse was maybe not what you thought it to be at the time.

x.   Mark or highlight. Pick a highlight scheme with colors for different verses. For example, I use a red highlighter when there is a warning about conduct, punishment, consequences or God's judgement; a warm yellow highlighter for the attributes and Character of God, a bright yellow highlighter for something God says that sticks out at the time of reading; I use a green highlighter for scenario facts e.g. 'Peter then asked Jesus'; 'So they flogged them and asked them not to preach anymore' are scenario facts which I highlight in green and so on.

xi.   When doing a Bible plan, or using a devotional, study the whole chapter, rather than just the few verses referenced.

xii.   Learn the known verses in all Books of the Word. For instance, John 3:16 is a known verse. Learn all the 3:16s from Genesis to Revelation. Genesis 1:1 is a known verse. Learn all the 1:1s from Genesis to Revelation. Psalm 23 is a known chapter. Read all chapter 23s of the books that have Chapter 23s.

xiii.   I believe everyone has a Bible character on whom they can pattern their lives. Yes, Jesus is Jesus, but we all have someone in the Bible whose life we see as similar to ours. We can study and pattern ourselves after that character, provided they had a strong finish. It could also just be that person you are drawn to, their personality, how they handled situations, their relationship with God, or their zeal, but find that person and be an expert on their lives. I found mine, a very perfect fit, and it is not hard guess who it is!

xiv.   This buttresses the previous point. God approved in our official Bibles only that which He desired, so there is information about which we might wonder, but will not find in Bibles; they are not inaccessible. I didn't find out that Apostle Paul was bald and 4'8" tall, or that Prophet Isaiah was hiding in a tree when the then-vicious Manasseh murdered him by ordering that the tree be sawed in half. I didn't know that Rebecca was supposedly three years old when Isaac took her to be his wife, although he did not marry her until she was 23. This was why there was a nurse (*the first Deborah*) who accompanied Abraham's servant, Eliezer (*whose name is also not in the Bible*) when he took Rebecca from her parent's home.

Especially when you find your character, learn random, interesting facts about their life. It helps to build your faith and fan your flames, knowing that these things happened on the same ground we walk on today.

Read about the events in the Bible, too. Read history! Was everybody a Christian? Why did the Christians have to hide, in order to meet? Where was Moses from age 40 to 80? What were those who weren't Christians doing? Why were they so adamant about not being Christian? Only one death of the disciples was recorded in the Holy Bible, but curiosity will arouse a true reader's interest to how the others ended up. There is so much more enlightening information, which puts the things we might not previously have understood, in clearer context when we read around events of the Bible using historical sources. The internet is a blessing in this regard, not a curse.

xv.   Okay, Christian, it is not all seriousness. Make the Bible a lifestyle! Pick up your lifestyle tips from there. The Bible is packed with so many funny stories, scenarios which when you burst out laughing at, do not render you unholy. You want comedy? Try God! You want suspense? Try the Unsearchable God. You want romance? Ohhh, try the Inventor of sex! You want new words and grammar? Try the Author and Finisher of the Holy Bible! You want tragedy? Try the God who wept! You want tips for that motivational speech or cute quotes, check the records of the God whose depths of wisdom are unfounded. I learned to ask about the well-being of people, and engage in the occasional small talk from Jacob in Genesis 29:1-14. I also learned to greet people name-by-name, not just generally, despite the position they occupy from Apostle Paul's respectful and caring letter in Romans 16. Finally, I got a new understanding about women's covering of hair and came to a resolution about it...and it is probably not what you think.

All in all, remember BALANCE! Read the New Testament in light of the Old Testament; when you see a reference in the New Testament to something in the Old Testament, don't brush over it. Go to the text so you see the correlation and how events played out exactly as they were predicted thousands of years before. Proverbs alone will make you a good motivational speaker; Psalms alone will make you a good poet or songwriter; Revelation and end-time prophecies alone will make you a bringer of "bad news." The Old Testament alone will make you a good historian and present a "warped" view of God. The New Testament alone will miss vital attributes about God, e.g. His justice.

A word of encouragement for anyone who has tried studying the Word, but still doesn't get it: Keep going. Don't stop drinking. It is an acquired taste and the moment the taste hits you, it comes together. Even what was tasteless before, comes alive in your soul. Keep building. The Word of God is that foundation which will not suffer your foot to be moved. He will not let you slip or stumble when you build on Him. Keep going. Keep falling, until you are broken to irredeemable pieces that only He can mend. Just never stop. The knowledge of Jesus Christ is a lovely fragrance worth diffusing everywhere. If reading it brings a bad smell to you, that is a good sign; it shows you were on your way to death and will be wise to save your soul by never stopping until you yourself begin oozing that sweet fragrance of Christ's saving grace everywhere you go (2 Corinthians 2:14-16). Please, do not stop. Until you are transformed from within, despite how white-washed you appear, your soul continues to ooze the smell of death. This is why all that attention is on you – it is a wonder where that bad smell is coming from. *Could it be you?*

Above all, let us all resolve in our hearts to never go a day without studying our Bibles.

When You Know...

When we know the Word of God, what do we do? Do we treasure these things in our hearts, obey them, lock them up and throw away the keys? Shortly before he died, Paul wrote two letters to Timothy. He encouraged Timothy to hold fast to the Truth he had been taught from his childhood, and to avoid false teachers. Paul told him about the usefulness and power of the Word of God, advised him to pray for authorities and leaders, stated how young and old widows should be cared for, and listed signs of the end-times. Every word of those letters we enjoy today. Suppose this young boy had torn up those letters, or folded them and kept them in his pockets; suppose he had said the letters were addressed to him and the signs of the end-times were his secret, we would be suffering for it today. What we enjoy in the Word of God is the diligence of faithful men who carried out a divine mandate with all seriousness. Jesus said to Peter in Luke 22:32, "when thou art converted, strengthen thy brethren."

In his letter, Jude was initially going to write about salvation but a more pressing issue was laid in his heart, and we know when God puts His word in our hearts, it burns until we release it. This was what was laid in Jude's, "contend for the faith." (Jude 3) Since the days of the Apostles, we've had bad yeast spreading among the body of Christ and in our generation, it is completely rotten. Many slander the Faith, many slanders the Holy Bible, they misinterpret God's word to suit their hedonistic lifestyles. Even Archangel Michael of warfare, with all his power, did not curse the false teachers who rightfully deserved to be cursed (Jude 9). He left them to God, knowing that such people would be rewarded with destruction (2 Peter 2:12). However, people unashamedly blaspheme, misinterpret, and misrepresent a blameless, mighty God with disdain and lies. This is why, if you are a Christian, if you love Jesus, if you remember His death and suffering, if you, *consider Him,* if you know Him, if you love Him, you must **PREACH!**

I have not hidden Your righteousness within my heart; I have declared Your faithfulness and Your salvation; I have not concealed Your lovingkindness and Your truth From the great assembly. (Psalm 40:10)

Jesus came to set us free and He set us free to spread His Good News, unceasingly and irrepressibly, because He will have all men come to the knowledge of the truth (1 Timothy 2:4), rather than the unintelligent assumption that we have been freed to live carefree or in the unseemly bondage of "human rights." In *Acts 5:19-20,* when the disciples were freed from prison, the angel of the Lord gave them one instruction, which they resolved to obey over any authority: *Go, stand and speak...* If they had disobeyed this directive, the new bondage in which they would have found themselves would have been far worse than physical chains. The same applies to us. If, after we have been set free, but lock the Good News in our hearts and throw away the keys, before long, we will be trapped in a greater bondage than that which bound us before coming to Christ (2 Peter 2:20-22), like a washed pig that goes back to the mud, *the Demas Disorder, the John666 Syndrome.*

We have been saved from darkness, but to stay saved is not just eliminating vices. It is replacing our old patterns of life with something new, our wide lifestyles with a narrow alternative. We must never be void under the guise of salvation. Nobody expects your personality to change if you become a Christian, at least God doesn't. It is a matter of channelling your strengths into something new, something true, something life, denouncing those sins that easily entangled you, and correcting them in others with love. Peter was always a talker and his mouth found him in awkward situations multiple times, but the moment that the breath of the Holy Spirit came upon him, his mouth was redirected into a fiery cause for the Kingdom, winning thousands of souls by simple Spirit-empowered messages. He remained a dedicated defender of the Faith until death.

In **Luke 9:51-56**, shortly after the Transfiguration, Jesus resolved to go to Jerusalem. As He passed through Samaria, the fury of James and John was kindled by the unkind reception given to our Lord by the Samarians. **They said, "Lord, do You want us to command fire to come down from heaven and consume them?"** Again, in John 13:21-23, Jesus was with His disciples, teaching, when in the midst of teaching, He became troubled in spirit, and said, **one of you will betray Me.** The disciples began looking at one another, wondering who was going to betray Him, but John, who was resting on the bosom of Jesus, spoke up and asked which one of them was going to do it. What Jesus did by not answering was to save Judas, because if Jesus had spoken, Judas would immediately have been roasted meat. However, as John grew in His knowledge of God, after the Holy Spirit had come upon them, he redirected that energy, fervency, and passion toward the things of God: the "son of thunder" became the "apostle of love." He was no longer asking if he should call down fire, but spurring us into love, encouraging us not to love the world or the things in it, but to love God and our brethren.

Some might say they are naturally introverted people. Even when they were in sin, they sinned in introversion. The God who created each unique individual still urges, "go and I will be with thy mouth and teach thee what thou shalt say." (Exodus 4:12) Their preaching could very well be within their sphere of influence. Aquila and Priscilla were not public speakers but were private evangelists who used their home to preach and did so as a couple (Romans 16:5). We are all without excuse, especially when empowered by the Spirit. In the book, *"70 Great Christians,"* Geoffrey Hanks says, *"...whatever the case, it is certain the church in Britain was not founded as a result of an evangelistic mission but because ordinary people shared the Good News of Jesus with their friends and neighbours."* Paul set forth an example of preaching all seasons, with many tears, preaching the truth whether publicly or in private (Acts 20:19-20). We are all without excuse.

Preaching is not a calling. "Preacher" is not one of the offices or "members" of the body of Christ listed in **1 Corinthians 12: 27-31**, which identifies the Holy Spirit's gifts. He empowers every Christian to preach. It is a calling for each person who identifies as Christian to defend our faith against these teachings of today from satan's bowels. Jesus put trust in His disciples to do this, and they faithfully passed it on to us. Preach. Don't bother if somebody has done it. We cannot modernize the Gospel, but we must "remain faithful to what you have been taught from the beginning" (1 John 2:24). We can't be creative with the Gospel. It is the same, immutable Message. We complement each other in this Kingdom, rather than adopting the pagan practice of outdoing and outshining each other: "I (Paul) planted, Apollos watered, but God gave the increase" (1 Corinthians 3:6). Besides, if we are looking to Jesus in our race, we are under an instruction to keep our eyes on our Coxswain and not our fellow runners. (Galatians 6:4) When it becomes a task to figure out what to say, we must be careful that we don't lean into heresy. The Word is the Word. "And every day, in the Temple and from house to house, they continued to teach and preach this message: "Jesus is the Messiah." (Acts 5:42)

When you know it, you won't be able to help it, "For we cannot but speak the things which we have seen and heard" (Acts 4:20)... Except you don't believe what you have known. In 2 Corinthians 4:13, however, in the face of death, Paul said, *we continue to preach because we have the same kind of faith the psalmist had when he said, "I believed therefore I spoke"*[179] *We also believe and therefore speak.*

Christian, do you believe? Do you love what you believe? If you do, then guard Jesus fiercely and jealously with your heart and with your voice. As your Saviour, Redeemer, Friend, Lover and Elder Brother, Jesus is family. Do not tolerate heresy or slander from anyone concerning Him. Only genuine passion and love for Him, by the empowerment of the Holy Spirit, can enable you to do this, even in the face of opposition. Never forget that love itself has its side of vehemence and passion. The intensity of love toward a person or a cause may be measured by the intensity of antagonism and disdain toward those who oppose and contradict that which is loved. There are many reflections in the Gospel of John and in his epistles, which display this energy of hatred toward the work of the devil and toward those dispositions under the influence of the father of lies.

Jesus didn't look away from us, even as we chanted, **Crucify Him!** He was not ashamed of us. Are we ashamed of the Gospel? He prayed for us on the cross. Pray for them, but correct any false talk about our Lord Jesus. The insult is spreading too fast in our generation. God does not take kindly to such slander about Jesus. He is a consuming fire. Let us not nail our Elder Brother to the cross again. *It is finished!*

Remember this, lest you be weary in your preaching: It is never the duty of

---

[179] Psalm 116:10.

any man to change people's hearts or produce conviction; my work is to share the Good News and pray for God to change hearts that are desperately wicked by nature. As Gideon's army declared, "for the Lord and for Gideon." (Judges 7:20) When I preach, I have done my part; the Lord will do His. Faithful and truthful preaching is all that is required of me, in season and out of season. If I only preach when I see results, I will be frustrated, because I am expecting my words to do the Lord's work of salvation, which is the pungent, rising smell of sin.

Preach, answer questions which you can answer truthfully and in line with Scriptures. For other questions, a simple response of *"I don't know"* is fine. "Anyone who claims to know all the answers doesn't really know very much." (1 Corinthians 8:2) The great Apostle Paul, with all his revelation and direct teaching from God, knew only in part (1 Corinthians 13:12). These are instances when applying the *"I am human"* excuse is justified and legitimate. I do not know all the mysteries of the Kingdom and will be in the bondage of spiritual pride if I present myself as if I do. Our hearts must remain pure and as transparent as glass. Paul declared, "But you, Timothy, certainly know what I teach, and how I live, and what my purpose in life is. You know my faith, my patience, my love, and my endurance." (2 Timothy 3:10)

How do we preach? What do we preach? "Mightily, publicly AND with Scriptures ABOUT Jesus." (Acts 18:28) There is no non-disclosure agreement in this Kingdom. **PREACH!**

I Will Not!

Christian, by and by, our preaching is for our credit and good. The Word *will continue* to spread with or without us. It was here before we were; it will be here long after we are gone. We can only wisely key into it and add our names to the list of contributors of spreading the Word. Who knows if we were born for our Gospel–filled voices to be as loud as those horns blown at Jericho for such perverse times as these? (Esther 4:14). Who is silencing us? WHO CAN silence us? (2 Corinthians 11:10) We have freedom and that means we are also at liberty to *choose* to be silent about the Gospel, but we should recall that in Acts 12:24, while pride destroyed Herod and worms were busy eating him up in death, the account the Bible gives is, **MEANWHILE, the Word of God continued to spread, and there were many new believers...** At any given time on earth, people are hearing the Good News and coming to Christ.

While we are boasting, fornicating, cheating, planning evil schemes, drinking and partying, shooting up drugs and smoking, piling up wealth and monitoring stock markets or simply minding our business *but* leaving The Great Commission out of our "to do lists," remember, *"meanwhile."* Our preaching is just to key into a cause to which we personally decide to contribute and is of nominal but not essential effect (1 Corinthians 15:11), because The Message is the same worldwide in its simplicity: "Christ died for our sins... He was buried, and He was raised from the dead on the third day..." (1 Corinthians 15:3-4). Christian, we are to the Gospel of Jesus Christ what Brother Sosthenes is to 1 Corinthians.

*Writer's Note: *Sosthenes was the writer of 1 Corinthians on behalf of Paul, as Paul probably dictated to him. Not that Paul could not write, Sosthenes was only helping)*

Ponder on this possible message on your gravestone:

"*Insert name* born ____, died _____ left behind _____ number of properties, stocks and shares in _____, fully loaded bank account in Asia, Europe and beyond; and multiple social media accounts with millions of followers to be inherited by the highest bidder.

MEANWHILE: *The Word of God continues to spread... "*

Brother and sister, when we return to dust, six feet under, the Word, in triple-quick speed, *continues* to grow. Charles Spurgeon said, *"We have received much by means of the efforts and sufferings of the saints in years gone by, and if we do not make some return to the church of Christ by giving her our best energies, we are unworthy to be enrolled in her ranks."*[180] It is the least act of gratitude we can do for Jesus Christ. It is the only lasting thing we can do for ourselves (1 Corinthians 15:58). Even without any human being doing it, if all believers had a conference and came to an agreement that no one will preach the Good News of Jesus Christ, stones and animals will do the work of spreading the Gospel. Scarves, ties, and shoes will spread The Message of Hope, Truth and Everlasting Life. Let us not test God Almighty (Luke 19:40).

Paul declared, "my life is worth nothing to me until I complete the task of testifying the Gospel of the grace of God." (Acts 20:2) Have we been saved? Have we been delivered from darkness? Do we know God? Have we felt the power of His love and enjoyed His mercies? Do we have breath? If so, we have a task of spreading the Good News, a duty to carry the torch of the Gospel handed to us, and to run with it, keeping the flames burning for our children and generations to come.

---

[180] C.H Spurgeon Morning & Evening Devotional.

Paul also declared, "And because I preach this Good News, I am suffering and have been chained like a criminal. But the word of God cannot be chained" (2 Timothy 2:9). Indeed, 2,000 years later, it is still free, growing bigger and spreading faster. Any individual's indecision is of no effect to the never-ending, ever-increasing, exponential spread of the Gospel. Let us be wise.

> *Jesus said unto him, 'Forbid him not: for he that is not against us is for us.'* Luke 9:50

Christian, pick your side but here is a prayer for you: "God perhaps will grant (you) repentance, so that (you) may know the truth and (you) may come to your senses and escape the snare of the devil, having been taken captive by him to do his will" (2 Timothy 2:25-26).

As for me, Eunice-Pauline, **"woe is me if I do not preach the gospel" (1 Corinthians 9:16).**

Finally, Brethren...

This is from me, a sister in Christ to you:

> *Humbly accept the word God has planted in your hearts for it has the power to save your souls.* **James 1:21**

Please know, love, delight, meditate, discuss, think about, ponder, memorize, store up, and treasure the Word of God. So much has been given to us, and so much is expected of us. We are without excuse. Desire the sincere milk of the Word, and let it build your faith and help you grow. You will be eternally grateful to God that you did. Break the Chinese Whispers for the sake of Paul and the many faithful, who carried this out and dutifully handed it to us, "For what I received I passed on to you as of first importance..." (1 Corinthians 15:3); and died for this cause.

I beg you, know God for yourself. Know God for yourself. Again, with tears in my eyes and on bended knees, know God for yourself. Don't look to church, cell-groups and fellowships, pastor, friend, social media, or even the Apostles to know God. How can we die for a Faith we don't know? How can we live if we don't die? (Romans 6:7-8)

Wisdom for us all in Jesus' name. Amen.

CHAPTER 3

DO!

If you know these things, blessed are ye if ye do them.

John 13:17

SoulTune: For the One[181]

---

[181] Bethel Music & Jenn Johnson; (2017); *For the One*; Bethel Music.

I
s it possible to disturb Jesus? Can we sound like buzzing bees in His ear? Can we frustrate Him?

> *But WHY do you call Me 'Lord, Lord,' and not do the things which I say?* Luke 6:46

During a conversation with a brother, he asked, *"What do Christians do for people in need? All they want to do is pray and say, 'All is well,' without any practical help."* My response was, *"Unfortunately, such people are not Christians."*

> *But be ye doers of the word, and not hearers only, deceiving yourselves.* James 1:22

When we listed reasons to know the Word of God personally, and stated that it is the way to true success, it was not without cognizance of the possibility that some know the Word and are faithful readers of the Word; *"Walking Bibles,"* we may call them. However, we listed one major part of knowing as a determinant to success, and took out, "that thou mayest observe to do according to all that is written therein" (Joshua 1:8), the reliant caveat of **DOING.**

> *Keep His statutes and commandments, which I am giving you today, so that you and your children after you may prosper, and that you may live long in the land the LORD your God is giving you for all time.* Deuteronomy 4:40

God's Words are our life (Deuteronomy 32:47). The devil is a thief and murderer, constantly on the prowl to steal the Word of God from our hearts. He does not care if we read and know it, his only goal is to hinder us from believing The Word that is able to save us. (Luke 8:12) He throws fiery darts which our shield of faith ought to quench. When we keep hearing the Word of God, we are building faith but the enemy's fiery darts are to keep us from **doing** those things which we know; "Show me your faith without your works, and I will show you my faith by my works" (James 2:18) His attack strategy is shooting flaming arrows of pride, doubt, despondency, temptation, lust, anger, frustration, depression, sloth, and every vice that stands against what we know about an unchanging God. *What do we know about God?*

To listen to God's Word is to stare at a solid foundation. While we are listening, we are only staring; to *build* on that Rock is to respond, to obey that which we know to be Truth. (Matthew 7:24) We should understand this, Christian: Our Faith *without* works is a corpse. (James 2:20) We are not to hear the Words of God, treasure them in our hearts and leave them there. Our hearts are not safe. Even just preaching is not sufficient; we will be, at best, unrewarded workers of Jesus, who will send people to Heaven but have no place there ourselves. Our preaching might be five minutes, but our ministry is 60 seconds, 1 minute, 24 hours, 7 days, 4 weeks, 12 months, work, home, abroad, bed, bathroom, airplane, internet, books, friends, walk, and pose.

It is appalling, painful, distressing, disheartening and simply unfair to Jesus, when so-called carriers of the Gospel, and those who relish the title of "religious influencer," bask in the limelight and attention that come with it; then come forward to cry "human" when exposed in their hideous, unthinkable sins. For those were not human mistakes, but abominable lifestyles to which they subscribed and enjoyed. They are quick to condemn people that judge them; they tell those who have unfortunately made them their gods not to make them role models, because that puts them under "pressure." James 3:1 warns us not to be quick to be teachers, because those who parade themselves as such *will* be judged more harshly than the ordinary Christian. Apostle Paul had many things he could boast about, whether by earthly or spiritual standards; he was no average citizen. However, as an ambassador of Christ, he threw away all of that away and said he did not want anyone to think of him above what firstly, "He sees me to be" *then* "hears from me." (2 Corinthians 12:6) Our conduct is first and above what we say.

Our godly conduct is sufficient for any person outside of Christ to approach us and ask how and why we are the way we are, which will make room for us to preach the Gospel of Jesus to them. 1 Peter 3:15 tells us to *always* be ready for such times. Readiness is not merely our excessive knowledge of Scripture and theology, but in our conduct at *all* times. Like Paul, every Christian should and must be able to say, "Imitate me, just as I also imitate Christ" (1 Corinthians 11:1). In 1 Corinthians 4:16, he not only said we should follow his conduct but *urged* us to, meaning, he *begged* us to copy him. Every true Christian has the Holy Spirit working in them (Romans 8:9), therefore, we must boldly make the same statement, or train ourselves under the leadership of the Holy Spirit to do so where, without doubt to all, there is a work happening in us - "But they were hearing only, He who formerly persecuted us now preaches the faith which he once tried to destroy" therefore, "they glorified God because of me" (Galatians 1:23&24) – but enjoy crying sinful *"human"* wolf, then we simply should release the unforced Christian tag. Such individuals are NOT Christians (Romans 8:14). What did we formerly do? What do we now do? Who is hearing it? Who is praising God because of us? This religion has rules and we must follow the rules if we must have peace. (Galatians 6:16)

If you love Me, keep My commandments... John 14:15

...And stop clanging cymbals into the Ear of Jesus, **"Lord, Lord"**, as He is *not* listening (1 Peter 3:12). This is why some people preach being good over religion; they prefer to call their religion "love and light," rather than come to Christ. This is why Christianity is slandered. Once upon a time, people struggled and faked being Christian, so that they could enjoy the kind treatment Christians showed each other and people around them. This was the trend during Constantine The Great's empire which made Christianity fashionable. Why must we call ourselves Christians if we are not willing to **be** Christians? Is this fair? What is fun about being a Christian? How can wickedness be found in anyone who claims to be a Christian, driving people away from the Kingdom of God!? *"If that is how Christians are, I do not want to be a Christian."* How many people have made such statements due to the conduct of an ambassador of satan parading as 'Christian'? God will judge such people and calls them fools (James 2:20).

> *Let your light SO shine before men, that they may see your good works and glorify your Father in heaven.* Matthew 5:16

Did Jesus say to let our lights shine? Did He tell us, "for God loved the world?" No, there is a thin line between __ and SO; there is a *world* of difference. "For God **SO** loved the world that He gave..." (Please refer to the breakdown of this in Chapter 1). "Let your light **SO** shine..." When your light is **SO** shining, there is no doubt whether there is a light or not. There is not "maybe" or "maybe not" about whether you are a Christian. It is without doubt to all and sundry, especially to those who are not Christians: "Be careful to live properly among your unbelieving neighbors. Then even if they accuse you of doing wrong, they will see your honorable behavior, and they will give honor to God when He judges the world." (1 Peter 2:12) IF you **must** be a Christian, this provision is **without** repentance.

Are we just to go about, announcing ourselves, shining our lights, when anyone can claim to be SO shining with good works? Good question. Even demons appear as angels of light, (2 Corinthians. 11:14-15) but for a Christian, the difference is never in the works, but the root of which those works are produced, the intention, the motivation.

> *And immediately, His fame spread throughout all the region around Galilee.*
> Mark 1:28

Jesus despised the fame that came with Him. He could not help doing good works. His exercise was good works. He burned calories when he "went around doing good... BECAUSE God was with Him." (Acts 10:38) If we *cannot* help but do good, *even* when we do not want to, we do NOT know God! If we *must* do good, we do NOT know God! If we must count the cost to ourselves before we help another, we do NOT know God. The only cost we are told to count is the cost of becoming a Christian – of taking up our crosses daily and following Him. Even more, if we must be recognized for our good, hello, Pharisee! We do NOT know God. "And He did not allow the demons to speak, because they knew Him." (Mark 1:34) How come this Jesus, whose fame spread abroad; whose works the whole world is not enough to contain, was only identifiable by someone in His circle with a kiss? How did those soldiers and Jewish leaders *not* know who they knew? Was He not popular? Was His light not shining? Was it dim or off?

According to Luke 6:47-48, when our deeds are out of obedience to Jesus' teaching, we are digging deep on a solid foundation; even when the worst storms come, we will remain unshaken. On the other hand, someone who is doing good works without the solid foundation of the Word of God will find themselves in a crisis when the tests and trials come. On the surface, ordinary man may not be able to discern the motive between acts done out of Jesus and those done out of self, but Jesus' Words from His throne, **I know thy works...** will judge between cattle and cattle.

When William Wilberforce (1759-1833), was saved and studied the Bible, he was going to leave his prestigious public office career, because he did not imagine that a Christian could work in the public sector. With encouragement from Christian friends and his constant digging into Scripture, he dedicated his life to fighting for two causes if he was going to remain a politician: Abolition of the slave trade, and social/moral reform. This was during a time when the profligate King George IV was in power. Wilberforce also chose not to be in any political party, remaining as an independent Member of Parliament from the Kingdom of Heaven, motivated by a desire to put his Christian principles into action and to serve God in public life. With severe health issues and strong opposition from Members of Parliament, he stood on the foundation of the Word; for the remainder of his life, he fought for the abolition of the slave trade until he was told, on his death bed, that the approval of the Abolition of Slavery Act 1833 had been passed. After hearing the news, he died just three days later.

He never used violence, he never gave up, saying, he was a white man *(who, by the way, was from a wealthy home but distributed all his wealth)*, and therefore did not need to fight for the blacks in the face of fierce opposition. By the end of his life, British morals, manners, and sense of social responsibility had increased, paving the way for future changes in societal conventions and attitudes during the succeeding era.

Only the Word of God could have kept a loving husband and doting father resilient for something in which he had no direct gain in until death. In such busy times of his life, he still maintained decorum and respect to all humans; he personally responded to all the letters he received, no matter how long it took him. He wasn't too busy fighting for the good of the people that he did not have time for the people. A 21st Century social media influencer, on the other hand, might say they are too busy and have too many messages so they cannot respond. Almost 200 years later, Wilberforce's sacrifice and dedication to the lives of humans, out of the strength of the Word of God, is still being enjoyed today. He is honored as a *"Christian hero, a statesman-saint, held up as a role model for putting his faith into action."*[182] Seasons, trials, and perhaps chance, will distinguish the solid Christian from the sandy worm. Time vindicates intention, purpose, and value... *'wisdom is justified by her children (Matthew 11:19).*

Our light SO shining is whether we have The Light, Himself, His Spirit, shining through us and not our human efforts enabling us to shine   (Romans 8:10). Human efforts will render one a nice person, but Jesus renders a Christian a kind heart. Remember, to be rendered as something means you have no control over the effect; lack of money renders you broke; lack of faith renders you hopeless; lack of Jesus renders you dead. Never in the Bible are we told to be nice; several times we are warned as Christians to be kind. (Romans 12:10; Ephesians 4:32; Colossians 3:12;   2 Peter 1:7). It is a fruit of the Holy Spirit. (Galatians 5:22) Not all Christians are nice, but all Christians must be kind. As the hymn writer said, 'Take my hands and let them move, at the impulse of Thy love.' This is a classic picture of an individual *rendered* kind. Does the impulse of God's love ever stop? Should our hands then ever stop moving in good works?

As Thomas á Kempis said,

> *We ought to have charity for all men but familiarity with all is not expedient.*

Niceness determines who benefits from their niceness. A nice person is fully in control of themselves. A kind person is absolutely not. A kind God will chastise the Son He loves with one hand but draw Him back in love with both hands. A kind God will strip you of everything you have but restore you a thousand-fold. A kind God will make a king an animal for seven years but restore him to his throne with even greater honor. A kind God will tell you in advance, *'of every tree of the garden you may freely eat; but of the tree of the knowledge of good and evil you shall not eat, for...you shall surely die'*,[183] and He will leave you

---

[182] Hague, William (2007), William Wilberforce: The Life of the Great Anti-Slave Trade Campaigner, London: Harper Press.
[183] Genesis 2:16-17.

to your freedom to do as you wish. A nice god will tell you, *'you will not surely die…your eyes will be opened, and you will be like God knowing good and evil'*,[184] but will not leave you to make your decision; he will stay there to convince you and ensure you eat the fruit which, by that act, will cause destruction for billions of generations by introducing sin and death.

A kind God makes one rich and adds no sorrow to it. (Proverbs 10:22) There is no catch to Him; His gifts and calling are without repentance; He is pure and brighter than the sun. A nice god will lead you to the highest mountain, show you the best things the world can offer, and promise it all to you IF you bow down to him first, *but* will not advise you that you are about to pierce your own life with many sorrows. Only when you do get to the end of your life, on your deathbed, and are asked for your will, does it dawn on you that it is all over, your money, beauty, estates, friends, cars, clothes, shoes, bags, followers, career, which you gathered in surplus at the expense of Christ, are all garbage, unnecessary weights, and items fit only for a septic tank. You realize that the nice god gave you your Heaven on earth. The abundance of those things which you enjoyed is the closest you will ever get to heaven. As tears run down your face, as your estate administrator asks, yet again in your final moments of life, *"HOW would you like to share your vast wealth?"* you reply, with your last breath, *"Firstly, I bequeath my own soul to the devil — for being so greedy for the muck of this world! Secondly, I bequeath my wife's soul to the devil — for persuading me to this worldly course of life. Thirdly, I bequeath my pastor's soul to the devil — because he did not show me the danger I lived in, nor reprove me for it."*[185] A nice pastor will preach to your ears, beautiful face, shoes, bags, career, and net worth. A kind pastor will preach to your heart.

The following passage is a summary of Chapter 5 of John Bunyan's
The Pilgrim's Progress (pub. 1678 & 1684)

Talkative, of Prating Row

As Brother Christian[186] progressed in his pilgrimage with his fellow-pilgrim, Faithful, and discussed their experiences along the journey, they came across a man who walked along the same Way heading to the Celestial City. He was

---

[184] Genesis 3:4-5.

[185] https://gracegems.org/2017/06/I%20bequeath%20my%20pastor's%20soul%20to%20the%20devil.html

[186] Bunyan, J. ThePilgrim's Progress (1861) American Tract Society, New York.

a tall man who looked much better from afar than when Faithful came closer to him to ask if he was by any chance heading to the same destination as the Pilgrims. The man proclaimed that he was and Faithful was very delighted and invited him to accompany him and Christian, because Pilgrims always rejoice when they meet their kind as they can talk of profitable things.

As they spoke, Faithful found out that this man knew everything about the Kingdom of Heaven that any Pilgrim could know. He knew about repentance, belief in Jesus, constant prayer, the comfort and joys which the Gospel provided. Faithful was so impressed by this man's knowledge of what it meant to be a Pilgrim and said to him that this Heavenly knowledge which this man possessed could only have been a gift from God, Himself. The man proudly attested to this with the correct Bible verse, which says a man can receive nothing from God except it is given to him. *(John 3:27).* The man out-spoke Faithful, who was keen on having fruitful talk, so much so that Faithful was not sure what other topic to discuss, for the man had vast and almost threatening knowledge, probably making him question his own salvation.

All the while, Christian had been quietly observing their confabulation, but did not make any comment until Faithful, who was so impressed by this man, urged Christian to say something. Finally, Christian modestly smiled and said to his Brother, *"This man with whom you are so taken will deceive with this tongue of his, twenty of them that know him not."* Faithful was surprised by this rather bold statement of Brother Christian and asked if he knew him to state such. Christian affirmed that he knew this man even better than the man knew himself and explained to him that this man is a popular man from his town called Talkative, the son of Say-well, who lived at Prating Row. He was known to have a fine tongue and speech but was actually a sorry fellow. Faithful was not convinced of this claim by Christian and accused him of joking because he smiled. Christian clarified to Faithful that God forbid if his smile was that of jest for this man who was comparable to a *"painter, whose pictures show best at a distance, but, very near, more unpleasing,"* and assured Faithful that he was not lying. He told him about how this man, Talkative, was for any company and any talk - whether in the midst of Christians or whether in the midst of drunkards, he was the orator of the moment; his religion was not in his heart but started in his head and ended in his tongue for the sole purpose of wasteful spewing of verbiage.

If anyone among you thinks he is religious, and does not bridle his tongue but deceives his own heart, this one's religion is useless. James 1:26

Faithful bemoaned that he had fallen for the man's deceit and Christian ascertained that indeed, he had, reminding him of the Proverb which says, "They say and do not," even though the Bible tells us that the Kingdom of God is not in word but in power (1 Corinthians 4:20). All Talkative's speech about prayer, repentance and new birth was worthless, because Christian knew him from back home, the City of Destruction, and his religion was as full as the taste of savor in an egg white. He described more about Talkative: He was not a man of prayer or repentance and even a beast would make a better Pilgrim than him; he was a reproach, stain and shame to everyone who was truly a Pilgrim; to his family, he was *"a saint abroad and devil at home,"* a fault finder who mistreated his servants; for those who did business with him, they found that it was better to deal with a Turk   (Moslem) than him, because this ~~Christian~~ Talkative cheated, defrauded and beguiled all his business partners; he raised up his sons to have no conscience and was quick to call them "fools" and "blockheads" if they showed any sign of having a tender conscience and also spoke badly about them to outsiders; because of him, so many people had stumbled, fallen and turned away from the Faith(without regard for and in direct contravention of Jesus' warning in Matthew 18:6-7); but for God's mercy, many will still be ruined because of this seemingly religious man.

We put no stumbling block in anyone's path, so that our ministry will not be discredited. 2 Corinthians 6:3

Christian was known to speak truth so Faithful knew this seemingly severe testimony of Talkative was trustworthy and more so, to warn Faithful who was easily impressed by this man's professions which had tainted that of genuine Pilgrims. He counselled Faithful that saying and doing are two different things and just as the body without the soul is dead, so religion is a carcass without its practical part of the soul. On the surface, Talkative is knowledgeable, well-spoken and even polite. In theological discuss, he will outshine any scholar with his seamless interpretation of difficult doctrines and this makes his superficial religion the perfectly curated façade for covering up his shameful lifestyle to undiscerning people so because of this man, "the name of God is blasphemed among the Gentiles." (Romans 2:24) Faithful, who was initially intrigued by Talkative's presence, becomes sickened to his stomach and wanted to get rid of this bad yeast of a man immediately but did not know how. Christian knew it was no hard task to rid the tares from the wheat, more so, Talkative, the tare, would equally be sick of Faithful's company through a simple process: *'enter into some serious discourse about the power of religion – to change hearts and lives-; and ask him plainly (when he has approved of it, for that, he will) whether this things which he speaks are set up in his heart, house or conversation.'*

187

The Fruit

Faithful heeds this advice of going into 'serious discourse' with the eager Talkative and asks him what the *evidence* is of saving grace in the heart of an individual. This particular question throws Talkative off balance as it is not his preferred route of talk but he goes ahead and answers, '*an outcry against sin*'. Faithful corrects him that an 'outcry' is not enough but we are to *flee* sin and every appearance of it. Potiphar's wife made an 'outcry' of sin over Joseph but her heart was really after the sin. To speak out against sin is not sufficient to *hate* sin and he gave Talkative the example of a mother who cuddles her baby, embraces and adores that child until the child causes some form of trouble or embarrassment and then the same mother speaks up and scolds the child.

Talkative begins to become suspicious of Faithful and questions his intention by asking him these questions. Faithful pointed out that he was only, as a fellow Pilgrim, trying to set things right and asked him what other evidence proves that grace is at work in the heart. Talkative responds, '*great knowledge of Gospel mysteries*'. This answer, Faithful points out, should have come first but that knowledge of mysteries is not enough because 1 Corinthians 13:2 says "though I understand all mysteries and all knowledge....and have not charity, I am nothing." Talkative was a classic example of someone who had vast knowledge of Gospel because the person God blesses is not the person who knows the law but he who keeps them (John 13:17); i.e. Knowledge accompanied with the grace of faith (*action*) and love. Without that, any knowledge is for talkers and boasters. Talkative tells faithful that this conversation is a trap for him and is '*not profitable*' so refuses to give any other evidence of salvation. Regardless, Faithful goes ahead and tells Talkative that when God works in a soul, that person knows this by how he sees and feels their personal sin; and others around such a person notice that the person is beginning to live a life of doing right in the sight of God. Faithful then asks Talkative if he has felt his own sins and if his life and conduct to people prove that he has or his religion is just in tongue and urges him not to lie since he is a 'Pilgrim,' for his conscience sake.

Talkative began to blush and told Faithful he did not engage in such discussions and was not bound to reply to his questions because he was not his judge. He then asked Faithful what moved him to ask such questions. Faithful told him that he was that he noticed that he was quick to talk and he sensed that his talk was all there was to his religion, because his life was in direct contradiction to everything he spoke of, he caused great pain to true Christians and because of his ungodly conduct, many people who came to the Faith had stumbled and many more are in danger because of his wickedness. Faithful there and then called him, *'a shame to all he members of the church'* and as Christian rightly predicted, Talkative responded, *'Since you are ready to take up reports and judge so rashly as you do, I cannot but conclude you are some peevish or cross man, not fit to be talked with; and so adieu!'*[187]

And this was how Talkative turned back and walked away, leaving Faithful and Christian to continue on their pilgrimage.

Test Yourself

Talkative is an incredible representation of many "Christians" today. We are happy to talk the talk but flee walking the walk. We want to bask in God's love but scorn His justice, and that smelly talk of *"stop judging me"* to any question asked is nothing but an echo of that individual's conscience. Yes, God loves us; yes, nothing can separate us from His love; yes, He SO loved us that He gave his only Son… We know this and the case of God's love is closed. We have abused that phrase so much that nobody believes it. People who really need to know that God loves them do not believe it because of how Christians have represented a God they claim loves them.

Let us now face a more serious question each heart should consider: ***"Do I love God?"***

Again and slower, ***Do I love God?***

> *Let us hear the conclusion of the whole matter: Fear God, and keep His commandments: for this is the whole duty of man.* Ecclesiastes 12:13

The duty of man does not include to "love" God. In the Ten Commandments, concerning our relationship with Him, God said," I am the Lord thy God; Thou shalt have no other gods before me; Thou shalt not make unto thee any graven image; Thou shalt not take the name of the Lord thy God in vain." (Exodus 20:2-4) Again, there was no command to "love" Him, but as the Pharisees approached Jesus with their evil motive of "trapping" Him, one of them, "an expert in the law," asked Jesus which of the Laws Moses provided was the most important. Jesus quoted Moses from Deuteronomy 6:5, "You shall love the Lord your God with all your heart, with all your soul and

---

[187] Ibid.

with all your strength" and Jesus stated an equally important verse which God Himself spoke directly to Moses at **Leviticus 19:18, You shall love your neighbor as yourself.** When we obey these two, we have obeyed all the other laws.

The channels of loving God are our heart, soul, and strength. Nowhere in His Word are we told to love Him with our lips. Our music of love with a heart, soul, and energy, void of personal love for God, is personal entertainment but certainly not reaching Heaven's Gates. Shortly before His crucifixion, Jesus was giving the disciples a heads-up that they were all going to desert Him that night, but nevertheless, after He rose, He would meet them in Galilee. Nobody said anything but Peter, the life of the party, *"Though all men shall be offended because of thee, yet will I never be offended."* Jesus then expressly told Peter, *"This very night, before the rooster crows, you will deny three times that you even know me."* Peter still insisted, *"Even if I have to die with you, I will never deny you!"* His boldness made all the other disciples say the same. His passionate speech had convinced them that they could also die with Jesus. However, wise Jesus made no response to His wordy promise. A few verses later, we read, *"Then he began to curse and swear, saying, I do not know the Man!"* The rooster then crowed, Holy Ghost-unfilled-Peter found himself indeed entangled in the web as Jesus had predicted, and "he went out and wept bitterly." (Matthew 26:31-35; 74&75)

After the resurrection, Jesus has just had breakfast with His disciples and He asks Peter expressly this time, **"Simon, Son of Jonah[188], do you love me?"** and Peter is back at it, affirming his love for Jesus and he even gets upset because Jesus asked him thrice. Peter says, *"Lord, You know all things, You know that I love You."* On all three occasions, Jesus tells him to "walk his talk," because from experience, we know that Peter's verbal affirmations were just that *(The same way positivists tell people to solve their problems by chanting "positive" psychobabbles.)* So, to prove this verbal love, Jesus says, "Feed my Lambs; Take care of My sheep, and Feed my Sheep." (John 21:15-17)

According to commentaries[189], the first love Jesus asked him about, from the original Greek texts, translates to *agape*, i.e., sacrificial, unconditional love, above all the other disciples; the second was also *agape*, but this time not in comparison to any of the disciples but by himself alone; and the third was *phileo* i.e., brotherly love, love for one's neighbors. Jesus then predicted Peter's death by crucifixion to him. In Peter fashion, he didn't comment on his own death which Jesus had foretold but wanted to know how John was going

---

[188] NKJV states Jonah. Other versions have John or Jonas.
[189] NLT Life Application Study Bible.

to die.

Now, Jesus had ascended to His throne and Peter was left on earth, but did he prove his love for Jesus? In Acts 2, the Holy Spirit came on Peter, and this man became unstoppable for the Gospel, both in word and deed. He preached boldly and publicly, winning thousands of souls and baptizing them (Acts 2:41); he had compassion on the disabled, and even though he did not have money, he gave what money could not buy. He stopped and healed, even though he was on his way to a 'church program'.

Even though people were amazed at this miracle, Peter took no credit for it, instead he turned it into an opportunity to publicly preach about the Jesus whom they crucified, but by whose name the miracle which amazed them was performed (Acts 3). The religious leaders had Peter arrested, but there was no denying Jesus here; by the power of the Holy Spirit in him, he spoke boldly that the miracles were by Jesus, whom they had crucified, but was now risen, and only by this same Jesus was salvation possible. This boldness of ordinary, uneducated men surprised these leaders and they commanded him and the disciples never to speak about Jesus again, but Peter *(and John)* did not say okay and leave. Peter responded to them, **"whether it is right in the sight of God to listen to you more than to God, you judge. For we cannot but speak the things which we have seen and heard",** as he and the others went back. He was not intimidated and went back to fishing, instead, he went back to his brethren and they prayed mightily. They received a fresh infilling of the Holy Spirit and continued preaching with boldness, alongside the other believers; they shared their possession and there was not a needy person among them (Acts 4).

This mighty ministry was filled with persecution and imprisonment, but it was backed up with signs and wonders and it continued. By the time Peter was nearing the end of his life as Jesus had revealed to him, he said, "So I will work hard to make sure you always remember these things after I am gone" (2 Peter 1:14-15). This was somebody who was about to die, but he kept working hard for the Gospel, not for his benefit, but for the benefit of us, who continue to read his work and are being transformed daily. Like a good leader, Peter passed on the mantle before his departure, "Feed the flock of God" (1 Peter 5:2). While not recorded in the official Bible, research shows that he was martyred in AD 68, crucified upside down at his own request, because he did not feel worthy to be crucified as the One he loved. Peter, by the help of the Holy Spirit, finally proved his talk. Simon Peter, Son of Jonah, LOVED Jesus.

So, Christian, do we love God volitionally, more than the next person? Do we love Him personally, such that we will sacrifice all that we have for Him? Do we love Him without condition, despite the seasons of our lives, both the good and bad? Do we love Him by loving every other person around us?

In *Luke 10:25 - 37*, a religious lawyer was back at it, trying to capture Jesus in a religious web with crafty questions. He asked Jesus what to do to inherit eternal life. Jesus redirected his question back to him, asking what the provision of the Mosaic Law was. The lawyer responded likewise, to love God with *your heart, soul, strength and mind* and *love your neighbor as yourself.* He answered correctly and Jesus told him to go and do the same, however, the man was looking for a way to justify himself, so he asked Jesus, *who is my neighbor?* Jesus then told the known parable of "The Good Samaritan:"

A Jewish man on a journey to Jericho had been robbed, beaten and left for dead by bandits. Coincidentally, a priest (a version adds 'of the Great House of God') happened to be passing along that road, but when he saw this man lying in agony, he crossed to the other side of the road. Next, a Levite (a Temple assistant) came to the man, looked at him, crossed over to the other side, and continued his journey. Then a "despised' Samaritan," i.e., a foreigner, came along, saw the attacked man's condition and had compassion on him. He put his travel plans on hold, started nursing this Jew's wounds with wine and oil, put him on his donkey, and checked him into an inn to be taken care of. The Samaritan didn't stop there. He came back the next day, paid the innkeeper two silver coins (the equivalent of a full day's wage) for the previous day, and encouraged him to take care of the man as needed; he promised he was going to return to reimburse him for all extra expenses incurred. After Jesus told this parable, he finally asked the religious lawyer His own question, and this Jewish lawyer would not even call the man a Samaritan but simply replied, *He who showed him mercy.* Jesus told him to go and to the same to others.

Christian, where do we begin? This Jewish lawyer who was a religious "expert" will not even address the Samaritan by his identity. The best acknowledgement was *"he."* The Jews had a long-standing rift with the Samaritans, since long before the days of Nehemiah and the rebuilding of the Temple. However, ethnic rivalry was of no importance to Jesus who, in no Parable but in reality, asked a (i) **Samaritan,** then (ii) **a woman** to give Him water out of her dipper which she had drawn from a well that was accessible to all. (John 4:4-7) Jesus set this standard for Christians and He expects us to do the same toward all people. We must soberly, individually, internally, and truthfully consider if we love God, remembering that, "If someone says, "I love God," and hates his brother, he is a liar; for he who does not love his brother whom he has seen, how can he love God whom he has not seen?" (1 John 4:2)

Three-Way Love

GOD: Despite what we profess, to prove we truly possess love for God is determined by a simple test:

You that love the LORD, hate evil. Psalm 97:10

There is a two-part question to satisfy this test:

1. How do I FEEL about sin?

In myself: If we look at Peter's life, the way he felt about sin in himself was that it was not possible for him to sin by denying Jesus, even if the others did. Peter had the right attitude to sin. He saw it as something which was wrong and which he was never going to do. So how do we feel about sin in our lives? Do we outcry it, but secretly enjoy it in our lives like Potiphar's wife? Or is there a genuine holy antipathy toward it? It is either we cannot stand sin or we can. 1 John 5:1 says, **whoever is born of God does not sin.** Sin is the only chain that keeps anyone bound, despite how small it may seem (Galatians 3:22). If we have come into the love and freedom that Jesus gives, holiness is a simultaneous effect. Spurgeon says, *"Conscious enjoyment of our Lord's love is a delicate thing. It is far more sensitive to sin and holiness than mercury is to cold and heat."*

Holiness might seem like some unreasonably pious concept no human can achieve, but God who commanded us to be holy (Leviticus 11:45), cannot lie (Titus 1:2). He knows we can be holy. Again, Peter, who had been converted by the Holy Spirit, called us to be holy (1 Peter 1:15); so if Peter, our tutor for this cause, could come to holiness, we also can. Peter gave us the formula as converted Christians:

- **Prepare your minds for action:** Let your mind know that something is about to change. We are no more living that care-free, liberal, old way of life, we are now led by the Spirit of God. We must be self-controlled and listen to what the Holy Spirit tells us in every situation. We cannot make decisions off the top of our heads anymore. We are now under a new Rulership which will require a lot of "slowing down."

193

- **Put all your hope in the Revelation of Jesus:** Every single passing moment, we must always think about Jesus and His return, which will be as a thief comes unannounced in the night (Revelation 16:15). All our thoughts, words and action should always be viewed in the light of *"Will I go back with Jesus if He comes now?"* About that thing which may seem pleasurable for the moment, and which we imagine we might be able to ask for forgiveness after, we should be able to ask ourselves, "What if I don't get a chance to ask for forgiveness, whether from God or whether from another human?"

- **Lock up your old lifestyle:** Throw away the keys into hell fire where you have no intention of going back to retrieve. As Peter tells us, we have enjoyed the pagan life of drunkenness, sexual escapades, self-centeredness, idol and material worship, wild partying, and reckless living, enough! Yes, we must expect scorn and slander by our old friends, but we must encourage ourselves with the coming Judgement Day, which both parties will face (1 Peter 4:3-5). As we find the offerings of this world of no interest to us, we must also be found of no use to them, either. The break-up must be mutual (Galatians 6:14).

  If we say, we are now walking with Christ and loving Him, transformation is a non-negotiable effect. However, it is not just throwing off these weights, the categories of which are broken down in Chapter 1, but it is replacing them with something new, and that is being "anxious to do the will of God" (1 Peter 4:2).

- **Be sober:** To be sober does not mean to be sad. It simply champions placidity over excessive display of emotion. It is greeting "Good Morning," i.e., the morning is good *but* we are aware of and daily mourning for sin and leaning on God's mercies to comfort us (Matthew 5:4). The devil can attack us when we are overly excited and when we are overly downcast. We must learn to neutralize our feelings. If we are to be watchful of the roaring lion and his schemes, we must be alert. We cannot afford to throw our heads up in prolonged laughter and miss the flaming arrow or blur our vision with endless tears and again, miss the flaming arrow. To be sober *certainly* means not being drunk!

- **Pray:** This is the only way to remain sober. Soberness is not a natural human ability. It can only be achieved through prayer. When we are constantly praying, we can maintain balance. When we are excited, we must pray. When we are sad, we must pray. When we are neutral, we must pray. Besides, how can we bear lack of communication with a God whom we say we love over any period of time? Do we not give all our cares to Him who cares for us? Is it all asking? Do we not tell Him how incredible He is? Don't we tell Him we cannot wait to finally meet Him? Don't we tell Him how perfect He is? Don't we thank Him just because? Is He not the first thing on our mind when we wake up? Is He not on our minds throughout the day? Do we not kiss Him goodnight when we lay down to sleep? For David, the man after God's own heart, this is his record, *My heart says of you,* *"seek His face!"* Immediately he responded, "Your face, Lord I will seek" (Psalm 27:8). How do our hearts feel about seeking His face?

Spurgeon sums up holiness as, *"Tender of heart, careful in thought, lip and life to honor our Lord Jesus."*[190] It is personal conscientiousness and intentionality summed up, "Pure and undefiled religion before God and the Father is this: … to keep oneself unspotted from the world" (James 1:27). We must place every jot and tittle of our lives on a megaphone-enabled billboard; as it plays out for the world to see, we must determine if we will be able to face Jesus when He comes, or if we will shrink away in shame because we refused to abide in Him (1 John 2:28). Before Nathanael was officially made a disciple, as he walked toward Jesus, He said of him in the presence of others, "Behold, an Israelite indeed, in whom is no deceit!" (John 1:47) Other versions say, *"a man of complete integrity:" "not a false bone in his body;" "in whom there is no guile nor deceit nor duplicity."* Nathanael, who had been invited by Philip to see the promised Messiah, was reluctant because Philip had mentioned that Jesus was from Nazareth. Nathaniel had intentionally been keeping himself unspotted from the Nazarenes, so he exclaimed before following Philip, *Nazareth! … Can anything good come from Nazareth?*

However, he gave his close friend the benefit of the doubt and followed him. When Jesus made this public commendation of Nathanael, aka Bartholomew, he must have been embarrassed and blushed for a Nazarene to say such about him, but he knew this good testimony of himself was true. He didn't say, *"Me? Man of integrity? Oh, stop it! I am only human and trying my best."* He knew the intentional life he had lived so he asked Jesus, *How do You know me?* and Jesus said to him, "Before Philip called you, when you were under the fig tree, I saw you" (John 1:45-48).

Wow! The first time we are introduced to the fig tree in the Bible is when Adam and Eve used its leaves as garments for covering themselves

---

[190] C.H Spurgeon Morning & Evening Devotional).

(Genesis 3:7). However, this man was under the fig tree, what exactly he was doing, we are not told, but Jesus saw him there and knew him as a man of integrity. Whatever we do in secret, whatever is in our hearts, we can hide in our closets, guard it by passcodes, or deny it, but God who sees, knows them who are His – children of complete integrity.

In others: In the lives of others, how do we feel about sin? Are we indifferent, as long as *we* keep ourselves holy? When we hear that Christians have turned from the faith, does that move anything in our hearts? Are we genuinely concerned? In *2 Peter 2:7-8,* we see how Lot, a righteous man, felt about the sins of his people; he was, ***oppressed/vexed/distressed by the filthy conversation of the wicked*** and ***was a righteous man who was tormented in his soul from day to day with their unlawful deeds.*** Lot was a resident of Sodom and was restless, not just in his head but in his soul, about the sins of those around him. He was not indifferent about it; he was not comfortable about it. It greatly affected him. How do we feel about the depravity and immorality going on in our world, which has far surpassed what those destroyed cities could think of today? When we go on social media and we see the counsel of satan trending, and lewdness which is commonplace, are our hearts moved with pain? Are we restless in our souls or have we become either indifferent about it or so used to it, attributing it to the 'age' we live in and evolving, that even our devices themselves have become branches of Sodom and Gomorrah?

In Luke 19:41, Jesus was approaching Jerusalem, and even before He got there, just as He saw the city ahead, he began to weep, because the people had turned; they had rejected the way of peace, but it was too late, because their eyes had already been "shut." Have we ever wept for our generation, knowing that some have truly been abandoned by God, because He is a God of free will? Have we wept because He gave them over to their heart's desires of immorality, nakedness, pornography, fraud, homosexuality, selfishness, personal branding, pride, shameful displays of "riches?" Because God has abandoned them, they begin to say there is no God, even though God is coming in His justice for us all, and they encourage even Christians to join them (Romans 1:18-32).

What about our fellow Christians, who say they know God but deny even knowing the name of His Son, not to mention the cross of Calvary, by the way the dress? When we see a Bible verse completely taken out of a context and being used to back up demonic gospel, do we fall on our knees with tears? Are we distressed by the fact that two Christians cannot have a Bible-based conversation without one losing interest? Have our tummies turned, or have we thrown-up after sitting through a sermon and not once was the name of Jesus mentioned? How do we feel about the fact that most are not wise or farsighted, people despise prayers, curse words are regular language, most frighteningly, that people have no fear of God? (Romans 3:11-18)

2. How do I REACT to sin?

Liar! You who say you are a perfect Christian without any sin, you are a liar! That is exactly what the Bible calls you (1 John 1:8) .Not only are you a liar, you also are calling the God you say you love with your heart, soul and mind a liar (1 John 1:10). Not only that, you also are denying that Jesus Christ ever came to the world, or even if He did, His propitiation is a legend. You are a liar because you have freely signed your name as a volunteer for eternal damnation in hell.

While we remain in these burdensome, fleshly suits, we all have sinned and continually fall short of God's glorious standard (Romans 3:23). Peter, who was a "chief apostle," was not without sin, even after all those men he had been empowered to convert and the boldness of standing up to authorities. In Galatians 2:11-13, Peter was found guilty of "eye-service" in his ministry. Peter knew and believed that when people come to Christ, we are all one family, our only ethnicity is "heavenly." So when he, a Jew, went to Antioch, he ate freely with the uncircumcised Gentile Christians.

However, James sent more Jewish Christians to join him in the Gentile city, and as soon as they arrived, Peter turned his back on his lunchmates. He, as the Rock of the Church, stopped eating with them. Peter had influence, so if he had remained there, these newly arrived men who were not official disciples but just representatives of James, even if they had reservations, would have joined him. Peter did it the other way; he turned his back on his brothers and the other Jewish Christians, even Barnabas, followed his pattern of hypocrisy which was against everything the Gospel of Jesus provided for.

There are those who claim to love God but are really His enemies, separated from Him by their evil thoughts and actions (Colossians 1:21). They comfortably and continually fellowship with the forces and friends of darkness; they are known in such circles and are heartily welcomed; they have built habits in which they regularly engage and enjoy with others or by themselves under their sheets; they are also liars (1 John 1:6); and yet to come to Christ. You can deceive your congregation, delude your co-workers, double-cross your spouse, hoodwink your family, and even fool yourself BUT don't be misled, child of Adam, you cannot mock the justice of God. As you plant satisfaction into your sinful, despicable desires, you will harvest decay and death (Galatians 6:7-8).

How do those who love God with their heart, soul and mind, those known by Him, (1 Corinthians 8:3) react when they have done the very thing the One they love hates; those who have genuinely sinned?

By Myself

*For we do not have a High Priest who cannot sympathize with our weaknesses, but was in all points tempted as we are...*Hebrews **4:15**

The story was told of a popular evangelistic preacher of the 20th Century who turned away from the Faith for about 25 years and met with Billy Graham toward the end of his life. The revivalist asked the preacher how he felt about God, now that his time was almost up, and the man's response was, *"I miss Him."* We never have to "miss" God. Do you turn away from a spouse after you hurt them? Do you pack up and leave, thereby punishing yourself for 25 years because your heart truly longs for that person? Sin has the immense ability to render the heart of a beloved child of God heavy, sad, and ashamed, but this is a tactic of satan. 1 John 3:20 tells us that if our hearts or feelings condemn us, God is greater than our hearts and He knows all things. The love He has for us is perfect in that it casts out all fear, so when we feel afraid of approaching God for punishment of sin, we are yet to know and believe God's boundless love (1 John 4:18). If for God's justice, we are punished for our sin, it is only an expression of His love for His children and we should endure it with hope, as only bastards are not chastised for wrongdoing (Hebrews 12:6-8).

Several times in His word, God tells us that He is not man, does not think like man, does not take counsel from man, and does not consider time as man does. In his classic, *"The Knowledge of The Holy,"* A.W Tozer says, the most insidious and deadly type of heresy is the sort of idolatry where we believe God to be different from who He truly is. If we attribute God's reaction to our sin the way we would have treated someone who offended us, or the way those we know, maybe earthly parents, have treated us when we offended them, we are leaning towards heresy and adding more insult to injury. In **Psalm 51:17**, we are assured that a broken and contrite heart, the Lord will never reject. He says if the wicked repent, He will forgive and heal their land. Jonah, with his manly heart, was ready to die than to see Nineveh forgiven.

God who sent Him to warn them of their destruction, said He had no desire

198

for even one of them to perish, but Jonah was depressed at the mercy of God. Again, when Peter struck the ear of Malchus at the Garden of Gethsemane, Jesus rebuked Peter who saw this as a way of defending his Master. God forgives sins and forgets. Man, in their nature, will torment you with your sin for the rest of your life. He turns our crimson to snow white and this is why He made this proviso known to us in *Ephesians 3:17*, that there is forgiveness of sins for His own children, whom He has accepted through the blood of Jesus, according to the riches of His grace. He knows how and indeed loves to forgive His children. It is only one who understands this that can say, even after committing the most heinous crime, "I am in great distress. Please let us fall into the hand of the LORD, for His mercies are great; but do not let me fall into the hand of man" (2 Samuel 24:14). Would we rather know God or man? Let God be true and every man a liar.

Let us examine our reaction when we sin:

- Do we, like this once powerful man of God, runaway for years and torture our hearts by missing the fellowship of God? Do we leave the church? 1 John 2:18-19 tells us that only an antichrist will leave the church and was never, in the first place, really God's own. Our salvation is proven only during such times as these. True and feigned salvation is distinguished when we really need to call on that salvation and we say we have.

- Do we, like Adam and Eve, hide and cover ourselves with fig leaves, perhaps so God will not see us? Even if we opted to go to hell and make our beds there, condemning ourselves that we have no hope of redemption, we will meet God there (Psalm 139:8). Once we have been adopted into the family of God, there is no escaping His Spirit. Our thoughts, movements, travels, resting, words, everything is known by God, even before we say or do it. He goes before and follows after us. David described this mystery thus, "such knowledge is too wonderful for me; It is high, I cannot attain it" (Psalm 139:6). It is futile to play hide and seek with the Owner of the four corners of the earth and the Creator of light and darkness, peace and calamity, good and evil (Isaiah 45:7). We shouldn't bother embarking on an already lost battle.

- Do we, like Ananias and Saphira, deny it? This one is particularly dangerous. This couple connived to lie to whom they thought was flesh and blood. Peter had lied about knowing Jesus, so they probably thought it was okay for them to lie to Peter, but it was not Peter they were lying to; it was the Holy Spirit. We must know that whenever we lie, we have said yes to satan. We have formally asked him to be our father. Running away from church or hiding are some-what childish acts, which some discipline and shaking up could solve; to lie about sin is to consent to being in the family of satan. It is to bow down to satan.

Spurgeon perfectly states, *"Hidden, unfelt, unconfessed iniquity is the true leprosy, but when sin is seen and felt it has received its death blow, and the Lord looks with eyes of mercy upon the soul afflicted with it."* Christian, we must learn from the ultimate man after God's heart, David. As Prophet Nathan confronted him about his sin, *immediately*, David began to weep. He knew exactly Whom he had sinned against. His hands had murdered Uriah, but the sin was against God. He penned the *Miserere* from the broken heart of a lover. Peter *immediately* wept bitterly. The Prodigal Son came back to his senses and *immediately* went back to his loving Father's arms to be a slave.

> *If we confess our sins, He is faithful and just to forgive us our sins and to cleanse us from all unrighteousness.* 1 John 1:9

When we confess sin, we have struck a defeating blow to satan. We have broken chains tying us up. We have lifted a huge burden from our hearts. We have opened our eyes. We have found ourselves. We have humbled ourselves before God, who Himself will restore us to even greater fortune. Denial, which is really pride disguised, is another trademark owned by satan's corpo-ration. To hide sin is to run when no one is pursuing. It is signing up for a job that we are not trained to do.

David's heart posture was, "I acknowledged my sin unto thee, and mine in-iquity have I not hid. I said, I will confess my transgressions unto the Lord; and thou forgavest the iniquity of my sin." (Psalm 32:5) When we make God our Friend, Father, Lover and All-in-All, it becomes a reflex action to imme-diately confess and deal with sin. God and David's hearts were so intertwined with inseparable love for each other that God gave David punishment op-tions to pick from when he sinned and David, knowing his Lover, chose to fall into his Lover's wrath. God then sent His angel of death to kill about 70,000 Israelites but not David. He came back to God to ask why he, David, who had sinned, was not being punished alongside his family but innocent people. God then offered him a "slap on the wrist" punishment by asking him to build an altar. David built this altar, offered offerings and he was forgiven. (2 Samuel 24)

We also see in Peter, after having had denied Jesus, just three days after, when he was told that Jesus' body was missing, he was the first amongst the disci-ples to run to the tomb. He was also the first disciple who stepped into the tomb to check if Jesus' body was really missing (John 20:1-7). He had no fear of rejection after denying Jesus, because Jesus had told him in advance that He had prayed for him over his betrayal (Luke 22:32). Jesus also showed that He loved Peter and there were no hard feelings after the denial by giving him another miracle of catching 153 large fish after the resurrection (John 21:1-10). Like such displayed between David and God, or Jesus and Peter, we must strive to adopt such models of intense, sealed, and perfect love between God and man.

Whether we are like the publican who stood afar, would not look up, but beat his chest pleading for mercy, or like our Elder Brother, Jesus, who boldly cried out to our Father, *"why have You forsaken me?"* Matthew 27:46, we must never fall to the devil's tactic of covering sin. This is also bringing to remembrance that God is just, so if after weeping, fasting, and pleading with God for mercy, we are told on the 7th day, that the child is dead, we are to get up from the ground, wash ourselves, put on lotion, and change our clothes, after which we go into the Lord's House, worship Him for *still* being the God we know Him to be, and then we return home, eat and expectantly wait for the arrival of our Solomon. (2 Samuel 12)

> *Now no chastening seems to be joyful for the present, but painful; nevertheless, afterward it yields the peaceable fruit of righteousness to those who have been trained by it. Therefore, strengthen the hands which hang down, and the feeble knees, and make straight paths for your feet, so that what is lame may not be dislocated, but rather be healed.* Hebrews 12:11-13

When we are confronted by other Christians for our sin, how do we react? Do we plead the *"only God can judge me"* defense under the falsehood of being "free," displaying the very conceit we are warned against in *Galatians 5:26?* When "least disciple," Paul, publicly rebuked "Chief disciple," Peter for his hypocrisy, there is no record that Peter, who was very outspoken and could stand up to *any* authority, rejected the authority of Paul, *"the murderer of Christians,"* who was confronting him (Galatians 2:11-16). Do we feel nobody who has not been saved as long as we have been, or possesses the Spiritual gifts which we do, nor has performed the miracles God has empowered us to perform, has any right to correct us?

Most important, how do we handle the aftermath of our sin? David shows us in Psalm 51:13 that we are to "teach transgressors thy ways and sinners shall be converted unto thee." Jesus told Peter also in Luke 22:32, "when thou art converted, strengthen thy brethren." We must never be ashamed of sin from which God has delivered us. The essence is that we were chosen before we were even born to show forth the praises of Him who called us out of darkness into His marvelous light (1 Peter 2:9). We must share our testimonies freely, through which we defeat satan[191] and cause people to glorify God for His saving grace in our lives. The Cross of Jesus Christ is boast-worthy (Galatians 6:14). When God, in Acts 9: 10 – 15, told Ananias to go and meet Paul after his conversion on his way to Damascus, Ananias was wary of meeting Paul, because he had heard about the evil Paul had done in his past life. Yet God vindicated Paul and commanded Ananias to go, because Paul had been chosen, even before he was born, to spread the Good News, which was not going to be without his own trials. Paul also was destined to suffer pain for the name of Jesus and truly, Paul said, "I bear in my body the marks of the Lord Jesus" (Galatian 6:17). In the places he went, he introduced himself with his past identity and how God had saved him. He constantly warned us to flee the works of the flesh, to which he had enslaved himself before coming to Christ and to pursue righteousness and godliness.

Peter also showed forth God's glory by warning us against the very things he did: Speaking against denying Jesus in the face of suffering he said, "if any man suffer as a Christian, let him not be ashamed;" (1 Peter 4:16) second, speaking against hypocrisy, he said, "rid yourselves of…hypocrisies;" (1 Peter 2:1) third, speaking against misleading weaker Christians by our actions he called it the way of false prophets who are under God's curse when they, "delight in deception even as they eat with you in your fellowship meals…lure unstable people into sin" (2 Peter 2:13-14); and told elders how to lead "but being examples to the flock" (1 Peter 5:3).

He had learned from his own experience the sensitivity of the role of leadership and was not ashamed of his error by warning against it. That is whole-hearted repentance. We must be proud of God's power in our lives, and strengthen others entangled in sins from which we have been freed. Everything we have been through, *even our sins*, have a purpose, so we must manifest the mercies of the Miracle Manufacturer, who turned our messes into a message for the masses. The race will certainly not be as ardent for the "good" ones as it is for us, wretches, who stand in front of a mirror and marvel at the wonder of being saved by Amazing Grace! *Thank You, Jesus!*

---

[191] Revelation 12:111.

By Others

How do we react to the sins of others? Do we look away? Join the bandwagon of gossip?

First, for those who are not Christians, we must pray for them. Jesus, on the Cross, gave us this humbling example when He was soaked in His blood, sweat, and tears and looked down from that Cross of Calvary at our faces as we insulted, spited, rejected, and left Him for dead. Yet at that moment, He said, "Father, forgive them, for they do not know what they do" (Luke 23:34). Again, Stephen, as he was being stoned to death, prayed for his murderers just before he died, saying, "Lord, do not charge them with this sin" (Acts 7:60). It so happened that unconverted Paul, aka Saul of Tarsus, was an important figure in that murder and benefited from Stephen's intercession of forgiveness, and shortly after, met Jesus himself.

We must understand that sinners are doing what they are bound to do by nature before experiencing new birth. Being born of a woman renders one a sinner (Romans 5:16; Ephesians 2:3). There is nothing abnormal about sin to such people; they might feel a certain emptiness if they do not sin. In his autobiography, *"Confessions."* Augustine described his relationship with sin when he recalled an incident in which he and his friends stole fruit from someone's garden, not because he was hungry, but because *"it was not permitted...It was foul, and I loved it. I loved my own error—not that for which I erred, but the error itself."* Sin was his way of life and delight. The very fact he did things that were wrong made it right to him. How did his mother, Monica, a devout Christian, married *(by the arrangement of her parents)* to a violent pagan and serial adulterer, handle the lifestyle of her son? She prayed earnestly for her son and reputedly wept every night over him. She was consoled by a bishop who assured her, *"The child of those tears shall never perish."* Shortly before she died, she told her now converted son, who would eventually be venerated as a saint, *"Son nothing in this world now affords me delight. I do not know that there is now left for me to do or why I am still here, all my hopes in this world being now fulfilled."* Her purpose in life was to pray until her son came to Christ. The current Californian city Santa Monica is named after her and in there resides a spring called, "The Tears of Santa Monica," to commemorate the sacrifice of tears that this Christian mother offered over her son.

Not only did her son become one of the most influential theologians of Christianity, but her unbelieving husband came to Christ a year before his death. Is the power of a mother's prayers over erring children only effective in past times? No, the Christian mother of the writer of these words you now read will give you a heart-wrenching account of how her once-degenerate daughter, Eunice became Eunice-Pauline over her day-by-day, year-by-year. *and still ongoing,* tearful, unrelenting importunities before God.

With Christians who sin, our reaction should be based on two categories: Those within our sphere of influence, and those outside our sphere of influence.

> *If anyone sees his fellow Christian committing a sin not resulting in death, he should ask, and God will grant life to the person who commits a sin not resulting in death.* 1 John 5:16

Regarding believers outside our sphere of influence, we must pray for them. This we have an obligation to do. We might not be able to reach out to them directly, supposing we are in different locations, or speak different earthly languages, but God, who knows all men's hearts, will hear us. If Jesus is alive and constantly interceding for us from His throne forever (Hebrews 7:25), we must do the same for our brethren. When we hear about genuine children of God who have fallen into sin, especially church leaders, we must consider them by putting ourselves into their shoes and genuinely praying for God to restore them to life. He will hear us. For those who still parade themselves as Christians, but even to pagans live questionable and antichrist lifestyles, we must note that Hebrews 10:26 tells us, "If we deliberately go on sinning after we have received the knowledge of the truth, no further sacrifice for sins remains."

How do we react to sins of Christians within our sphere of influence?

> *If another believer is overcome by some sin, you who are godly should gently and humbly help that person back onto the right path...Share each other's burdens, and in this way obey the law of Christ.* Galatians 6:1-2

Even when it hurts to correct the person, when it appears that it might be rather harsh to do so, depending on the intensity of sin, as long as our correction is from a sincere heart and with love, we must correct them. In 2 Corinthians 7:8-10, Paul expressed his initial regret at the seemingly harsh tone of his letter to the Corinthians, but realized it was worth it, because it produced godly sorrow in them; that led to their repentance and eventual apology to him (v.7). Besides, the sorts of sins that were going on in their church, including sexual immorality, suing one another, spiritual pride, etc., would be heart-breaking for anyone who genuinely cared about the salvation of souls.

Thousands of years later, we are still benefitting from these letters. Lessons such as "bad company corrupts good manners;" we should "not be unequally yoked with unbelievers;" we should "flee sexual immorality;" and the true characteristics of love, spiritual gifts and their uses amongst others, are some of the invaluable lessons we have had the opportunity to learn through Paul's "harsh" tone to erring believers. He gives us insight into how he felt when he penned the words, "I wrote that letter in great anguish, with a troubled heart and many tears. I didn't want to grieve you but I wanted to let you know how much love I have for you." (2 Corinthians 2:4)

Wounds from a friend can be trusted, but an enemy multiplies kisses. Proverbs 27:6

We must remember that we are not God; we cannot do His work of salvation on His behalf. The latter part of Galatians 6:1 reads "and be careful not to fall into the same temptation yourself." Nehemiah, when he returned to Jerusalem to find not a one-off of sins, but a track-record and evidence of delightfulness in disobeying God; intermarriage with pagans *(failing to learn from Solomon's mistake in this regard)*; an abuse of His Temple and exploitation of the welfare of the Temple workers, after laborious dedication to the rebuilding of the Temple, handled different categories of people according to their ability: The Levites he restored, after they purified themselves; those who had married pagans, he cursed, beat, pulled out their hair, and made them swear that their children would not repeat their mistake. High Priest Eliashib, his grandson, who had married a pagan woman and who ought to have been in charge of the affairs in Nehemiah's absence, was the very person who encouraged these acts by leasing a room in the Temple to Tobiah (a forbidden Ammonite). Nehemiah completely banished him from the Temple for his treachery (Nehemiah 13). To whom much is given, much is expected.

After Moses dealt with the Israelites for their idolatry, he went before God and put himself on the line for his people, "Yet now, if thou wilt forgive their sin, and if not, blot me, I pray thee, out of thy book which thou hast written." (Exodus 32:32)

As stated, Nehemiah tactfully handled different people who were all in his sphere of influence according to the kind of sin and their position, and these found him favorable in God's sight, according to His prayer. Moses also handled his people then went before God in prayer, and God repented of His initial plan of destroying His people. However, to not make any attempt to help, to cut ourselves off from Christians who sin, to torment another over their sin, to be too busy to carry another's burden, Paul addresses, "If you think you are too important to help someone, you are only fooling yourself. You are not that important." (Galatians 6:3)

Ultimately, when God's forgives sin, it is not a pass for abuse of His grace. We must soberly recall this warning from the lover of God himself, "There is forgiveness with Thee that Thou may be feared;" (Psalm 130:4) to **fear** the One in whose hands it is a terrible thing to fall; (Hebrews 10:31); yet, chooses to lavish us with the rich mercies of His forgiveness. We fear Him *and* sin no more.

Love of Self: Jesus commands us to love our neighbors as we love ourselves, so to effectively love *Him* by keeping this commandment, we should establish *how* we are to love ourselves. We must do this by considering whether the "love of self" is the same idea as the trendy, worldly, common notion of "self-love." The default conclusion of this is, if the 21st Century social media concept of self-love is anything to go by, that command will be a terror to the "self-loving" person.

The "self-loving" person cannot love another person. Their god is themselves. They see no other, hear no other, and account to no other. *Deny what?* Deny the beautiful piece of *(fading dust)* art they consider themselves to be? *Joke!* Deny themselves anything their eyes desire when it is *their* money for which *they* worked hard? *Impossible!* Deny their need to show-off their perfectly curated closets of the best, most expensive, and most exclusive items in the world? *Unthinkable!* Deny themselves the best meals from which their gold-plated toilets will benefit in a few hours? *Impracticable!* Deny themselves their personal brand's standard by sharing the Message of the Gospel of Christ, which is "not what the public wants to hear" and could injure their brand? *Unbankable!*

The love of self to which Jesus referred is summed up in the Golden Rule: "Do unto others as you will have others do unto you." This is simply the way we carry ourselves, the way we work, the way we speak, the way we react, the way we listen, the way we give, the way we offend etc. all, as if it was someone else that was interacting with us, working for us, speaking to us, listening to us, reacting to us, giving to us, offended by us, etc. In essence, it is how we live day after day, our conduct, which matters above all. Just as we can identify a tree by the fruits it produces, we identify people by their actions. (Matthew 7:20) We are what we *do*, not who we *say* we are.

With tears in his eyes, Paul wrote:

> *...there are many whose conduct shows they are really enemies of the cross of Christ.* Philippians 3:18

We may well declare something, but our conduct will either corroborate what we profess or condemn it. There is a story about a manager in a company who took the blame for another staff-member who was well-trained for the job at which she had committed a fatal error. During the board meeting, they called up the lady who could potentially lose her job due to this error. The manager took the blame, completely absolving her of all fault and liability. After the meeting, she went into his office to ask why he did that; it made "no sense." He wouldn't answer her, but the lady, who was not a believer, kept pressing. Finally, he said, *"This is the only time I will say this: I am a Christian."*

We do not need to go about saying we are Christian, our works, manner of speech, and conduct do the professing. We cannot possibly list the way every individual should live every second of their lives, such as how much toothpaste they should use to brush their teeth, how a man should cut his hair, or how many footsteps a woman should walk every day. However, there are principles which, whether we apply them to walking, bathing, making our beds, peeling carrots, or responding to an email that ensures we do not deny the Cross we believe in:

Conscientiously: Do EVERYTHING out of "love from a pure heart, from a good conscience, and from sincere faith." (1 Timothy 1:5) This is where we separate cattle from cattle. Only root, motive, and reason should guide our actions. God has made every food clean; there is absolutely nothing in this world a Christian is forbidden to eat because the "earth is the Lord's and everything in it" (1 Corinthians 10:26). However, Paul went on to warn that if, as a believer, you are invited to the house of an unbeliever to eat, you can eat anything, but if you are offered meat which they have "graciously" told you has been offered to idols, do not eat it, even if your conscience has nothing against it, but for the conscience of the other person (1 Corinthians 10:27-33).

This is how delicate and important conscience is to God, whether ours or that of another. Everything we do must be, *"to the glory of God."*[192] Now do we say, "I am being selfish", "ignoring the needs of another", or "killing somebody" (as some have done), to the glory of God? Paul, who went about killing Christians in "good conscience" and for "God's glory," before he came to the knowledge of truth testified, "don't be concerned for your own good but for the good of others" (1 Corinthians 10:24). Is it good for the other person? Does it bring glory to God? Do it!

> For our boasting is this: the testimony of our conscience that we conducted ourselves in the world in simplicity and godly sincerity, not with fleshly wisdom but by the grace of God, and more abundantly toward you. 2 Corinthians 1:12

What does our conscience testify about us? Most important, how do we build

---

[192] 1 Corinthians 10:31.

conscience? Without the Holy Spirit guiding our actions through God's Words, we are moralists, legalists, or conformists ready to be tossed around by every passing trend. A good conscience toward God brings peace. A good conscience toward God brings satisfaction and hope.

Diligence: This watchword appears repeatedly in the Bible. In keeping God's commands (Deuteronomy 6:17); in doing our business if we expect to rise to the top (Proverbs 22:29); guarding our hearts (Proverbs 4:23); twice in 2 Timothy 4, where, in the space of a verse, Paul repeatedly told Timothy to be diligent in coming to him (21&23); in leadership (Romans 12:8); *in a rather frightening one,* making sure that God has called us as His own (2 Peter 1:10); and in many other places of Scripture.

Diligence is a distinguishing principle guiding a Christian's conduct. Diligence is consistency, patience, and whole-hearted endeavor. From the mundane things, like home cleaning, to regular things, like our jobs or managing calendars to acknowledge important dates in people's lives year after year, to the one eternal: carrying out our calling as Christians, diligence is not getting lazy in order to inherit the promise of salvation (Hebrews 6:11). We are to grow in diligence (2 Corinthians 8:7). David found favor with Saul and all the people, including servants, because he "went out whithersoever Saul sent him and behaved himself wisely" (1 Samuel 18:5). How diligent are we in building our lives, whether or not there is foreseeable profit attached to it? In **Daniel 1:4,** after King Nebuchadnezzar had captured some men from Judah, he ordered his chief of staff to select only strong and healthy men who were versed in *every* branch of learning and gifted with knowledge and good judgment to serve in the royal palace. There was a precondition for selection, and that was the personal work that each man had done on themselves; those who had dogmatically built themselves up in every branch of learning, not just in their educational field, and after they selected them, they were going to be trained again in the Babylonian culture. We cannot sit back until there is some opportunity before we realize that we need to work on ourselves.

Opportunity meets preparation. Despite the work these young men had already put into themselves, they were still going to be trained. We should be diligent in building up ourselves daily. Ordinarily, people decide to become diligent when they see a short-term personal benefit, such as losing weight before a big event, writing an exam, or even in courtship. When we know that there is certainly something we see coming out of the need to be diligent, the fit body, the excellent result which might open career doors, the marriage, we give it our all. But as a Christian, we are to be diligent in all things, in season and out of season, especially in seeking God, because His reward is for those who **diligently** seek Him (Hebrews 11:6). This means when we are waiting on Him for a specific thing, it does not affect our relationship with Him; we are still worshipping, studying, praying and on the other hand, when we have things "going" for us, we are still who we are with Him, "Lest I be full and deny You, And say, 'Who is the LORD?' Or lest I be poor and steal, and profane the name of my God" (Proverbs 30:9). Whether poor, whether rich, we remain consistent with Him. This builds trust with us in other people too, when they know that we will show up in season and out of season, finish the good we start, and do so wholeheartedly. Diligence is the parent of excellence, and when coupled with care, it is the producer of virtue.

Discipline: In such times as we live in, where the world dictates how we spend our time, tells us we *must* have social media profiles on every platform, and considers us abnormal if we do not, discipline is of utmost importance to every Christian. Without discipline, there can be no diligence. So many things are competing for our time and hearts, and without casting blows to our bodies and bringing it under subjection to our authority, we become zombies, ruled by our senses. The common discipline every Christian should engage in should be starting each day with prayer and Bible study. This should be a delight, not a burden for any child of God, and alongside giving to others, the only things that should be done by "default" for any Christian. Every other thing needs to be thought through. Have we learned to discern? Do we know when to say yes and when to say no, not just to other people but also to our stomachs, our tongues, and our eyes? How do we spend each day? Do we filter what entertains us? What are our daily "rituals"? How do we manage time? Do we "hate" the same "early mornings," in which Jesus rose up to pray? When do we fast personally? What spiritual disciplines do we engage in to build our spiritual stamina?

Of these things called devices: phones, tablets, laptops, television, games etc., do we realize their power? Hours on end scrolling away our lives? Look at all *that* time we spend with them, only feeling empty and a notch "un-smarter" each time. This is why we will hardly ever be greater than history, especially intellectually. It is almost impossible to imagine any individual, currently living or yet to live, who will ever outsmart or outthink the great people of history. In the past, all they had was their brain, so they had no other choice but to use it. Forced to apply it, they came up with many great and lasting inventions, theories, books, films, philosophies, and more.

Today, the average brain is redundant. Intelligent and fruitful conversations are non-existent; people with absolutely no credibility, wisdom or shame figure out how to navigate the internet, are considered influencers, and go on to influence naïve minds into destruction. If we must be addicted to anything outside our Bibles, it should be books, intentionally selected books. Apostle

Paul asked for his books and especially his parchments (2 Timothy 4:13). Reading is endorsed in the Word of God, "give thyself to reading" (1 Timothy 4:13); despite that, Ecclesiastes 12:12 says "excessive devotion to books is wearying…"

What does moderation mean to us, regarding portions of our food, how we spend money, how we dress? Is eating a default activity for us, daily remembering that "if any would not work neither should he eat" 2 Thessalonians 3:10? What about our personal hygiene? What is the state of our "secret places"? Without intentional discipline in these regards, we will never get it done, because technology in all its existence will not absolve us of the responsibility to keep ourselves and the places we live and work clean. God, in His holiness, commands perfect cleanliness within ourselves *and* our surroundings (Deuteronomy 23:14). Without discipline, it will be impossible to embark on spiritual exercises that kill the flesh or yield to the Holy Spirit's promptings. *"The excellence of a free mind is gained through prayer rather than by study,"* writes Thomas á Kempis in *Imitations of Christ.*

Timeliness: "Redeeming the time because the days are evil. Wherefore be ye not unwise but understand what the will of the Lord is." (Ephesians 5:16-17) *"It feels like only yesterday when…"* is a statement usually made when referring to an event which happened in time gone by. Time goes by faster than our watches tell us. When a baby is born, the speed at which their face changes and they develop habits is usually surprising to those around the baby. This is a function of time and how we spend our time is paramount. What satisfaction do we feel at the end of each day when we see that we have been productive with our gifts? In a world of influencers, if we do not know what God has planned for each individual, we will search for whatever is popular and embark on it. The sense of individual purpose is mostly lacking, because parents, friends, and artificial intelligence is what people rely on to decide what they should do with their gifts. We will never find fulfilling purpose outside God and His word. The One who created us knows what it is that we will do that will bring Him glory and bring satisfaction to our hearts. The days are too evil, too fleeting, too short, to try our hands at what he have *not* been called to do. Also, it is unfortunate that keeping to and managing time is still impossible for some. Discipline eradicates clumsiness. Once we can account for every hour of our day, we will lead better lives.

Integrity: "Private and public life": The very destruction of the great society once looked up to. Listen Christian, we have no private and public life. David said, "I will give heed to the blameless way. When will You come to me? *I will walk within my house in the integrity of my heart*" (Psalm 101:2). If anything, our private lives should be a pleasant surprise to all. *"Oh I didn't* *know you read so many books;"* or *"I didn't know you were so organized,'"* sounds better than, *"I cannot believe he was capable of such a thing, he seemed so gentle;"* or *"I couldn't believe the things I saw on their phone."* Will our search and browsing history be a disgrace? We say it is wrong to steal, commit adultery and condemn idolatry, but do we do them?[193] Are we trustworthy with resources? "For we are taking pains to do what is right, not only in the eyes of the Lord but also in the eyes of man." (2 Corinthians 8:21) We must go out of our way to prove our integrity. *"I don't have to prove anything to anyone,"* is quite the foolish statement. We *do* have something to prove and that is character. "You know how Timothy had proved himself…" (Philippians 2:22)

Saying, *"God knows the truth,"* also is foolish when it is in our hands to show the truth. Even to God, we are told to study, to show ourselves approved. In picture perfect 21st Century, we *certainly* have something to prove, beyond all that paint on faces, material items, and filters. Paul was handling the offerings that had been gathered by the Corinthian church when he made that statement. He took every precaution to ensure that he was found blameless in the trust given to him. Also, in **Acts 16:1-3,** Paul went out of convenience and necessity to circumcise Timothy, who was an already grown and reputable man, but before his ministry began, he took pains to "unspot" Timothy before the Jews.

Of course, circumcision is of no effect to God, neither does it account for 0.1% toward our salvation, but for the sake of Jewish men, he became a Jew. We must go out of our way to present ourselves spotless, blameless, and faultless before God and man, in every way that is outside sin. Nathanael did not know he was being watched under the fig tree. We must conduct ourselves always knowing that we are being played on the big screens in Heaven and will one day be shown on the big screens on earth. Nothing is hidden under the sun that will not be made known. It is only a matter of time. What will we do for money? If we must use passcodes on our devices, it should be because of willingness, not a matter of necessity. If we have to think twice before another person can use such private things that belong to us, for fear that something potentially damaging to our public image might be found, we only fool ourselves. Time *will* catch you unannounced. Pilate turned to the leading priests and to the crowd and said, "I find nothing wrong with this man" (Luke 23:4). When we are assessed, what will be found wrong with us?

We live in such a way that no one will find fault with our ministry. 2 Corinthians 6:3

---

[193] (Romans 2:20-22).

211

Accountability: "Tychicus, a beloved brother, faithful minister, and fellow servant in the Lord, will tell you all the news about me" Colossians 4:7. Who can tell the world all the news about us? Who knows us? Who will put their name and reputation on the line for us? Who will beat their chest about us? Who *knows* us? Integrity and accountability belong to the same family. When we have built accountability with genuine Christians over time, on the day when our integrity is beckoned, we are a name away: "If anyone asks about Titus, say that he is my partner who works with me…" (2 Corinthians 8:23). Also, are we credible enough that when anyone is said to be associated with us, they can be at rest? Paul knew the weight and trust his name carried, so Titus was heartily welcome in Corinth. In positions of trust, to whom are we accountable? With the offerings the Corinthians had generously gathered for the Jerusalem Church, Paul travelled with Titus and another brother who was known by the Churches "to guard against any criticism for the way we are handling this generous gift. For we have regard for what is honorable, not only in the sight of the Lord, but also in the sight of men" (2 Corinthians 8:20-21). After taking these steps, he put it in a letter in order for the Church to be in the loop of all their activities. Even when we are doing the right thing, we must keep honorable persons in the loop, for the sake of transparency. We must work for our hearts to be as clear as glass.

Discretion: Oh, sad generation of social media, you hide what should be exposed and expose what should be hidden; "do not let your left hand know what your right hand is doing, that your charitable deed may be in secret; and your Father who sees in secret will Himself reward you openly" (Matthew 6:3-4). We must keep our senses under the subjection of God's Word when our itchy fingers and uncontrollable tongues want to announce the charity we do. What really is there to make known? Is it so unusual to us that we must announce the strange good we do? Let us learn from Jesus, "then He commanded them that they should tell no one…" (Mark 7:36) This was His heart's position. Regarding anything that could give Him favor before man, His default stance was to keep it secret. While people were rejoicing over miracles He did, He slipped away.

Of course, we cannot help it if people go ahead and proclaim what we have done, "…the more He commanded them, the more widely they proclaimed it" (Mark 7:37). If for any reason we are found out, first we must never take to heart whatever commendation people say, because in a wink, man will turn against us, but most important, it is an opportunity to give glory to God and never self (Psalm 29:2), and boast about the Good News of Jesus (2

Corinthians 10:17). If we desire commendation, let it be from God.[194]

Heartily: "…as unto the Lord and not unto men" (Colossians 3:23). This is not going about smiling in an evil world. This is a heart's position. Those who presumptuously judge the next person because they *don't smile*, should desire a greater cause to fight for. If we went about thinking only those who smiled with their lips were those right in heart, unfortunately, such naivety would cost us. Could satan have been frowning when he spoke to Eve in the garden? Could Jesus have hated those people He whipped in the temple? Would we sell our souls for a smile? Where in the Bible are we told to smile? The case here is not to go about frowning, or with a mean look, because that is against the basic requirements of social courtesy; the Bible tells us to live in peace with all men, but whatever we do, we should position our hearts as, *"Thank You, Lord, that I am able to do this. I pray that I do this in a way that pleases You,"* rather than smiling when we know we are cursing people in our hearts. Our duty is to ensure that what our hands find to do, despite who has employed us, we should keep God as our Employer and work as if He is the One directly managing us. We must stop promoting artificiality. A straight face with a heart somersaulting with joy in the Lord is better than smiling lips communing with the devil in heart. An insult from an enemy is better than a friendly bear hug.

Minding your own business: "If I will that he remains till I come, what is that to you? You follow me" (John 21:22). Jesus was in serious discourse with Peter, asking whether he loved Him and giving him his earthly assignment, as His ascension was imminent. He had just predicted to Peter the manner of death by which he was going to leave this world, and Peter, being Peter, in all that he had just heard, was more concerned about how John was going to die. We fail to appreciate the freedom that history has given us in our generation. Our free movement, free speech, free association which we abuse today, did not come about as a birth-right. Thank God we see in Scripture how even God Himself, will not let just anybody approach Him. Even His close friend Moses could not see God face to face. Thank God for Jesus; He has given us freedom; thank God for the men and women of history who gave their lives, many of them so brief, for us; we are truly free. Christian, we must be wise. The race is too delicate to take our eyes off Jesus for one second.

Technology has worsened this fact, due to its easy accessibility by all and sundry. We will be wise to learn from Peter, whose faith started failing and he began to sink when He took his eyes off Jesus. When we cease to focus

---

[194] 2 Corinthians 10:18.

on the race set before us, when we begin to meddle with civilian affairs, it won't be long before we find ourselves becoming lukewarm in our faith. If it has nothing to do with building our faith, if it is not something God has commanded us to do, such as praying for sinners, if it is not bearing fruit for the Kingdom, if it is not casting a blow to our body, we should stay away from it. Meddlers are fools (Proverbs 20:3). Remove the log in your eye before the speck in another's eye. Social media is a curse in this regard, with its "comment" option. Who are we to comment? We must avoid needless curiosity. Are we going to answer for anyone or give account for only ourselves?

Some may disguise prying by making enquiry about Christianity. Always learning and never able to come to the knowledge of truth,[195] *"Is it a sin if...?"* *"What if I mix it with juice"' "Is gambling bad?" "How far should we go?"* The narrow-minded path of Christianity is widened in our lives, as we begin to listen to old wives' fables and tell-tales of cunning men. Everything we need to know about God, His ways, His requirement, *is* in His Word. The rest He will reveal if He so desires.

Minding our business also includes minding our own possessions and resources. Covetousness is explicit idolatry (Colossians 3:5). Thomas á Kempis, in *"Imitation of Christ,"* said on avoiding curious inquiry, *"Do not be anxious for the shadow of a great name, for the close friendship of many or for the particular affection of men. These things cause distraction and cast great darkness about the heart."*

However, if we see the slightest appearance of contempt against Jesus, and walk away thinking we are minding our business, we have walked away from the faith. That is the time to comment. When the Bible is insulted, misquoted, and misinterpreted, that *is* the time to talk. We are appointed as defenders of the faith. It *is* necessary to point out the error when God is referred to as "god." There is a difference. The use of a lower-case letter in place of an upper-case letter is the thin line between blasphemy and Truth, and if an educated[196] Christian should notice this error without an affected conscience, such Christianity is questionable. Worse still, if your conscience *is* affected but you do nothing, you have sinned.[197] "But let none of you suffer as a murderer, a thief, an evildoer, or as a busybody in other people's matters" (1 Peter 4:15).

Without expectation: "When you have done all those things which you commanded say, 'We are unprofitable servants. We have done what was our

---

[195] 2 Timothy 3:7.

[196] 'Educated' because another Christian who has not been trained to know such differences has no reason to be affected in conscience by this.

[197] James 4:17.

duty to do'" (Luke 17:10). We must see the fallacy of the lady who thought remaining a virgin until marriage entitled her to have children immediately, and insulted God for making her and her equally chaste husband wait for two years before giving them a child. Does the commandment to avoid fornication come with a promise of children when married? Anything God commands us to do is for our own good, not for His satisfaction or reward. Our immorality is of no effect to God. Our service is of no effect to Him. He gives us commandments for us to live free from sin in this present world and avoid piercing ourselves with sorrows and eventual death. Does this mean we are working and denying ourselves for nothing? Absolutely not! God has never owed one man.

Amongst multi-billions and trillions of people who have walked this earth, God has owed none. Let us rather work with endurance and patience toward obtaining the crown that lasts forever. In our daily endeavors for men, we also must be patient and consistent, even when they are mean and cruel, because "God is pleased when because of conscience toward God, you patiently endure unjust treatment" 1 Peter 2:18-19. Little drops of water make a mighty ocean. Rather than get frustrated when people don't notice or acknowledge our good deeds and hard work, our belief and hope should rest in God and only God. We must not be weary, we must not be faint in working with all our heart and maintaining good conduct, keeping his commandments, and remaining unspotted in the world. It is for our good and only ours. Man's commendation should not arouse our affections. Worse, we must not commend ourselves. "For not he who commends himself is approved but whom the Lord commends" 2 Corinthians 10:18.

Lovingly: "Now these three remain: faith, hope and love; but the greatest of these is love" 1 Corinthians 13:13. Christian, we are sheep, we are doves, and we are ambassadors of Jesus Christ, living in a dog-eat-dog world. Our mandate is upside down to the carnal mind and Jesus warned so, *"But among you, it will be different"* (Matthew 20:26). Our rules and guidelines include: turn the other cheek when slapped; go two miles when forced to go one mile; allow ourselves to be defrauded; humble ourselves to be lifted; regard all men as better than ourselves; be the least if we want to be great; sit at the back until called forward; rejoice when persecuted; bless those who curse us; forgive seventy times seven times in a day; do not bother about what we will wear or eat, and so on. These are guidelines by God Himself to guide us in a world filled with ravenous wolves. We can never wage war the way the world does. The only way we can have peace is to love God and love man. The only trademark we have in this corporation is love. Our religion is the only one guided by love. Another religion might say their religion is peace, so if need be, they will kill anyone who disturbs or threatens such peace.

Our commandments are encompassed only by one rule: LOVE. Love your enemies, love your friends, love the poor, love the sick, love the rich, love the simple, greet with a kiss of love. This is the only distinguishing feature of a Christian from a demon. We love because He first loved us. Christian, why do we not love? Do we not understand what God has done for us through His Son, Jesus? Do we not believe? Nothing we read is a lie. Jesus did come, Jesus did die, Jesus did rise, Jesus did ascend, and Jesus is coming back. Please, let us not love only those who are good to us. We cannot be Christian without love. They are synonymous (Romans 13:10). This is why introducing ourselves as Christians should break down all barriers, because we have said so many other things about us in one word. Christianity is not about faith or hope; it is about love. Love feeds the other two, love is useful for this life and the life after, faith and hope are only useful for earthly survival. Whether correcting another, angry at another, giving to another, rejecting another, forgiving, resolving quarrels, saying no, saying yes, sharing, singing, cooking, hosting, all we do … "do everything with love" (1 Corinthians 16:14).

It is not love that we try to build alone in ourselves with a worldly checklist or recipe, it is the love that comes from personally knowing God. It is that love we experience which renders us kind and loving. Until there is genuine love for God out of which everything else we do flows - even the very air we breathe, breathing with love - the Christian race will be a burden and absolutely impossible. On the other hand, when the love flows from God, to love others will be the burden in our hearts. Self-love is a curse. Self-love is satan's evolving strategy to destroy the 21st Century inhabitants; he has used different tactics in different generations and self-love is that which he has devised for our generation. Any preacher who preaches self-love is preaching an antichrist message; Jesus explicitly preached against the notion of self-love in Luke 14:26.

Please let us not be deceived. The Word of God has never evolved by a comma, but when we look into history, we see how different trends arose that destroyed those generations. If you pursue self-love, rest assured you are embarking on a suicide mission, but if you love God and out of that love, your neighbor, you will find peace and unspeakable joy of heart. It is freedom. The world will move on to the next best trend, but as Christians, we must not. Remain as loving to all and only seek to grow in it, but do not move on from love. We must be consistent in our love, even when nailed to a cross and in a pool of our blood, the way Our Master did.

Finally, brethren, above all, "Only **let your conduct be worthy of the Gospel of Christ**, so that whether I come and see you or am absent, I may hear of your affairs, that you stand fast in one spirit, with one mind striving together for the faith of the gospel" (Philippians 1:27).

Love Neighbor

A new command I give you: Love one another. As I have loved you, so you must love one another. By this everyone will know that you are my disciples, if you love one another.

John 13:34-35

Faith is undoubtedly the most preached topic today. Unfortunately, it also is the most mis-preached. As we do with everything, we have reduced faith to a transaction where we "just believe" and God will do something for us. This is why so many turn away from the Faith, are discouraged and slander the Faith, when they do not receive an earthly need within a specific period of time, in a certain quantity, and with a certain characteristic. Most Christians have begun and ended here on earth. If Abraham, the champion and model of Faith, had this notorious view about faith, should he not have rightly cursed God on his deathbed and died justified? "These all died in faith, not having received the promises, but having seen them afar off, and were persuaded of them, and embraced them and confessed that they were strangers and pilgrims on the earth" (Hebrews 13:13). Citizen of the world, why do we reduce God so much? When we pay tithes and offerings with the sole hope that we will receive ten times back, we have reduced God to the best investment banker. When we remain chaste with the hope that God will give us great spouses, we have reduced God to a matchmaker. When we attend church every Sunday, because if we do not, it is a sin or something bad will happen to us, we have reduced God to the most confrontational church member we know.

The champions of faith, none of whom received the promise which God gave to them, "saw from afar." When our faith has to do with holding our breath and waiting so God will give us some earthly need or satisfaction, we are only suffocating ourselves. If our faith has nothing to do with the fact that Jesus is coming back and we see that indeed, one day He will come back and whether we are alive or not, we will rise and reign with Him, so do all we can to ensure we are not counted unworthy for His ultimate salvation, we are

217

practicing everything but the Christian concept of Faith. "Without faith it is impossible to please God.... He is a rewarder of them that diligently seek Him" (Hebrews 11:6). Do we imagine that the Almighty God's reward comprises cars, better jobs, houses, money, status, and fame? *Oh dear.* That the Creator of all things will reward His creation with manmade creations? *Sigh.*

Christian, we are in this world, but not of this world. Our reward is not anything worldly or anything we have seen. They confessed that they were strangers and pilgrims of the earth and understood that their reward could only come from "a city which hath foundations, whose builder and maker is God" (Hebrews 11:10). Without understanding this reality, we will continue to hate God on earth with all our earthly service when we receive the things we wish for, because surely these earthly things can only be wishes and not hopes. Do we wish to get married or hope to get married? Do we wish to have children or hope to have children? Do we wish to have money or hope to have money? Do we wish to go to Heaven or hope to go to Heaven? When we turn anything earthly, which we can see another man already has, to a hope that we get it, we are dead.

We need to understand that it is okay to wish for earthly things. They are wishes because life goes on, even if we do not have them, but if we wish to go to Heaven, rather than hope, we are dead. Where there is no hope, there is no perseverance, no continuity nor encouragement to pursue that which is hoped for. When it is simply a wish, we will love for it to happen, but will not die for it to happen. With hope, we do or die. It is Heaven or hell. It is Jesus or nothing. It is *"Well done, good and faithful servant,"* or *"depart from me ye worker of lawlessness."* Dear Christian, your soul cries out to you, please listen. We are strangers on this earth. This world is not our home. We cannot afford to wish for Heaven. We must remain hopeful until we get into Heaven. That hope which we have is what is called faith. Forgive anybody who has taught you anything otherwise. *They knew not what they did.* If you wish for something that will encourage you on your earthly pilgrimage, seek God's Kingdom and His righteousness; you will be amazed how much He will bless you with every other thing, that even using it becomes unnecessary.

Now, about this Faith that fuels our hope of Heaven, how do we exercise it on earth? We do not need to be in church every Sunday to prove that we have faith. We do not need to give offerings to prove that we have faith. We do not need to empty our bank accounts to prove that we have faith. We do not need to deny ourselves of anything to prove that we have faith. We do not need to jump down from a high cliff to prove that we have faith. We do not need to go into the lion's den to prove that we have faith. We do not need to keep God's commandments to prove that we have faith. We do not need to do *anything* to *prove* that we have the faith which God rewards. It is done! God already made His promise to Abraham, and because He is not man that He should lie, He has "entangled" Himself in His own web (Galatians 3:17-18). So we must stop the legalism, mutilation, and self or instution–imposed burden; we have been freed from the need to do anything; anybody doing anything from the mind-set of proving the faith that God rewards, should ensure they keep all the commandments and rest assured that they have already received their reward. For they have rejected the propitiation of Christ and fallen from grace; they are cursed (Galatians 3:10).

Since we do not need to do anything, since we have believed in God, and have faith in Jesus and are justified and free "indeed," do we now sit back, relax and wait for our reward, i.e., that Christianity is a lazy religion? *Get thee behind us, satan!* That is a lie from the enemy. "Good for you! Even the demons believe this and they tremble in terror. How foolish! Can't you see that faith without good deeds is useless?" James 2:19-20

...What is important is faith expressing itself in love. Galatians 5:6

It is Faith that produces acts done *out of* the joy of Salvation, not making an exchange from God. Whether He blesses us on earth or not, we continue to do, because we love Him and have faith in the hope of the Son's return. Some of the things we will do out of this love will make no sense to the carnal mind, like the Galatians who, when they initially got saved by faith, were so joyful that they overlooked Paul's physical ailment; it ordinarily would have put them off, but they were joyful to the point that they were willing to give him their eyes (Galatians 4: 13-14). Only genuine faith could lead a person to offer such self-sacrifice to another, not as a matter of duty, but because understanding and accepting the gift of Jesus and coming into the family of God, renders one kind (3 John 1:11). Everything that is not needed in Heaven becomes useless to an understanding pilgrim. This love for another as oneself is the universal test in determining those who know God and those who do not, by seeing the good they do and **why** they do it. So, we don't have to do anything to prove faith, we have to prove faith by loving God through people (1 John 4:20). The difference? We have a say in one, we do not have a say in the other.

However, saved once is not saved all. Loving God once is not loving God all. The joy of salvation once is not the joy of salvation forever. (Psalm 51:12). These same Galatian churches lost the joy of their salvation when they started being religious by adhering to false teaching so soon after Paul had brought the Good News to them (Galatians 1:6).

You were running the race so well. Who has held you back from following the truth?

It certainly isn't God, for he is the one who called you to freedom. Galatians 5:7-8

This is why some who have been in church for years, erroneously imagine that their length of attendance and rule-keeping renders them right with God. We must renew our minds daily with the Word of God and prayer, if we are to build on solid ground where we can always rely on the joy of being saved. It is bewildering to hear some of the anti-Biblical rules which have sprung up in churches, which are so wide; that is a clear indication that Bibles are piling up dust. When we stray from the Word, we are bound by nature to devise man-made ideologies and parade them as God's. Only the Word can keep us straight, narrow, and unbending.

> *I can't stand your religious meetings. I'm fed up with your conferences and conventions. I want nothing to do with your religion projects, your pretentious slogans and goals. I'm sick of your fund-raising schemes, your public relations and image making. I've had all I can take of your noisy ego-music. When was the last time you sang to me? Do you know what I want? I want justice—oceans of it. I want fairness—rivers of it. That's what I want. That's all I want.* Amos 5:21-24

The Galatian churches had been "free" before being saved, in that they did not need to go through all the religious rituals of mutilation required by the Judaizers, so when they heard the Good News Apostle Paul personally brought to them, they were filled with the joy of salvation. Shortly after he left, however, they had begun listening to the bad yeast of religion that directly contravened the freedom found in Christ. The people who were "free" before getting saved, got saved and became bound. God forbid! That is not the message of Christ. This was the genesis of his confrontation to Peter, who was separating himself during meals from non-Jews; this was why he wrote the "harsh" letter to the Galatians.

Again, his blunt letter showed his genuine love for his "children," as he called them. He knew there was no other way he could communicate his message, if he did not apply "tough love." (Galatians 4:20)

> *For you have been called to live in freedom, my brothers and sisters but don't use your freedom to satisfy your sinful nature. Instead, use your freedom to serve one another in love.* Galatians 5:13

In Galatians, we are warned about two extremes which could arise from freedom found in Christ. The first extreme is not doing anything because we are "free" from the law, and the second is doing everything "right" to gain God's favor. This first extreme is the ride of heresy, which almost every modern "Christian" is aboard to hell. They claim freedom and dress like harlots and thugs, *even* in the church, in outfits that, at some time in history, would have automatically rendered one a candidate for mental institutionalizing. They claim freedom and ask, "Is it a sin?" or the audacious statement, "*I know who I am in Christ!*" I weep for you, my child. You need not bother to look too far or shout too loud. Stand in front of a mirror and let satan, your father, king, and lover, caress you with more sweet nothings. Then you can jump even further and won't dash your foot against a stone, since you are the "child of God."

How much longer are we going to claim freedom and keep acquiring the latest of the worldly things released day after day? Our eyeballs will not even leave this world with us! Why are we storing up treasures? Why do we want to enjoy all we will ever know of Heaven *on* earth? Do we not believe there is a greater glory? Do we not believe that there is really a Heaven, where those who are *really* the children of God are *really* heading, and where we will *really* have our personal mansions? Will you not ensure that you pursue godliness and ensure that, not by reason of the color of shoes, or an earthly month's salary, or a "lovestruck emoji" above a picture, that you sell your soul and miss this Heaven?

> ...*If it were not so I would have told you.* John 14:2

Who does not want to have any and everything? Who does not want the perfect figure, perfect skin, perfect marriage, perfect bank account, and even perfect death? It is not foolishness that anyone will give up the cares and thrills of this life to follow "something" we cannot see. We are not crazy, nor are we unenlightened. How perfect it would be if we could have this world and have Jesus too, but we cannot. The buffet is set out. The meals have been prepared by chefs from Heaven and earth. The menu options are "life and death, blessing and cursing" (Deuteronomy 30:19). The greatest gift that God ever gave to every individual is:

> **CHOOSE** *for yourselves this day whom you will serve.* Joshua 24:15

You cannot drink from the cup of the Lord and from the cup of devils; you cannot eat at the Lord 's Table and from the table of demons (1 Corinthians 10:21). You cannot serve God and yourself. You cannot serve God and your collection of items. You cannot serve God and your accomplishments. You cannot serve God and your family. You cannot serve God and your church. You cannot serve God and your social media profile. You cannot serve God and your addiction. You cannot serve God and your body. You cannot serve God and your stomach. You cannot serve God and your beauty. You cannot serve God and your reputation. You cannot serve God and your past. You cannot serve God and your tattered clothes. You cannot serve God and your charitable causes. You cannot serve God and your tithes and offerings.

Everything that is not God is *not* God. Everything that is not God is *not* life. Everything that is not God is *not* freedom. We cannot continue "having a form of godliness but denying its power" (2 Timothy 3:5). You say the God who has the power to save you does not have the power to change your desires, ambitions and appearance? Modern "Christian," you cannot continue lying to your heart that you are free, seed of Adam.

The second extreme is those who force children of God to do or not do anything. As Paul said, "*mutilate yourselves!*" (Galatians 5:12). "Don't do this," "don't do that," ... It is better for those people who have become slaves to their own pious ways to form their cult and cease tampering with a religion which has been done and settled before time began by Him who began it. Do we now serve God or serve man?

The anecdote to both unrewarding ends? Personally knowing God through Jesus, by understanding, as far as the human mind can take it, the price He paid on our behalf when He, a sinless God, descended from Heaven; was born by a woman into the world like us; lived liked a peasant amongst us; yielded to none of the temptations ensnaring us daily; was despised and beaten by us; became a curse and died for us on a Cross, *yet* loved us through it all; destroyed the laws and veil hindering us from directly accessing Him, and is still loving us unrepentantly. We cannot be taught this. Only God can teach individual hearts where learning is evidenced by the way we begin to look at and love other people, whom He equally loves as He loves us. This is true because every other individual is as close as we will physically ever get to God while on earth.

> *Verily I say unto you, inasmuch as ye have done it unto one of the least of these my brethren, ye have done it unto me.* Matthew 25:40

We become thankful individuals and cannot help but show this gratitude, even though nothing we do will ever be nearly sufficient, because it is an indescribable, unrepayable gift of Grace. However, if we are doing nothing, or see the need to love others as an unnecessary burden, we are either still unlearned, already abandoned by God, or predestined goats. The manifestation of that love is the evidence of the Holy Spirit in us, conforming us to the person of Jesus (1 John 4:7-17; Romans 8:26).

When we begin to love from a pure heart and sincere faith, our good conscience toward God then orders our conduct towards our neighbors. If we use our conduct to patronize our darkened hearts and blurred consciences that we are "good people," or that we have done something right, we have failed. If we use a person to determine whether we will do good toward them or not, we have failed. Conscience comes first. This way, even if we could have done something, but we genuinely did not have the means to do it, we are at peace. If someone is undeserving of good to them, but we go ahead and do it because we know it is the right thing to do, we go ahead and do it for Jesus' sake. We choose to live from the inside out and not outside in toward all, friend and foe. This reframes us from deceitful niceness to God-produced kindness, which transcends will, understanding, desire and commendation.

We are also not conscious of when we are doing good, because we can't help it. It is a lifestyle. We are to be RICH in good works (1 Timothy 6:18). Can we count or name all the meals we have eaten since birth? This is why Jesus needed to be identified. He did good as He moved about, without waiting for any form of applause. As His fame spread far, people brought their sicknesses and diseases for healing, and He healed every one of them. There was no "good" budget or healing quota to be maintained. Thomas á Kempis, in urging us to shun familiarity said, *"Sometimes, it happens that a person enjoys a good reputation among those who do not know him but at the same time is held in slight regard by those who do. Frequently we think we are pleasing others by our presence and we begin rather to displease them by the faults they find in us."*[198] We do good and move on.

How?

- **Love with PRAYER**: This is the greatest display of neighborly love. "Ever since I heard of your strong faith in the Lord Jesus and your love for God's people everywhere, I have not stopped thanking God for you. I pray for you constantly" (Ephesians 1:15-16). The first and most important thing we can do for any other person is to pray for them, especially when we hear that people have come to Christ. For anyone to accept the true Christ in the world we live in today is a miracle and as believers, we are to intercede for them that their faith will not fail, that they will receive wisdom and grow in the knowledge of God. If we have direct access to them, we must encourage them by letting them know we are glad they have come to the knowledge of Truth, and that we are praying for them. Intercession is the ultimate display of spiritual humility and love; it is calling the names of others and lifting them up in constant prayer.

---

[198] Thomas A Kempis, 'The Imitations of Christ'.

A common prayer we all say to encourage ourselves is, "He who has begun a good work…will complete it" Philippians 1:6. However, this prayer came from another man's humble intercession for a group of believers who had come to Christ, Paul to the Philippian church, and his praying for them to continue to grow. He was very glad about their salvation, and even though he was in prison while he wrote the letter to them, their continuity in spreading the gospel made the chains worth it. Jesus told Peter, "I have prayed for you that your faith will not fail" (Luke 22:32). We must pray for those who have not come to Christ and especially for those who have, it is especially encouraging when we let them know we are praying for them. We would not have had these letters to key into, if Paul had kept to himself the fact that he was praying for these churches. Intercession is the greatest display of love, *especially* to another believer.

- **Love with RESOURCES**: This is the most practical display of neighborly love. There are two ways of doing this: "Suppose a brother or a sister is without clothes and daily food. If one of you says to them, "Go in peace; keep warm and well fed," but does nothing about their physical needs, what good is it?" (James 2:16)

The first is intentionality. Christian, it is a shame if we have ever said, "**no**" to anybody in need, who asked us for any material thing. Scripture tells us not to withhold good from those deserving, as long as it is in our *power* to act. Not so fast! You don't have it in your hand at that moment, but do you know someone who does? Power is all encompassing. Power is not just what we *can* do, but what we *are able* to do. Can we make a phone call that will solve the problem? Can we take them somewhere that will solve the problem? We must realize that it is an honor for anyone to ask us a favor for anything. Whatever the motive is, that is nothing to us. Can we help? Then let us help. What reason is there to say no? Of the multitude of people Jesus healed, not one did He turn back. Did all of them believe in Him? Were they all silent when shouting, "***Crucify Him!***" Did they fight for this Man who healed them from lifelong infirmities?

As long as it is in our **power** to help others, because we are ambassadors of Christ, even if it might cause some inconvenience to us, *especially* if it will cause an inconvenience to us, we must help others. We must be prepared to help others. This was part of the cost we ought to have counted before following Jesus. The instructions to the believers in Crete, "…be always ready to do what is good…devote themselves to doing good…learn to do good by meeting the urgent needs of others" (Titus 3:1,8 & 14). Three times in a short letter Paul reminded Titus about the importance of this. There was no room for, *"I didn't plan for this,"* or *"This is not in my monthly budget,"* because we are to meet even the urgent needs of others. We ought to have budgeted before accepting Christ. He certainly did not give us just some hair strands or His fingernails. He gave us *all* of Him. Is it then earthly needs of others that will stop us from thanking Him? We must note that it is just not a one-off thing where we play the Good Samaritan for this one person in need; "… shew a pattern of good works" (Titus 2:7). This can only be a track-record as a result of consistency.

The second way of practically loving is unintentionally, randomly. Some plead the case of *"they didn't ask me."* Jesus is coming back for only those "zealous of good works" (Titus 2:14). If we wait until our proud looks are approached for help, we stand no chance of pleasing God. Jesus went about doing good. He carried Himself to where need was and when it came to Him, He did not cast out. We are blessed to be a blessing for people to give praise to God, not us (2 Corinthians 9:11-14). If what we do for others can only make them say, "Thank you." rather than, "Thank God," or "I thank God for you," we need to do a bit more. Do we see someone we can help? Are we in a hurry? We *must* stop and help. We are only in a hurry because we are privileged to be alive; "…you fool! Tonight, your soul shall be required of you" (Luke 12:20). Where will you then hurry to?

Remember, the Good Samaritan was also on a journey when he stopped to help the Jew that two religious Jews had earlier avoided. He didn't cancel his itinerary for the whole day. He simply went out of his way, used his power to hand him over to someone, and returned at a more convenient time. Do we really need to collect that *"change due"* when we shop? We would have paid the same price if the change price was added to the price due. Is it impossible to pay for the next person's fuel or grocery? Let us go about doing good, not to boost already obese egos but to say, *"I love You Lord. Let Your Kingdom come."*

Pure and undefiled religion before God and the Father is this: to visit orphans and widows in their trouble. James 1:27

- **Love with SELVES**: This is the most believable display of neighborly love. We cannot just *"throw the money at the problem."* Sometimes,

225

all we need to love another person is ourselves. Our presence. Our communication. For goodness sake, we know that the Almighty God hears us **every time** we come to Him in prayer. He does not sleep or slumber; He will always hear us. What fraction of that can we do for our neighbors? This is the ultimate way to be salt and light. Our presence itself should be a blessing, "since I was sure of your understanding and trust, I wanted to give you a double blessing by visiting you twice" (2 Corinthians 1:15). What does our presence mean to others? Does our absence bring relief? Is there emptiness when we are not around? Do people notice something is missing when they haven't seen or heard from us?

This is no display of pride. Nobody wants to be around someone who makes their presence all about themselves, except with a sigh of relief and mockery. They notice when we have made our presence not about ourselves but about those we are with. We listen to them, we encourage them. We hold their hands; like John and Jesus, they can rest on us. "For I remember your tears as we parted and I will be filled with joy when we are together again" (2 Timothy 1:4). Is the clock being watched when we are around others? Do they wish we would stay longer? Do they hold back, or don't hold back tears? Do they give us genuine hugs of love when we have to separate?

Christian, are you salt and light? Or are you pepper or sugar: too harsh that they don't want to be around us or too sweet, they see through our flattery and lies? After the hurt, betrayal, and years of loneliness, despite what his human nature would have done, Joseph spake kindly to his brothers (Genesis 50:21). We can't fake this. The only way he could have done that was because he saw the situation and the people through God's lens. Despite what people have done to us, can we still speak kindly to them, because Jesus also died for them? If anything, Joseph attempted to feign anger but could not sustain it. Knowing God and keeping himself unspotted from the world had rendered him kind, even in such a position of power and authority.

The only way our love *is* believable is when we love with ourselves. Prayers can be replaced by another believer, better help can be provided by another individual, nobody can replace the unique fingerprint that we are. Let our absence leave the clouds dark (Matthew 27:45).

Order of Priority

...whatever you did for one of the least of these brothers and sisters of mine, you did for me. **Matthew 25:40**

We are admonished to love and help all men, as long as it in our power to do so, but there is an order of priority as to whom we help, and that is Christians first. Jesus said, what we do for His brothers and sisters we do for Him, so is every human in the family of Jesus? "For whoever does the will of My Father in heaven is My brother and sister and mother." (Matthew 12:50)

People of this world who have rejected Christ *will* pass away, and their death is their end, but God's own will reign with Him forever. The point is not to help unbelievers for that will be sin, but if there are two people soaked in rain and you have an umbrella to give, give it to the one who says they are a Christian. *If* the person is a true Christian anyway, they will either share with the other person or give it up completely for them.

> *Whenever we have the opportunity, we should do good to everyone—**especially** to those in the family of faith.* Galatians 6:10

Christians first, because that is our family. We speak the same language; we have the same hope, same faith, and same blood. Jesus made it clear that only those who do God's will are His family. Despite this, He helped all that came to Him, but were all of them believers? He turned no one back, but there was an order of priority. He made that statement when His biological mother and brothers had come to where He was teaching, and the people expected Him to put His teaching on hold to attend to them. It is not just Christians with whom we are personally familiar, it is more profitable when it is Christians who are strangers to us, as long as they are Christian.

> *Dear friend, you are acting faithfully in whatever you do for the brothers and sisters, especially when they are strangers.* 3 John 1:5

We are told again: "*Share with the Lord's people who are in need. Practice hospitality*" (Romans 12:13), and regarding prayer: "*Pray in the Spirit at all times ...be persistent in your prayers for all believers everywhere.*" (Ephesians 6:18)

Are we to love *all* men? Yes, we must. Is there a scale of preference? Yes, there is: ***Christians first.***

> *I exhort therefore, that, first of all, supplications, prayers, intercessions, and giving of thanks, be made for all men.* 1 Timothy 2:1

I Am Doing!

Do we consider ourselves to be doing already? Walking upright in our Faith? Loving God and our neighbors, even as we love ourselves?

Finally, then, brothers, we ask and urge you in the Lord Jesus, that as you received from us how you ought to walk and to please God, just as you are doing, that you do so more and more. 1 Thessalonians 4:1

....DO MORE! Good works build a reputation over time. It is drops of water that will make a mighty ocean, not even splashes. Drops. Tiny drops of good works are heaping up oceans of reward with God to come, whether in this life but certainly in the next. One day, we will be unable to trace where it all began. Never be weary in well-doing. We will reap a mighty harvest if we faint not (Galatians 6:9). Be rich in good works. Let us be known to consistently go about doing good without expectation of reward or commendation, but out of love, thankfulness, and a good conscience toward God. Every day is an opportunity to spread love through good works; one day, it will be called upon for reference. Make today count.

Also, if we consider ourselves doing, let us personally examine ourselves in a more excellent way, a way useful for our walk in this life and in the life to come, with this checklist against our names and determine if indeed we have attained being the person of love:

_____ is patient.

_____ is kind.

_____ does not envy.

_____ does not boast.

_____is not proud.

_____does not dishonor others.

_____is not self-seeking.

_____is not easily angered.

_____keeps no record of wrongs.

_____does not delight in evil but rejoices with the truth.

_____ always protects.

_____always trusts.

_____always hopes.

_____always perseveres.

(1 Corinthians 13:4-7)

Did we affirm all in ourselves? Are we perfect in Christ, becoming like Him or yet to know Him?

So, help us, God.

I Will Not!

If anyone does not love the Lord, that person is CURSED. Our Lord, come! 1 Corinthians 16:22

Do we consider ourselves to be Christian? We must remember, despite what we say, a tree is only known by its fruits. Jesus said, if you love Him, keep His commandments. Yes, He has saved you, but is He just Savior to you, or also Lord? If He is Lord, then acknowledge Him as that by keeping His commandments.

He who has My words and despises them has that which shall condemn him on the Last Day. John 12:48

Christian is an earthly name and earthly identity. Nobody is going to call another person Christian in Heaven. In the same way, nobody on earth who is not a believer calls themselves worldly, as they are in their world, in their home and of the world. It is status quo for everybody who walks this earth to be worldly, but once we say we are Christian, we have identified the fact that we are in this world, but not of this world; I am a Christian because of the things I do. We can have all the spiritual gifts, we can have all the blessings of God, we can be anything, but whosoever does not Love the way God has called us, does not know Jesus. There is no hard fact about that.

Christian by nomenclature, atheist by practice is pointless. If everybody using that word, "Christian" to identify their religion really practiced it, do we know what sort of world we would live in? We focus too much on doctrine and rules, but it is only love that will strengthen the Church (1 Corinthians 8:1), who will then go into the world to strengthen the world. We spend too much time asking God for things; He has given us principles so we can prosper in

229

soul, body and substance in this life. Jesus is coming back to repay each and every one of us, believing and non-believing, according to our deeds not our professions or church prominence (Revelation 22:12). We are better off if we do not identify with anything, because judgement starts in the church and you do not want to be found there with no works to show for it (1 Peter 4:17).

And I saw the dead, small and great, stand before God; and the books were opened: and another book was opened which is the book of life: and the dead were judged out of those things which were written in the books, according to their works…And whosoever was not found written in the book of life was cast into the lake of fire. Revelation 20:12,15

He who has ears should hear and think on these things. Wisdom for us all in Jesus' Name. Amen.

CHAPTER 4

WHY?

*The world is passing away, and also its lusts; but the one who does
the will of God lives forever.*
1 John 2:17

SoulTune: When It's All Been Said and Done[199]

---

[199] Don Moen (2004); When It's All Been Said and Done; Colorado, Integrity Music.

WHY?

It is appointed unto men once to die... Hebrews 9:27

We make plans, we carry out costly insurance policies about those things which we are not assured will happen, but that which we know *will* happen is a terror to us: we do not want to speak or hear about because it is "bad news". This is no appointment that anyone can cancel. If perhaps, as in the case of Hezekiah, it is postponed, one day, it will certainly come. We are not all appointed success, we are not all appointed fulfilment of destiny, or finding soulmates, or hitting financial goals, but this one appointment we are ascertained. It is comparable to a "you have been served" notice. Ignorance of notice of this appointment is no excuse, but what is more frightening is the addendum to this subpoena, *...but after this the judgment...* So, death is not the end, but the means to an end, which is judgment by the Righteous Judge (2 Timothy 4:18).

Charles Spurgeon said, *"May we regard death as the most weighty of all events, and be sobered by its approach. He who does not prepare for death is more than an ordinary fool, he is a madman."*

We are told to live each day like it is our last. Christian, every day *IS* our last. Paul said he faced death daily for Christ. Do we not wonder, when we sleep, those who sleep anyway, because the Lord gives sleep only to His beloved (Psalm 127:2), in all that vulnerability and darkness, and we wake up, carrying out our days like we had the power to wake ourselves up? Oh, we spoiled generation! We imagine our lives are rechargeable, like our phones, by being electrically powered to restore life? There is more hope for our little gods than us in coming back to life when dead. A phone which has been dead for years can be awakened with a battery. Who can restore that life that goes? Job 14:7-10 shows that even trees have more hope of sprouting again with new branches, but man, the greatest of all God's creations, the dominator and subduer of the earth, seas, and land, dies, but who can restore him? Jesus restored Lazarus to life? Where is Lazarus today?

The hymn writer said, "New every morning is thy love our wakening and uprising *prove*..." If we imagine that our alarm or body clocks are the reason by which we rise every day, we have misplaced trust. The hymn continues, "...through sleep and darkness safely brought, *restored* to life and power and thought,"[200] As we close our eyes to sleep each night, if we cannot smile at the thought of meeting Jesus that moment, we must restore ourselves to a position in which we can sleep in peace. The Bible tells us not to let the sun to go down on our anger, not to go to bed with anger in us, because anger is

---

[200] John Keble, New every morning is the love (1822).

232

classified amongst the works of the flesh in Galatians 5:19-21 which render us unfit for the Kingdom of God and can only send us directly to hell. Imagine running the race so well and just one on night of going to bed angry you died in your sleep and had to go to hell for just that 'one off' anger? God forbid! Moreover, surely, we do not want to meet Jesus with angry faces.

I laid me down and slept; I awaked; for the LORD sustained me. Psalm 3:5

Every morning we wake up is a miracle. That we go to sleep every night and can make plans, saying, *"See you tomorrow,"* is the greatest act of faith. Who guarantees tomorrow? Arthur Pink, in *The Attributes of God,* said the four things every individual must meditate on are: *"Death, which is most certain. Judgment, which is most strict. Hell, which is most doleful. Heaven, which is most delightful."*

Preparation

Only one life, 'T will soon be past, only what's done for Christ will last... —C.T. Studd

Christian, we are not our lives. Jim Eliot, who died for the Faith at the age of 29 said, *"He is no fool who gives what he cannot keep to gain what he cannot lose."* Most important, this world is not our home. It is not anybody's home. We are all leaving sooner or later, whether we know Jesus or whether we have chosen not to. Apostle Peter, in his first letter, addressed his readers thus: "This letter is from Peter, an apostle of Jesus Christ. I am writing to God's chosen people who are living as foreigners in the provinces of Pontus, Galatia, Cappadocia, Asia, and Bithynia. (1 Peter 1:1). Are we living as foreigners here, or are we comfortable here? Are we fond of making earthly plans, but failing to make the *one* plan? We are only as good as the legacy we create on earth. Every new day we are given is another chance to build a good legacy. Listen, we only know Jesus because of what He did while He was on earth, precisely during his **three-year** ministry, the space the world is unable to contain, and 2,000 years later, He is only getting more popular. Jesus is the most debated Subject in existence.

Are you one of those who say my Lord, Jesus Christ and Savior never existed? Take this as a promise before God and man, unless you repent, 2,000 years from now, NO ONE will be able to prove you existed. 2,000 years? 200 years from now, NO ONE will be able to prove you existed. 200 years? 20 years, 20 months, 20 weeks, 20 minutes, 20 seconds, TWO SECONDS from the moment you are buried, cremated, whatever it will be, in the name of my Lord Jesus Christ, the **risen and living** Savior, nobody on this earth will ever be able to prove you existed (Job 8:16-19; Obadiah 1:16). Not those closest to you, not those farthest from you, and unless you repent, this is a promise.

Death is not a function of age. Some, such as King Edward VI, who only ruled England for six years and died at age 15, left a legacy that made a lasting contribution to the English Reformation and the structure of the Church of England. How many more people have we seen die and we say they are *"gone too soon,"* because even though their years were short in number, they made a mark on earth that will never be forgotten. How about those who live for 969[201] years, yet died prematurely, because all they did was live? What are we building our lives on? The only solid ground on which we can build is Jesus. The only infinite legacy we can build on is Jesus. First, if anyone is without Jesus, such a person is hanging only by a thin thread, with their fate in their own hand, hitched to a spider web. Such persons have deliberately given up all hope of divine providence.

We must think of our deaths as often as we eat, especially what will happen the moment after we die. Death is not the end. When one is expecting to be called for an interview, preparation never ceases. The same applies to students who read and study right to the door of the exam room. Is our "house" in order at any given time the Angel of Death calls? In **Genesis 35:8**, we meet the first Deborah of the Bible, Rebekah's nurse, who was travelling with Jacob and his family and died during this travel. They wept for some days, buried her under an oak tree, and named it *"the place of weeping"*. We knew nothing about this woman, only that in the middle of a chapter, the Bible drops in the fact that this woman has died and we have to stop enjoying the story we were reading and join in her funeral. This woman was Rebekah's nurse and there is no record of Jacob ever going back to get this nurse Deborah from his mother's house after he had to run away from home the first time. So how did she come in? We do not know. All we know is that for her name to be mentioned in the middle of a chapter, and for us to stop a journey to weep for her for days and name the place in memorial of her, she must have been a woman of service. Serving generations from Rebekah's to Jacob's, and now her name will always be read forever. We would love to know more about her but the records are not much; all we know is that there was a first Deborah and not "Warrior-Princess-Judge Deborah." The old caring nurse Deborah, who had left Rebekah's house as a young girl with her (Genesis 24:59), and according to records, was buried by Jacob and his family

---

[201] Genesis 5:27.

about 120 years after we first heard of her.[202]

> *Therefore, my beloved brothers, be steadfast, immovable, always abounding in the work of the Lord, knowing that in the Lord your labor is not in vain.* 1 Corinthians 15:58

Only what we do for Christ will last, Christian. Some are so fixated on building empires, securing uncertain futures for their children, saving up money they will never spend, and doing all of this at the expense of anything for Christ. This tragically flawed mindset will become a snare, even for the children of such who will declare, "our ancestors left us a foolish heritage" (Jeremiah 16:19). They will realize it at some point, and either curse us for its emptiness and worthlessness, or bless us for its value and truth. Truth will always be truth. Another set will say, "We will not hide them from their children, but tell to the coming generation the glorious deeds of the LORD, and his might, and the wonders that he has done." (Psalm 78:4)

The best Christian books and resources are those that were written 500 or 1,000 year ago. They are still so alive and still so relevant. At the time John Bunyan died, his classic, *The Pilgrim's Progress,* which he wrote while he was imprisoned for public preaching, and his other written works, left him with an estate of £42. More than 350 years after his death, 1,300 editions have been produced, translated into more than 200 languages, and never has a copy been out of print. Bunyan had five children, but none of their descendants can be traced today. Regardless, his work is still impacting and changing lives and is considered one of the most important religious works.

Every other sector evolves. The best institutions in the world today were all founded on the Christian Faith, with strict Christian principles and morals. We cannot keep building on lies and vanity. This is why "purpose" is such a big topic today; it is because everyone is looking for purpose outside purpose. How do we imagine another human being can ever tell us what our purpose is? We will never find purpose outside of, *"through God, from God, by God and for God".* Purpose will only be found in the things we do which are *"to the glory of God,"* even if it is folding clothes.

Have we found and are we doing that which, if we died this very night, we will die knowing we did this for God? Ten years before William Tyndale was killed for his interpretation of the Bible, the Catholic priests were burning the first set of his New Testament translation and in his diary, he wrote: *"In burning the New Testament they did no other thing than I looked for; no more shall they do if they burn me also if it be God's will it shall be done. Nevertheless, in translating the New Testament I did my duty.* "[203] What is our duty? More important, are we *doing* our duty? Anything done outside of service to God and humanity, benefitting no one but ourselves, unfortunately dies with or before us.

Nehemiah's last words in his book were, "remember this in my favor, God" (Nehemiah 13:31). He had just finished dealing with those who had turned the Lord's Temple into a den of thieves, purged out everything, and restored order into the House of God. What can we ask God to remember in our favor? Are we lax toward sin in ourselves and others? When Hezekiah was told the first time by Isaiah that he was going to die from his illness, so he should set his house in order, Hezekiah went and prayed to God crying, "remember how I have walked before you in truth and with a perfect heart, and have done what is good in thy sight" (Isaiah 38:3). For whatever reason, Hezekiah wanted to remain in this strange land, he was given 15 more years by God, according to his own request. Those 15 years led him to produce one of the most wicked kings in Israel's history, Manasseh, who eventually went on to kill Prophet Isaiah amongst many heinous acts. Regardless, what can we call God to remember in our favor, which we have done out of *genuine* love for Him, and out of a perfect heart? Not out of duty, fear or pride?

> *They share freely and give generously to the poor. Their good deeds will be remembered forever.* 2 Corinthians 9:9

The incredible blessing we have from history is that we are all capable of living perfect lives by learning from the mistakes and the wise decisions of others. Those lessons, coupled with the Word of God (His Spirit) and prayers, give us more than we need to live perfect lives. Nothing is new under the sun. We can always check anything we want to do, and see where this ended up, despite how pleasing it might look *prima facie*. This was how Nehemiah learned from Solomon's mistakes. We have just too much given to us. We can learn from Abraham, Jezebel, Elisha, Daniel, Joseph, Nebuchadnezzar, Jonah, the disciples, satan, and most important, Jesus Himself. There are also records of great men and women who have lived purposeful lives and those who thought they were doing something right at the time but ended up terribly sorry for it. The internet is a great resource that hides absolutely nothing, neither does it forget. Even though there is so much good to learn from it, there is also so much evil we can expose ourselves to, but all in all, the greatest gift of love God has given to us is choice.

---

[203] Hanks G. 70 Great Christians.

To think of death, is a death to some men.

Oh sirs, meditate upon death.

Meditation on death, will put sin to death.

Death to the wicked, is the end of all comfort, and the beginning of all misery.

Death to the godly, is the outlet to sin and sorrow, and the inlet to peace and happiness.

When a saint dies, he leaves all his bad behind him, and carries his good with him.

When a sinner dies, he carries his bad with him, and leaves his good behind him.

The godly man goes from evil, to all good.

The wicked man goes from good, to all evil.

Oh sirs, meditate upon death!

—*Arthur Pink*

King George IV was born into everything the worldly mind could ever dream of. His annual allowance as a royal was £7,000,000. During his coronation as king, the ceremony cost about £22,000,000, while his father's had cost £10,000. His life was one of wild extravagance, involving heavy drinking and numerous mistresses, and he was known as the "First Gentleman of England." Naturally clever, bright, and eloquent, his laziness and gluttony led him to squander much of his talent. *The Times* wrote that he would always prefer *"a girl and a bottle to politics and a sermon."* The Duke of Wellington, during the Catholic emancipation, described him as, *"the worst man he ever fell in with his whole life, the most selfish, the most false, the most ill-natured, the most entirely without one redeeming quality."* One of his private senior aides confided in his diary about him, *"A more contemptible, cowardly, selfish, unfeeling dog does not exist ... There have been good and wise kings but not many of them ... and this I believe to be one of the worst."*

When death began knocking because of his declining health, he decided to become religious and confessed to an archdeacon that he repented of the dissolute life he lived, and hoped that mercy would be shown to him, but it was too late. When he died, *The Times* narrated public opinion on his life:

There never was an individual less regretted by his fellow-creatures than this deceased king. What eye has wept for him? What heart has heaved one throb of unmercenary sorrow? ... If he ever had a friend – a devoted friend in any rank of life – we protest that the name of him or her never reached us.[204]

It is not how we start matters, but how we end, and history, helps us to choose the kind of life we will have. There are those in the Bible who, without doubt, would have done things differently if they knew they'd be used as examples for lifetimes to come, such as Eutychus, who is known for dozing off during a sermon, falling out of the window, and eventually dying; Felix the indecisive governor, who was more interested in collecting a bribe from Paul than actually freeing him for not committing any crime; Herodias, for putting the blood of John the Baptist on her little, naïve daughter's hands; Judas Iscariot, who betrayed Jesus for 30 pieces of silver, not even a quarter of what was paid Delilah for betraying Samson; Potiphar's wife, who tried to seduce Joseph and cried wolf; the Roman believers in Romans 16, who helped Paul in their seemingly little way; Aquila and Priscilla who opened up their home for fellowship; the group of Jews in Acts 23:12, who took an oath not to eat or drink until they killed Paul, who must have starved to death, because more than ten years later, Paul was still alive and preaching.

No doubt, some of them would have done some things differently if they had known at the time that their lives were going to be played on big screens, as examples for us all. If the story of our lives were posted on a large billboard outside all the airports of the countries of world, where billions of travelers would see it and take a picture to post and share, would we be proud?

What Will It Be?

What will it be, Christian? We draw up 10- and 50-year vision boards, plan our next birthdays, schedule social media posts, and we even go to sleep freely. All of these we do without a thought about whether we will see the light of the next day. Why do we not make a priority that which we know *will* happen, and leave every other thing to the mercy of God? Will we be proud of the work we have done for God? Will we wish we did more? Not for humanity *but* for God?

Will we have a gallery of beautiful selfies, large bank accounts, best makeup portfolios, best collection of clothes, best career history, best marriage, best parenting? Will we still be so full of ourselves, that even though we are in our 100s, our death will still be regarded as untimely, while others in their 20s,

---

[204] https://archive.org/details/georgeivregentki00hibb

40s and 50s left us and we still say that they lived full lives, they fulfilled their destinies? Will we be biting our lips and trying to make reconciliation for the wrong things we did? Will we need to be calling on people to apologize to them? Will we be looking for pastors to bless our souls, or will our lives have been so fully poured out nothing is left to give but a faint smile of completion and our last breath? Will we be beyond persuasion and certain of where we will be headed? Will we know that finally, at last, our lives are about to begin and the party is just about to start? If nothing else will motivate us, let us give our death that honor of motivating us to be ready for it at any point. It is appointed unto man **once**....

A man's condition in this life may be honorable, and yet his state in eternity may be damnable.

Poor Lazarus goes to Heaven-- when rich Dives goes to Hell.

It is far better to go to Heaven poorly --than it is to go to Hell richly.

If once you drop into Hell--then after a thousand years:

You will be as far from coming out of Hell, as you were at your first entrance into Hell.

There is only one way to KEEP a man out of Hell --but there is no way to GET a man out of Hell.

In this world, the wheat and the chaff both grow together, but they shall not always both lie together.

In Hell, there shall not be a saint among those who are terrified.

In Heaven, there shall not be a sinner among those who are glorified.

Oh sirs, let us go to Hell by contemplation that we may never go to Hell by condemnation.

Oh sirs, meditate upon Hell!'

—*Arthur Pink*

In our generation, when two people meet, even before they have agreed to begin any kind of relationship, one is already dreaming of the wedding they will have, the caption, the wedding hashtag, where they will live, who will be the stay-at-home parent, and every other thing they are not guaranteed will ever happen. Meanwhile, some, while on earth, prepared themselves, had their personal epitaphs long and already written.

Kari Jobe said: "*The only thing I want in life is to be known for loving Christ to build His church; to love His bride and make His name known far and wide... I pray it's said about my life that I lived more to build Your name than mine.*"[205]

Steffany Gretzinger said: "*Let my children tell their children, let this be their memory, that all my treasure was in heaven and You were everything to me... And when I'm old and grey and all my days are numbered on the earth, let it be known in You alone, my joy was found.*"[206]

John Newton self-penned his epitaph long before he died, saying: "*JOHN NEWTON. Clerk. Once an infidel and libertine a servant of slaves in Africa was by the rich mercy of our LORD and SAVIOUR JESUS CHRIST preserved, restored, pardoned and appointed to preach the faith he had long labored to destroy. Near 16 years as Curate of this parish and 28 years as Rector of St. Mary Woolnoth.*"

John Knox's epitaph reads: "*Here lies one who feared God so much that he never feared the face of any man.*"

William Carey's reads*: Born August 17th, 1761: Died - -*

> "*A wretched, poor, and helpless worm*
>
> *On thy kind arms I fall.*"

This writer's epitaph currently reads*: "Eunice-Pauline, Friday 13th December 1991 —*

> *Once proud at heart, lived a life void of Truth and hope until saved by the Good News of the Gospel of her Lord Jesus Christ.*
>
> *Then poor in spirit, was driven through this present world fueled daily by an overwhelming supply of the Love and Mercies of Jesus Christ.*
>
> *Gone to finally be with her Father, to receive that which is promised her kind.*
>
> *She pleads that you join. Will you?*"

The Apostle Paul's reads: "As for me, my life has already been poured out as an offering to God. The time of my death is near. I have fought the good fight, I have finished the race, and I have remained faithful. And now the prize awaits me—the crown of righteousness, which the Lord, the righteous Judge, will give me on the day of his return. And the prize is not just for me but for all who eagerly look forward to his appearing." (2 Timothy 4:6-8)

---

[205] Kari Jobe, The Cause of Christ (2012) Album: Where I find You.
[206] Steffany Gretzinger, No one ever cared for me Like Jesus (2020) Album: Forever Amen.

What will it be, Christian? Will we write it now and live lives to honor it, or will we leave it to the media, friends, and chance to come up with the words which will sum up what our lives were? Does death scare you? If you are a follower of Jesus, let the thought of death excite you, and keep it exciting you, for though it tarry, it will surely come.

> *Though death is a bitter cup, there is sugar at the bottom. Death is the believer's best friend; for it brings him to Christ, which is far better. "I desire to depart and be with Christ, which is better by far!"*

> *It is the desire of a true saint to be gone from this present world, "I desire to depart." What a wicked man fears — that a godly man hopes for! The worldling desires to live in this present world forever; he knows no other heaven but earth — and it is death to him to be turned out of his heaven.*

> *A wicked man does not go out of this world — but is dragged out!*

> *—William Carrey*

Ponder on the words from Charles Spurgeon, who prepared for his death before he left and left us with these words:

> *Be ready, servant of Christ, for thy Master comes on a sudden, when an ungodly world least expects him. See to it that thou be faithful in his work, for the grave shall soon be digged for thee. Be ready, parents, see that your children are brought up in the fear of God, for they must soon be orphans; be ready, men of business, take care that your affairs are correct, and that you serve God with all your hearts, for the days of your terrestrial service will soon be ended, and you will be called to give account for the deeds done in the body, whether they be good or whether they be evil. May we all prepare for the tribunal of the great King with a care which shall be rewarded with the gracious commendation, "Well done, good and faithful servant".*

Wisdom for us all, in Jesus' name. Amen.

CHAPTER 5

WHEN?

The time has come, he said. The kingdom of God has come near. Repent and believe the good news!
Mark 1:15

SoulTune: Softly and tenderly Jesus is calling[207]

---

[207] Will L. Thompson; (1880); Softly and Tenderly Jesus is calling; hymnary.org

The Gift of Now

The Lord is not slow in keeping his promise, as some understand slowness. Instead he is patient with you, not wanting anyone to perish, but everyone to come to repentance.
But the day of the Lord will come like a thief. The heavens will disappear with a roar; the elements will be destroyed by fire, and the earth and everything done in it will be laid bare. **2 Peter 3:9-10**

The Lord is not slow in keeping His promise, as some understand slowness. What does slowness of time mean to you? Is it a burden or a gift? In *The Knowledge of the Holy*, A.W Tozer said, *"Life is a sort of fevered rehearsal for a concert we cannot stay to give. Just when we appear to have attained some proficiency, we are forced to lay our instruments down."* We get nervous, we demand things, we are not hitting targets. We thought, by a certain age, things would have happened, but they are yet to happen. So, we ask God when it will come, when that vision He gave us will come.

Time, time, time. Time is going. We are ever looking forward, but never at **"now."** Friend, God gave each and every one of us a common vision which, though it tarry, it will *surely* come, and that vision is that Jesus *IS* coming back to judge all men. Do we understand that each day He tarries is a gift to us? It is almost a sigh of relief, but don't release your breath yet. In *The Knowledge of The Holy*, Tozer went on to exposit that eternal years lie God's heart, i.e. for Him, time does not pass, it remains. Are we going through a pandemic on earth and think this is a surprise to God? We think it became 2020 and God said, *"Let Us send man a pandemic?"* The only *"let Us"* or *"let there be,"* which God ever said was at the beginning of time, and the next time He will say it is in the context of *"let Us return to the world for judgement. It is time."*

Between now and then, whatever we go through is of no effect to God. Coronavirus? He has been there and done that. Whatever woe continues to betide us in these evil last days is simply us, experiencing events which God has ordained from the initial "let Us," and never an afterthought. We can only be wise to consider the times against the signs that were given foretime to us in 2 Timothy 3:1-9, when we begin to wonder when will God return. He is not in a hurry to do anything; there is no deadline against which He must work. Are you in Christ? Relax and remain in Him. Are you out of Christ? You do not believe, it is fake, ancient stuff that doesn't apply to you? Friend, time is a devouring beast for you.

We have only two times to consider, which are NOW and END. Anything in between, such as "in an hour," "tomorrow," "in six months," "five years from now," is a presumptuous declaration. What did the year 2020 teach us? All we know is now and the end, the thin line between life and death, life now and life eternal. The power, gift and essence of **NOW** is to **RE-PENT**, forsake your sin, and come Home.

And this is eternal life, that they may know You, the only true God, and Jesus Christ whom You have sent. John 17:3

The power of now should only be interpreted in the context of whether if you are alive now and have not fallen on Him to break you, you can and should do it **now**. Why should you linger? What more can this world *possibly* offer you? Does money still excite you? Do possessions and the accumulation of it make your heartbeat faster? Are you living for the gratification that now affords? Are you still hoping to develop yourself, to get further in your education, to "make it" in life? Please, friend, Jesus is calling you now. He is calling you first and now. Nothing should even come a close second to Him. It should not be Jesus first, then other things later, it is Jesus or nothing. Can God be deaf to the cries of a man? Yes, He can *and* **will**. The cries of a man from hell will never be heard by God.

I love them that love me; and those that seek me early shall find me. Proverbs 8:17

I say this with tears, friend, the only "early" we have is now. We can never be earlier and more diligent than now. Do NOT put your soul on hold. Do you know what living in sin does to a soul? How does the thought of cancer seem to you? To live without Christ is to be in a spiritual cancer. You are fatally sick and on your way to eternal destruction. There *IS* a cure for this cancer, and that is the blood of Jesus. Think on the end of your life and make a decision now. Listen, there is a time you are going to die. The day a solution is found to death, is the day I stop being a Christian, but as surely as Christ has and will be the only One to ever conquer death, I remain on His side, for death has no sting on me. But for anyone outside of Christ, when death sweeps you away, listen, that is the beginning of your end. You then begin to die every day.

Christians die every day on earth and live every day beyond death. The sinner lives every day on earth and dies every day beyond death. Those who seek Him early will certainly find Him and grow in Him; they will discover new mysteries, new joys, new hope, new strength and the better things that come with salvation (Hebrews 6:9). The world has NOTHING new to offer, nothing new that is good at least; maybe new viruses and quicker ways to die, but there is no happiness unfound on earth. Everything it can ever offer is an anti-climax. Heaven is the only offering of a climax at the end. Do you imagine this is a façade? You think death is the end? Stop the foolishness! Ignorance is over. Stop it!

And the times of this ignorance God winked at; but now COMMANDETH all men everywhere to REPENT. Acts 17:30

Why does the Word of God still exist today? Why do you close your eyes and deafen your ears to truth? How much longer? Your philosophy, your embarrassing liberalism, and deadly modern thought are driving you faster to your grave than your dead conscience is letting on. "I will destroy the wisdom of the wise; the intelligence of the intelligent I will frustrate" (1 Corinthians 1:19). You think you are wise? You think you have achieved and worked hard? You think you have attained and settled? Oh dear, good luck going face to face with God. Listen, when God says He will, *He **will**.* Are we not seeing the wisdom of the wise already being thwarted, frustrated, and brought to nought? Do we not see the way the earth and everything in it is in confusion? A convulsing child? How much longer will we continue to relish the delicacies of satan? We cannot ignore much longer, "if My people who are called by My name will humble themselves, and pray and seek My face, and turn from their wicked ways, THEN I will hear from heaven, and will forgive their sin and heal their land" 2 Chronicles 7:14. Why do we waste our time with medicine and concussion, when the cause, effect, and solution are right before our eyes, in our hands, on our lips, waiting only for us to act? What will money, brains, and books do for us? The solution is right here: humble ourselves, pray, seek His face, STOP the wickedness of heart, **THEN** God will hear from Heaven and forgive our sin and heal our land. Our prayers are misplaced. We are calling, "Lord, Lord," and not doing what He says! Clanging cymbals!

For He says: "In an acceptable time I have heard you, And in the day of salvation I have helped you." Behold, now is the accepted time; behold, NOW is the day of salvation. 2 Corinthians 6:2

Our solution, our salvation, our healing, are dependent on a decision, which we have been given the choice of making, but we must know, as certain as it is never too early to seek Jesus, ***Seek the LORD while He may be found, call upon Him while He is near;***[208] there is a time it becomes too late, there is a time He becomes far, there is a time He becomes lost, so the psalmist cried, "So teach us to number our days, that we may apply our hearts unto wisdom" (Psalm 90:12); and this is what we fail to do. We fail to number our

---

[208] Isaiah 55:6.

days, we like to hear that as our days grow, so will our strength, but Jesus warns perhaps to those who will not die before the time, "take heed to yourselves, lest at any time your hearts be overcharged with surfeiting, and drunkenness, and cares of this life, and so that day come upon you unawares" (Luke 21:34). Some have an appointment with death, others will be caught unawares.

Dear friend, it is far better to consider death and prepare for it, than to enjoy this fleeting life and be caught unawares. Let us learn from Esau, who gave up that which rightfully belonged to him for a fleeting moment of satisfaction. He came to his senses to claim that which belonged to him, but it "was too late even though he sought it carefully with tears." (Hebrews 12:17). Salvation is a gift which has been given to us with a choice of acceptance, but remember that when we give it up to enjoy this temporal life and its sinful offerings, our tears will only be useful for drinking in hell.

Heed this plaintive appeal, modern-day residents, the world has evolved, the end has not. The Truth surely has not. Consider the end. Place your life on the mirror of eternity and where will you end up. If you took your last breath now, would you welcome it with a smile or ask for an inhaler in a futile attempt to prolong it? When it was clear that King George IV was going to die, having lost sight in one eye, obese and confined to sitting upright in a chair for he was prone to attacks of breathlessness if he lay down, he fought doggedly for his life, to the admiration of those around him who he had scorned his whole life:

> His will to live and still-prodigious appetite astonished observers; in April 1830, the Duke of Wellington wrote the King had consumed for breakfast a Pidgeon and Beef Steak Pye ... Three parts of a bottle of Mozelle, a Glass of Dry Champagne, two Glasses of Port [and] a Glass of Brandy, followed by a large dose of laudanum. Writing to Maria Fitzherbert in June, the King's doctor, Sir Henry Halford, noted, "His Majesty's constitution is a gigantic one, and his elasticity under the most severe pressure exceeds what I have ever witnessed in thirty-eight years' experience.[209]

Will our fighting and clinging to dear life astonish those around us, and perhaps even ourselves? Will we boldly face the stones thrown at us and cry, **'Lord, into thy hands I commit my Spirit'**? We can run all we want but, "we are made for eternity as certainly as we are made for time and as responsible moral beings, we must deal with both."[210]

---

[209] P. Steven (2001). 'George IV: The Grand Entertainment'. London: John Murray Publishers.
[210] A.W. Tozer, The Knowledge of the Holy.

...and consider that the longsuffering of our Lord is salvation. 2 Peter 3:15

Time is relevant to only we humans and nothing to God. We are the ones who need morning and night, birthdays, legal age, retirement age, birth certificates and death certificates, certainly not God. Yet consider that He tarries so that we can repent, because He will wish no man be destroyed.

Three-Way Call

Blessed is he who shall eat bread in the kingdom of God! Luke 14:15

A man once gave a great banquet and sent the first notice of this feast through one of his messengers, Mr. Moses. When the time finally came for the banquet, He sent His best and closest Servant, Sir Jesus, to tell the invitees, "Come, for everything is now ready." But they all alike began to make excuses: *"I just married the woman of my dreams and my soulmate;" "I just got the promotion I had been working hard for;" "I just started a new business;" "I am finally getting famous – I must keep building my brand,"* and many more excuses, so they all sent their regrets but never came, even though they had been giving the notice long before the banquet began.

This is the call to feast at God's table. What will your response be?

1. **'I AM'** - You have accepted the invitation and are ready for the feast. You are part of the wise virgins[211] with your lamp and oil ready and have been preparing and continuously adjusting your appearance to ensure you present yourself perfect and spotless at the table. You wait with eager expectation. You are free, you have been saved, you have found life. Oh, what joy. Continue to stand firm; you must take heed, lest you fall. You must continue to look in the mirror of the perfect Law of Liberty and adjust yourself to ensure that you are present to your Master, spotless and blameless. You are in this world but not of this world. You yearn for home. For you, it is far better to depart and be with Christ. If He says, "remain," you remain, but while you remain, what does He expect from you?

   You did not choose Me, but I chose you and appointed you that you should go and bear fruit, and that your fruit should remain, that whatever you ask the Father in My name He may give you. John 15:16

---

[211] Matthew 25:1-13.

Don't imagine that your salvation is owed to your wisdom, farsighted-ness, and strong-will. God Himself chose you and has commanded you to bear fruit. Remember, every branch that does not bear fruit, He cuts off. To be saved once is not to be saved all. When you take care of the work He has given to you, you can then ask for whatever you wish on earth and He will give it to you. You can then enjoy His blessings, be-cause you know the gifts He gives make us rich and add no sorrow. To whom much is given, much is expected; the more He blesses you and answers your *"whatever"* requests, the more He expects you to bear fruit.

Second, you must grow as you bear fruit for Him by increasing in your knowledge of Him (Colossians 1:10). We cannot remain babes in Christ forever. The six-month, two years, and beyond test should guide us. Je-sus told us we will do greater works than Him. Where are our greater works? Jesus raised the dead, have we? Jesus healed every sickness that was brought to Him, have we? We can only do greater works when we grow in our knowledge of God. In our prayers, in our faith, and as we walk closely, we must and we *will* grow, if we stand firm and aspire to please Him in *everything* we do. "Him we preach, warning every man and teaching every man in all wisdom, that we may present every man perfect in Christ Jesus" (Colossians 1:28). The disciples have done their work and departed to be with the Lord.

They have given us the Gospel which can help us grow, so that when we are presented, we are found perfect. We have no excuse not to grow and aspire to perfection in Christ. The Word is everywhere. How blessed are we! Christian, **GROW**.

2. **'I WAS'** - You were part of the 10 virgins. You knew it all, the mysteries of the Kingdom, had all the gifts of the Spirit; you were on fire for Christ. You had your lamp but no oil to sustain it, so you heeded the *John666* call and now suffer the syndrome. Perhaps you got tired of waiting for so long and willingly treaded the Demas Disorder path and are currently suffering from the insanity. You might still be regularly going to church, all might seem well on the outside, but between your spirit and Jesus, you know that all is *not* well. That is only because, "you have left your First Love" (Revelation 2:4). You let religion, the trends of the world, and carnal aspirations drive you far away from the One you love.

You were hot but you mixed with the cold, so you became lukewarm for a passing time and have now gone completely cold. The name, "Jesus" does not cause your heart to beat faster with excitement, as it once did. Why did you turn? Did a religious figure fail you? Surely, such a person

248

is *not* Jesus! Did you become religious? The rules were too many, so you just found yourself in a routine that caused no need for intentionality on your part? Were prayers not answered? Did you seek Him first, and His righteousness, or were you all about the prayer requests? Surely, you know you mean more to Him than the birds and flowers He cares for with splendor. Do you not miss Him? He misses you and wants His child back. We, your family members, miss you and want you back.

Your Father desires to throw His arms around His prodigal child who returns, but the onus is on you to, "remember from where you have fallen, and repent and do the deeds you did at first" (Revelation 2:5). All of those things you did were not in vain; the perseverance, the enduring, the ceaseless prayers, the sacrifice, He loved them. He wants you to return to your First Love and make love to Him the way you once did. He wants your love, your unashamed display of love for Him. You have cheated, but that is okay, He forgives and remembers no more. All *you* need to do is return. His arms are open. Nothing has changed with Him. Those warm, secure arms are still warm and secure. Come back into His rest.

Even if He disciplines you, when you return, remember it is only the ones He loves whom He disciplines. Surely, you know your Love; His discipline is His mercy; He disciplines with one hand but draws you back with both. He is known better for His lavish display of restoration than for His initial rescue (Jeremiah 16:14-15). There is hope for you! In all your neglect, "this is in your favor..." (Revelation 2:6) There is something that you know He hates, which you still hate, so your conscience is not dead. Come Home, come Home.

If you will not, but continue to revel in your vomit, take it from a man who almost fell into that snare, but for the mercy of Jesus, it would be better if you had never come to Jesus at all. It will be far worse for you than for those who never came to Christ. You knew Him once, enjoyed His light and freedom, but found living a holy life too much for you. You are headed for unspeakable, irredeemable destruction if you do not repent (2 Peter 2:20-22). Do not let Him remove your lampstand completely, throwing you into darkness and a dead conscience. Do not let Him abandon you. You *still* have hope. The blood of Jesus is still washing away sin and making black hearts white as snow. The blood is *still*. Search your heart and decide. The choice is yours.

3. **'I WILL'** - My dear friend, I admire your courage. You are one hell of a gambler. If it were money and possession you gambled with, it might be

considered fun and games, but with your life? You decide not yet; you are busy, you don't believe this religion stuff. You think Jesus Christ is a religion? Jesus does not even know what Christianity is! He never endorsed the word, *"Christian."* This was a derogatory term connoted by a group of flesh and blood mockers to followers of Jesus. You are being asked to accept Jesus and follow His teaching. If, as a result of that, you happened to be called a Christian, rejoice and be exceeding glad. A great reward awaits you in Heaven.

There is nothing that keeps wicked men at any one moment out of hell, but the mere pleasure of God. — A.W Tozer

Heaven, a place not open to all, is certainly closed to you who are yet to accept Jesus. You are the one who will hang on to dear life when the time comes, but you will be dragged out of the earth. Listen, you are going to die, perhaps tonight, perhaps in 50 years, but then what happens to you? Do you imagine it is the end? You say you are intelligent, so reason this out: You are born into a world into which you did not ask to be born. You go through it with choices that you are allowed to make, and then you die. You imagine that is the end? Come on! What will it feel like for you when you realize that all this was Truth, and you are finally ready to accept Jesus, but there is only one issue: You are no longer in the body. You are now out of the body and feeling the flames coming from hell. Oh yes, we can only accept Christ in the body, on earth, the place of choice. Listen, seed of Adam, it was not your decision that brought you into this earth. By divine providence, you found yourself in this sick, evil place, with its tears, sorrow and pain. It was also not your decision to have a sinful nature. You were born by a woman, so you inherited an already existing nature, but you are going somewhere, and you have a choice to choose where you are going. Do not be deceived, we shall not all "die." Earthly death is the beginning of life for some, and the beginning of the end for others. Don't reduce yourself to your flesh and blood. You are more than that. You are everything you do not see. You are everything you do not touch. Make a choice while you can. "He who watches the wind will not sow and he who looks at the clouds will not reap" (Ecclesiastes 11:4). Stop being ruled by reason. Make a decision for your soul, now.

"A wise person thinks a lot about death, while a fool thinks only about having a good time" (Ecclesiastes 7:4). Do you not see that you are living in a world of fools, drunk on social media and appearance, whose phones have more hope of life than they do when they die? Here today, gone tomorrow, perfectly laid out profiles will be left behind. Think about your end, make a decision about where you will end up, the Big H or the small "h;" your ordinary h, your home in this world, will be left behind. We either belong to Heaven or hell. When you decide where you want your home to be, then begin to live each day toward getting to that home.

Let the wicked forsake his way, And the unrighteous man his thoughts; Let him return to the LORD, And He will have mercy on him; And to our God, For He will abundantly pardon. Isaiah 55:7

If you decide on Heaven as your home, you have made a wise decision. No matter where you are now, a mansion, in prison (physically or emotionally), at work, in the kitchen, on a plane, and no matter what you have done, even the worst of sins, forget it. God will freely and abundantly pardon. He does not desire you to spend eternity elsewhere; hell is already congested with souls. Heaven is sparse, because few find the way. "Christians" might desire you to perish because they think Heaven is only for them. They are disturbed by the spirit of Jonah but my friend, God does not desire that you perish. I have no desire for you to perish. I was once bound by sin like you.

My conscience was dead. I stole, I lied, I fornicated, I was a drunkard, a hard partier and, if I dare say, the very life of the party. I cheated, I was proud, I was selfish, I was untrustworthy, I killed, I lived life on the edge, and was extremely arrogant, but I found life. Now I see so many of you and feel such pity at the chains binding you, and at the weights pressing hard on your souls. It does not have to be that way. First, you need to think about your end, your death. Where do you want to end up when you take that final breath? Have you made Heaven your home? Then decide you *will* get there, regardless of any temporary price.

Are you wondering what The Way to Heaven is? Here's what I found: *Jesus said to him, "I am the way, the truth, and the life. No one comes to the Father except through* **Me**. John 14:6

I once was lost, but now am found, was blind but now I see "...grace and truth came through Jesus Christ" (John 1:17). Jesus is calling for you, sinner, to come home. He came to shed His blood for you and me. Not even for angels. The angels who fell were fallen forever: meet Lucifer, now satan, but even if you fall seven times, He will forgive you if you repent. Listen, Jesus loves you. The more rebellious, stained, guilty, accused, and wretched you are, the better it is for Him. He wants to have mercy on *whom* He will have mercy. You are no better candidate for His transforming, saving grace and a boastful display of His sovereign love.

"Herein is love, not that we loved God, but that He loved us, and sent His Son to be the atoning sacrifice for our sins." (1 John 4:10)

His strength is made perfect in your weakness. His blood will wash the dirtiest vessel white as snow, oh, try Him! *Try* Him. Every tongue that rises up against you, based on what you have done, is already condemned by the One who will fight all your battles for you and vindicate you with His own testimony over you.

He called me home and although dead for years, His grace found me, and I accepted Him. He saved me and I forsook my wicked ways. I am now on a narrow path on which I carry my cross daily to remain on that path. For me, it is Heaven to be with my Love, or nothing. What will it be for you?

I say to you that likewise there will **be more joy in heaven over one sinner who repents** *than over ninety-nine just persons who need no repentance.* Luke 15:7

Meditate

Well done, good and faithful servant. Enter into the joy of your Lord. Matthew 25:21

Heaven is a place where all joy is enjoyed.

In Heaven, there will be: Mirth without sadness, light without darkness, sweetness without bitterness, life without death, rest without labor, plenty without poverty.

Oh, what joy enters into the believer when the believer enters into the joy of his Lord.

Oh, what glories are there in glory! Thrones of glory, crowns of glory, vessels of glory, a weight of glory, a kingdom of glory. Here on earth, Christ puts His grace upon His spouse. There in Heaven, He puts His glory upon His spouse. In Heaven the crown is made for them, and in Heaven the crown shall be worn by them. In this life, believers have some good things, but the rest and best are reserved for the life to come.

Oh sirs, meditate upon Heaven, for meditation on Heaven will make us Heavenly.

Heaven is not only a possession promised by Christ, but a possession purchased by Christ. When our contemplations and minds are in Heaven, then we enjoy Heaven upon earth.

To be IN Christ is Heaven below; to be WITH Him is Heaven above.

Let our condition now be ever so great, it is hell without Christ. Let our condition now be ever so bad, it is Heaven with Christ.

"I had rather be in Hell with Christ than in Heaven without Him," said Luther. Hell, itself would be Heaven if Christ was in it. Heaven would be Hell if Christ was out of it.

> *That which makes Heaven so full of joy, is that which is above all fear. That which makes Hell so full of horror, is that which is beyond all hope.*[212]

"When I think of the goodness of Jesus, and what he has done for me, my soul cries out, 'Hallelujah! Praise God for saving me!'"

My name is Eunice Pauline Hephzibah, a vessel of God's mercy, an apostle to the Christians. As long as I remain in this world, I am not of this world; let no man trouble me again, for I bear on my body, heart, and soul the marks of Jesus Christ.

Now all has been heard; here is the conclusion of the matter: fear God and keep his commandments, for this is the duty of all mankind. For God will bring every deed into judgment, including every hidden thing, whether it is good or evil. Ecclesiastes 12:13-14

To Him be glory forever! Amen.

---

[212] A. Pink, 'The Attributes of God' Chapter 14: The MERCY of God. Retrieved from www.gracegems.com.

Appendix

"I PLEDGE TO TOUCH"

We have come to the end of the book, *The Untouched Part*, but it is the beginning of a journey to touch that in ourselves we do not touch: our hearts. If God will show me mercy and cause this book to bless you, the oath below is one between each individual and God. It is to begin a journey toward inner beauty by letting Him work in our hearts, while we stay off cosmetics and the need to look good, as we know that counts for nothing with God. If you are serious about this, you can pledge a minimum of six months to completely abstain from those weights: make up for some women, for other women, it might be the need to shop, acquire new things, and so on. For men, it might be an addiction to some investment, games, movies or whatever each individual knows is what easily besets them. These are merely some of the encumbrances which slow us down, in order for us to allow God to begin His work. Of course, we know His work will never be completed within any period, as long as we are on earth. Use the time to declutter material things and to know God and love people. Think nothing of yourself and be quick to forgive. Most importantly, share the Good News of Jesus Christ and grow in your knowledge of Him.

God BLESS you.

Inner Beauty Oath

I, _____ pledge
this _____ day of _____, 20_____

in witness of God, the Father, God the Son, Jesus Christ, and God the Holy
Spirit that for the next ___ months/year(s), I will pay no mind to cosmetic
and beautification needs and the weights that hinder me from running my
race. I pledge to give my heart wholly to God for Him to work on me until
my inner beauty begins to shine through. My heart will be the most beautiful
part about me and I will love will God with all my heart, soul, and strength,
and love all humans equally.

I pledge from this day not to call myself a Christian until I become a   Christian.

So help me, God.

*"In that day the Branch of the LORD will be beautiful and glorious, and the fruit of the
earth will be the pride and the adornment of the survivors of Israel."*
(Isaiah 4:2)

Christian, YOU are the Branch of the Lord (John 15:5). Be beautiful.

May the grace of our Lord, Jesus Christ, be with your spirit. Amen.

ABOUT
KHARIS PUBLISHING

KHARIS PUBLISHING is an independent, traditional publishing house with a core mission to publish impactful books, and channel proceeds into establishing mini-libraries or resource centers for orphanages in developing countries, so these kids will learn to read, dream, and grow. Every time you purchase a book from Kharis Publishing or partner as an author, you are helping give these kids an amazing opportunity to read, dream, and grow. Kharis Publishing is an imprint of Kharis Media LLC. Learn more at https://www.kharispublishing.com.

CPSIA information can be obtained
at www.ICGtesting.com
Printed in the USA
BVHW080552260421
605848BV00009B/790